The New Managed Account Solutions Handbook

HOW TO BUILD YOUR FINANCIAL ADVISORY PRACTICE USING MANAGED ACCOUNT SOLUTIONS

Stephen D. Gresham
Arlen S. Oransky

John Wiley & Sons, Inc.

Published by John Wiley & Sons, Inc., Hoboken, New Jersey.
Published simultaneously in Canada.

Wiley Bicentennial Logo: Richard J. Pacifico.

For general information on our other products and services or for technical support, please contact our Customer Care Department within the United States at (800) 762-2974, outside the United States at (317) 572-3993 or fax (317) 572-4002.

Wiley also publishes its books in a variety of electronic formats. Some content that appears in print may not be available in electronic books. For more information about Wiley products, visit our web site at www.wiley.com.

Library of Congress Cataloging-in-Publication Data:
Gresham, Stephen D.
   The new managed account solutions handbook : how to build your financial advisory practice using managed account solutions / Stephen D. Gresham, Arlen S. Oransky.
      p.   cm.
      Rev. ed. of: The managed account handbook. c2002. Includes bibliographical references and index.
      ISBN 978-0-470-22278-2 (cloth) ISBN 978-1-119-16160-8 (paperback)
      1. Financial planners—Handbooks, manuals, etc. 2. Investment advisors—Handbooks, manuals, etc. 3. Portfolio management. I. Oransky, Arlen S., 1956- II. Gresham, Stephen D. Managed account handbook. III. Title.
   HG179.5.G742 2008
   332.6—dc22
                                                                           2007032146

10 9 8 7 6 5 4 3 2 1

To Phyllis and Glen Gresham, for a lifetime of guidance, inspiration, and love

—S.G.

To my wife, Christine—your patience and support have been unending

—A.O.

Contents

Foreword

Over the past five years, the amount of assets held in separately managed accounts has more than doubled, to $805 billion. This growth, impressive as it is, pales in comparison to the growth that lies ahead. Over the next five years, the first wave of baby boomers—the richest class of people in world history—will begin to retire, initiating a decades-long transfer of wealth estimated at up to $40 trillion.

These baby boomers have spent their professional lives accumulating wealth in employer-sponsored retirement plans, individual retirement accounts (IRAs), and other investment vehicles. When the time comes for them to transfer their accounts and begin disbursement, many are going to seek the aid of financial advisors who can provide them with all of the services they require: Account consolidation. Innovative investments. Risk management. Tax efficiency. The only platform that can provide all of these services—and more—is the managed account. Advisors who have established themselves as providers of managed account solutions will reap the benefits of this historic wealth transfer.

In 1997, a group of money management visionaries realized that the future of the financial advisory profession lay in separately managed accounts. They formed a group, the Money Management Institute (MMI), to serve as a forum for industry leaders to meet, discuss issues of mutual concern, and advocate on behalf of their members on legislative and regulatory issues. Today the MMI membership represents 95 percent of the industry's assets under management. The organization is the nation's foremost authority on managed account solutions.

Steve Gresham, a member of the MMI Board of Governors, and Arlen Oransky, MMI vice president, are uniquely suited to write the book on managed account solutions.

Steve, executive vice president of Phoenix Investment Partners, helped create some of the industry's first fee-based accounts back in 1984, and he's been an integral part of the managed account story ever since. His expertise has been sought by CNN, PBS, Bloomberg Radio and TV, and many other media outlets, including the *New York Times*, *Fortune*, and *BusinessWeek*. In addition, Steve is in constant demand as a speaker at financial conferences, educating advisors on using managed account solutions to transform their practices from the outdated, commission-driven model to the fee-based, professional practice of the future.

Arlen has more than 25 years' experience in the financial services industry. He directs the member acquisition and retention efforts for the MMI and leads the development of the Institute's conferences and web-based meetings. Arlen has worked with leading advisors across the country and outside of the United States, and has served as senior vice president for Weiss, Peck & Greer Investments and as vice president and product manager for TIAA-CREF.

In preparing the second edition of this book, Steve and Arlen sought advice and input from many members of the MMI's Board of Governors, all of whom are acknowledged experts in the field of money management, financial services technology, and managed account solutions.

The future of the financial services industry lies in managed accounts. On behalf of the Money Management Institute, I invite you to be a part of that future. The book you are holding in your hands will tell you nearly everything you need to know.

—CHRISTOPHER L. DAVIS
President, The Money Management Institute

Preface

When we published the first edition of this book back in 2002, U.S. capital markets were still reeling from the double whammy of the tech wreck of 2000 and the events of September 11, 2001. The roaring bull market of the 1990s had taught many investors (or led them to believe, anyway) that they knew how to make money, but the subsequent bear market demonstrated that they didn't know how to protect it. Millions of investors realized they needed help, and they scrambled to find a financial advisor who could provide them with a wealth management solution.

In many ways, this was a case of history repeating itself. Managed accounts were first introduced in the 1980s, but didn't really take off until after the market crash of 1987. In the 1990s, the managed account industry evolved and expanded, but many affluent investors didn't notice because they were too focused on making money to give much thought to managing it. As a result, they lost sizable chunks of their portfolios because they had failed to properly diversify. Those who ignore history are doomed to repeat it, as George Santayana observed.

Today, with millions of baby boomers on the eve of retirement and the imminent onset of the greatest wealth transfer in human history, more investors than ever are clamoring for financial advice. Many of those investors will be best served by a managed account solution. The industry has changed dramatically since the first edition of this book was published, with new products and services being introduced and technological innovations expanding the advisor's ability to serve clients.

Managed account solutions are ideal for a wide range of clients, but they are also essential for financial advisors who wish to change from the erratic, transaction- and commission-driven approach of the past to a model built on consistent, recurring revenue that enables them to build equity in their practices. How can you as an advisor benefit by providing managed account solutions to your clients? This book seeks to provide you with a personal answer. We have gathered the strategies of advisors who successfully adopted managed account solutions into their businesses as well as insight from the undisputed leaders of the managed account industry, including many members of the Money Management Institute's Board of Governors.

The book covers three general areas of four chapters each. The first quartet provides an overview of the managed account industry from its origins in pension reform legislation to the new options being offered today. The middle quartet details the advantages of managed account solutions and advice on how to determine if managed accounts are right for your practice and, if so, how to implement them. The final quarter of the book is forward looking and outlines ways to build on your managed account success and what the future holds for the industry.

Consider each chapter to be a drawer in a filing cabinet filled with the best practices of investment management consultants to which you may return many times for consultation. If you are unfamiliar with managed account solutions, you may wish to start with the first chapter and work your way through the book. If you are familiar with managed accounts but are uncertain of the advantages to you, the advisor, then you may wish to start with Chapter 5, "Key Benefits of Managed Accounts and Recurring Revenues," or Chapter 6, "How to Tell If Managed Account Solutions Are Right for Your Practice." If you are already a provider of managed account solutions but wish to take your practice to the next level, then an ideal starting point would be Chapter 8, "Developing Your Managed Account Solutions Business."

By reading this book, you are taking an important step forward in the development of your practice. Managed account solutions represent a higher level of service for the investment side of your client relationships, allowing you to focus more time on the vital areas of client service and attending to the overall wealth needs of your best clients. The world of managed accounts is complex, and each advisor has his or her own approach to the business. Take your time to find a path that is right for you, knowing that even the most accomplished practitioners had to start at the beginning.

—STEPHEN D. GRESHAM
Phoenix Investment Partners, Ltd.

—ARLEN S. ORANSKY
The Money Management Institute

Acknowledgments

*T*he *New Managed Account Solutions Handbook* is hardly in the league of Harry Potter, *Shrek*, or *Pirates of the Caribbean*, but the challenge is the same: how to refresh a familiar topic and hold the attention of a discriminating audience. From that perspective, the team assembled exceeded all of our expectations. We hope you agree.

The original *Managed Account Handbook* was a team project involving professionals from all corners of the managed account world. The revised version casts an even wider net, drawing in more players and concepts from a bigger managed account solutions industry. Some of the new faces are from overlay and platform companies sponsoring unified managed accounts (UMAs), while others are from the distribution side, notably banks. New content providers discuss exchange-traded funds and other product choices. Mike Lynch of Twenty-First Securities organized an entire section for this book (and for *Advisor for Life*) on the importance of nontraditional investments to risk-adjusted returns. We are grateful for the support of Lee Chertavian, Randy Bullard, Valerie Petrone Corradini, Anthony Rochte, Larry Sinsimer, Lidiette Ratiani, J. Reed Murphy, and Chip Walker.

Managed account solutions are increasingly a part of a broader wealth management solution, and the new text responds with more discussion and analysis of overall financial advice and tactics for helping affluent families take on the practical challenges of retirement planning. Transitioning both clients and advisors to managed account solutions and wealth management remains a central theme of the book, and we appreciate the experience and expertise contributed by Jim Miklas, David Wadley, Don Berryman, Ed Friderici, and Jim Tracy.

Practice management is the third leg of the stool, supporting not just the transition to managed account solutions, but also the marketing, prospecting, and organizing of a solid financial advisory practice. The ultimate test of any book is the relevance of its content to the practitioner, and many top advisors have contributed their ideas and opinions—John Rafal, Steve Hiorns, George Kempf, John McCormack, Gerry Dubey, and Louis Chiavacci. We also appreciate the expertise of Mark Tibergien, Joe Lukacs, and Don Trone.

Industry leaders rallied around the project, particularly those with ties to the Money Management Institute (MMI), whose president, Christopher L. Davis, was a visionary 10 years ago for the potential of the modern-day managed accounts solutions business. Current MMI chair Kevin Hunt, immediate past chair Len Reinhart, and chairman ex-officio Mark Pennington all played a role, as did Jim Patrick, Frank Campanale, Charles Widger, and Jay Link.

No project of this breadth could move forward without the strength of its past, and we were able to tap the knowledge of industry veterans and pioneers Peter Muratore and Richard "Dick" Schilffarth. We also asked our colleagues to look ahead and give us their perspective on the future of the industry not only in the United States, but also overseas. We are grateful for the support of Mark Fetting, Ed Blodgett, Mike Evans, Terry Shimizu, Tina Wilkinson, Lisa Langley, and Martijn Duijnstee.

The editorial team was the anchor. The team at Cape Cod Compositors once again exceeded expectations. Kim Dombek pulled graphic rabbits out of her hat at the last minute. The Wiley team led by David Pugh moved quickly and decisively once the project was outlined. The MVP award goes to editor Tom Johnson, in whom we found the ideal steward to guide the previous work into the modern age. His knowledge and industry perspective were invaluable to developing a book much expanded but also refined as to its mission and specific content. Tom brought the book in on time and with class. Evan Cooper, thank you for referring us to Tom.

Our final acknowledgment is to you, the reader. We hope that this book becomes a valuable ally as you further develop your financial advisory practice. We are grateful for the time you devote to exploring its contents.

—Stephen D. Gresham
Phoenix Investment Partners, Ltd.

—Arlen S. Oransky
The Money Management Institute

1

The Evolution of Managed Accounts

The managed account industry, which began amid pension reform, has mushroomed in response to clients' demands for a consistent process to manage their investments.

Managed accounts have been getting so much attention lately that it's easy to forget that the concept has been around for quite some time. Recent years have seen the introduction of innovative elements such as unified managed accounts (UMAs), mutual fund advisor accounts, and unified managed household accounts (all of which are discussed in detail elsewhere in this book), but the industry itself can trace its origins to the social turmoil of the late 1950s and early 1960s. Pension reform legislation passed in that most turbulent of times laid the foundation upon which the modern managed account industry was built.

Financial advisors and wealth managers serving high-net-worth clients may question the relevance of pension reform to their practices. However, it's quite possible there would be no managed account industry today were it not for the strategies and services—and legislation—first developed to address the investment management needs of institutional clients. Equally important, advances in technology have led to economies of scale, making the managed account approach no longer the exclusive domain of billion-dollar pension funds and megarich individuals. Thus, an overview of the evolution of managed accounts is in order. (See Figure 1.1.)

In 1958, Congress passed the Welfare and Pension Plan Disclosure Act, the first of several key legislative landmarks that would lead to the creation of the managed account platform. At the time, more than 40 percent of all nongovernment American workers were covered by an employer-sponsored

1963

Straus merges with Dempsey-Tegeler and James Lockwood becomes the largest mutual fund producer at the firm. Ellis and Lockwood team up with Tom Gorman.

1967

U.S. population reaches 200 million.

Merrill Lynch enters the performance measurement business for institutional clients.

1970

Dempsey-Tegeler closes and Lockwood, Ellis, and partner Tom Gorman join Dean Witter.

Butcher and Singer becomes one of the first financial services firms offering consulting services through its autonomous Butcher Consulting Group.

1973

James Lockwood proposes new business model, but Dean Witter turns him down, rejecting Dean Witter Plus. Lockwood's team approaches Hutton and offers the concept that later becomes E.F. Hutton Suggests.

Hutton forms its Consulting Group.

Hutton broker John Vann opens the first separately managed account (SMA) for Hilda Peck.

1950

James Lockwood joins Chicago-based brokerage firm of Straus, Bosser & McDowell in the mid-1950s, where he meets future partner John Ellis.

1965

Harvard professor Michael C. Jensen conducts the first major study on the performance of mutual funds.

1968

Edwin Callan, a leader in the institutional consulting business, forms the investment measurement division of Mitchum, Jones & Templeton.

A.G. Becker Corp. conducts the first major study of institutional plans.

1972

The Dow Jones Industrial Average closes above 1,000 for the first time.

Vic Rosasco joins Bache and later organizes the Senior Consulting Group after Prudential acquires Bache. He provides innovative training and support for interested brokers.

1974

The Employee Retirement Income Security Act (ERISA) of 1974 is enacted, making way for the Prudent Man Rule.

The Dow closes at 577 in December 1974 (45% off its peak), its lowest level since October 1962.

Hutton offers investment consulting services to retail clients.

1975

May 1, "May Day," the Big Board's fixed commission rates are abolished and brokerage commissions become negotiable.

Hutton introduces Hutton Investment Management (HIM) in October.

1977

John Calamos founds Calamos Asset Management—the first unique style manager with convertibles strategy for SMA sector.

1979

Hutton sales force grows to 6,000 under the leadership of George Ball and Peter Muratore.

1985

The Investment Management Consultants Association (IMCA) is launched under the guidance of Jim Owen and Dan Bott.

In the mid-1980s, Mobius and Security APL begin offering technology solutions.

1976

First Hutton SMA training program begins.

1978

Len Reinhart joins Jim Lockwood at Hutton as an analyst.

1981

Assets in Hutton's Consulting Group exceed $1 billion.

1986

Shearson Lehman Brothers launches its Portfolio Management (PM) programs.

Figure 1.1 Managed Accounts Historical Time Line, 1950–2006

Source: Money Management Institute. Concept and design: Wechsler Ross & Partners Inc., New York and London.

The Dow falls
508 points, or 23%,
to close at 1,739
on October 19,
known as Black
Monday.

An SEC report
deems compensating
brokers based on
client assets under
management instead
of by the number of
trades executed to
be a best practice
by firms.

Merrill Lynch
enters the
managed accounts
business with its
Consults program.

Prudential and
PaineWebber test
SMA waters.

Major firms establish
their own trading
desks for managed
accounts. Jim
Lockwood retires.

Shearson introduces
its TRAK program,
the first SMA program
employing mutual
funds. On January 2,
the Dow closes
above 2,800.

Equitable Life
Assurance Society
offers SMAs
to investors.

Shearson launches
its Guided Portfolio
Management
(GPM) program.

On November 11,
the Dow closes
for the first time
above 5,000.
Phoenix Investment
Partners enters the
SMA business.

1987	1989	1992	1995

1988	1990	1994	1996

Shearson Lehman
acquires Hutton.

Dan Bott launches
the Institute for
Investment
Management
Consultants (IIMC).

The Association
for Investment
Management
and Research
(AIMR) springs to
life from the merger
of the Financial
Analysts Federation
(FAF) and the
Institute of
Chartered Financial
Analysts (ICFA).

At year-end,
Shearson boasts
assets totaling
$4 billion.

The Securities and
Exchange Commission
(SEC) releases
the "Large Firm
Report" of industry
compensation
practices headed by
Merrill chairman
Dan Tulley.

Jim Lockwood
passes away at
age 77.

CheckFree purchases
Security APL—further
enhancing technology
offerings.

Figure 1.1   (Continued)

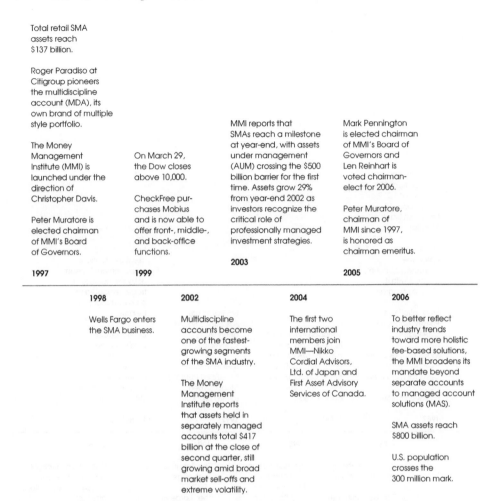

Total retail SMA assets reach $137 billion.

Roger Paradiso at Citigroup pioneers the multidiscipline account (MDA), its own brand of multiple style portfolio.

The Money Management Institute (MMI) is launched under the direction of Christopher Davis.

Peter Muratore is elected chairman of MMI's Board of Governors.

1997

On March 29, the Dow closes above 10,000.

CheckFree purchases Mobius and is now able to offer front-, middle-, and back-office functions.

1999

MMI reports that SMAs reach a milestone at year-end, with assets under management (AUM) crossing the $500 billion barrier for the first time. Assets grow 29% from year-end 2002 as investors recognize the critical role of professionally managed investment strategies.

2003

Mark Pennington is elected chairman of MMI's Board of Governors and Len Reinhart is voted chairman-elect for 2006.

Peter Muratore, chairman of MMI since 1997, is honored as chairman emeritus.

2005

1998

Wells Fargo enters the SMA business.

2002

Multidiscipline accounts become one of the fastest-growing segments of the SMA industry.

The Money Management Institute reports that assets held in separately managed accounts total $417 billion at the close of second quarter, still growing amid broad market sell-offs and extreme volatility.

2004

The first two international members join MMI—Nikko Cordial Advisors, Ltd. of Japan and First Asset Advisory Services of Canada.

2006

To better reflect industry trends toward more holistic fee-based solutions, the MMI broadens its mandate beyond separate accounts to managed account solutions (MAS).

SMA assets reach $800 billion.

U.S. population crosses the 300 million mark.

Figure 1.1   (Continued)

pension plan, according to the Employee Benefit Research Institute (EBRI), and fraud and mismanagement were widespread. The law was complex, but its purpose was simple: To thwart fiduciary abuse, pension plan sponsors had to meet new disclosure and reporting requirements. The act was amended in 1962 to transfer accountability for the protection of plan assets to the federal government.

Also in 1962, Congress passed the Self-Employed Individual Retirement Act, commonly called the Keogh Act, which made self-employed small business owners and their employees eligible for pension plan participation. These legislative steps were augmented by the Tax Reform Act of 1969, which spelled out the basic rules for creating and operating pension plans jointly managed by unions and employers.

Five years later, in the aftermath of the historic 1973–1974 stock market plunge, Congress passed the Employee Retirement Income Security Act (ERISA) to protect the benefits of participants in private pension plans. One particular aspect of ERISA spurred development of the modern consulting industry: Plan trustees were required to document their investment process and manage the assets prudently.

As a result of these regulatory directives, many corporate and municipal pension plan sponsors elected to have their assets managed by professional investment managers. The downside to this decision, however, was that many sponsors had no idea where to find suitable management experts. Prior to ERISA, major insurance companies and bank trust departments dominated the field of public and corporate funds, with the majority of assets concentrated in mutual funds rather than being actively managed. State-owned and corporate pension funds would initiate investments with little or no accountability, and value-based performance measurement was rare.

The ERISA legislation also called for the creation of the Pension Benefit Guaranty Corporation (PBGC), a federal organization charged with insuring, monitoring, and protecting the pensions of 44 million Americans. Each year the PBGC issues a state of the industry report on the fiscal health of U.S. pension plans, and the prognosis has not been positive. As of 2006, U.S. pension plans were underfunded by more than $340 billion, according to the PBGC. Fearful that the federal government might have to step in and subsidize these failing pension plans, Congress passed the Pension Protection Act of 2006, the most comprehensive pension reform legislation since ERISA. The Pension Protection Act requires employers with underfunded pension plans to make up their shortfall within the next seven years and to adopt a strategy of liability-driven investment to avoid the possibility of future shortfalls.

The Pension Protection Act will have a dramatic effect on the managed account solutions (MAS) industry for two reasons. First, in order to make up their funding shortfalls, many plan sponsors will have to invest more aggressively and creatively than ever before, moving beyond the familiar terrain of mutual funds and utilizing more complex financial instruments such as hedge funds, credit derivatives, and other alternative investments to maximize returns and minimize risk. Second, the focus on liability-driven investment—meaning returns must be based on future payout rather than some random, external benchmark—means these plans will require ongoing, active risk management and rebalancing. Gone are the days of pouring all of a plan's assets into a selection of mutual funds and hoping the funds' growth would at least keep pace with the plan's demands.

Not that this strategy was all that effective to begin with. In 1965, A.G. Becker Corporation (a forerunner of SEI Corporation) conducted one of the first major studies of mutual fund manager performance and discovered that most managers failed to meet—let alone beat—their relevant indexes.

Three years later, the firm undertook a review of institutional plan perform-ance and reached the same conclusion.

At first glance, the Becker findings might appear to support a case for passive investing. However, the firm noted that some managers were able to outperform their benchmarks and argued that these were the managers to whom investment assets should be entrusted. Becker published tables comparing plan performance, then approached select plan sponsors and encouraged them to utilize the report's tables to gauge the performance of the banks responsible for managing their pension funds. This practice opened the door to subsequent performance and portfolio management services that, in turn, provided ample opportunity for Becker to acquire sub-stantial institutional accounts, especially those whose trustees were uncom-fortable with the intricacies of quarterly performance comparison charts.

Other firms, engaged in developing their own research criteria relating to mutual fund and pension fund performance, began contacting plan spon-sors and offering their help in evaluating fresh research and management options for plan sponsors' funds. What began as a trickle became a flood as more and more firms climbed aboard the bandwagon. In exchange for investment policy statement guidance, asset allocation, and manager selec-tion, consulting firms negotiated to receive brokerage commissions for their recommendations. Important referral business also factored into the mix.

Niche firms emerged to capture a piece of the institutional consulting market, widening their sphere of influence to include nonprofits as poten-tial recipients for their advice. Soon middle markets opened up, allowing these participants to enjoy levels of management previously reserved for larger funds. The rush was on to meet the demand for institutional invest-ment management.

The Beginning of an Industry

The need for investment consultants gained added urgency in the early 1970s, when U.S. capital markets turned drastically bearish as political instability and the Arab oil embargo plunged the nation into a recession. By the time the Dow Jones Industrial Average bottomed out at 577.60 on December 6, 1974, the country had experienced its worst bear market since the Great Depression. Individual and institutional investors, including small and midsize pension plans, were clamoring for asset protection that could be realized only through sound investment management advice. The early investment management consultants were poised to step in and fill the niche.

Among the consultants now considered pioneers of the managed account industry are Jim Lockwood, Richard "Dick" Schilffarth, John Ellis, and Tom Gorman. The four had worked together in the early 1970s at Dean Witter, where they had launched a short-lived money management service for retail clients, but moved together to E.F. Hutton in 1973, frustrated over Dean Witter's failure to aggressively promote the program.

Peter Muratore, then E.F. Hutton's product manager and director of marketing, was immediately impressed with Lockwood's presentation. "At the time, Hutton was already looking for a way to generate revenues as well as make recommendations on how investors could benefit from investments in a falling stock market," Muratore recalls. "We'd moved toward mutual funds because they were an obvious choice, but had become disenchanted with the whole concept of rent-your-broker-out-for-a-commission, while the fund companies would end up with a 20-year fee structure. That's why we jumped into annuities, life insurance, direct investments, and other offerings. Hutton had built a very complex training system—one of the best in the industry, if not *the* best—and we were known as a firm that could roll out a new product very quickly. Jim's ideas satisfied our interest in building a fee-based organization. We welcomed him with open arms."

Muratore gave Lockwood and his colleagues the support they needed to establish a new consulting division, E.F. Hutton Suggests. The team set up the department to bring in corporate and government clients and provide management consulting services. It was a different way of approaching institutional sales. Instead of calling on money managers to sell investments, they called on clients to sell the money managers.

"This was a whole new way to talk to clients, because it put the broker on the same side of the desk as the client—he was more of a consultant than a salesperson," Muratore explains. "Our larger producers immediately saw this as a much better way to interact with clients and manage their own careers, because they weren't producing only dollars for today, but ongoing fee revenues for themselves and the firm. Rather than start every January 1 with a zero balance and a goal for the year, fee-based brokers started with a balance and built from there. The idea caught on very quickly and spread like wildfire."

Initially, the Hutton team focused on converting current clients to a fee-based structure rather than trying out the approach on new clients. "Retention of clients was our first goal, because at the time a lot of them were asking, 'What's wrong?'" says Muratore, referring to the catastrophic state of the U.S. capital markets in 1973 and 1974. "We would say to them, 'I would like to talk to you about a different way of investing. Large institutions that have thousands of employees don't bother employing someone to run their pension plans; they use a consultant to find someone to manage their money for them. We can offer you access to the same managers that General Motors, AT&T, and other large corporations use. That way, not only will we have the ability to shift assets and investments as your needs and desires change, but also we will be able to find managers to invest in different ways.' Our brokers had been giving ideas—good, sound ideas—but the market was not behaving well at the time. With this new approach, if the investment advisor wasn't doing a good job, we could move on to the next expert but still keep the client relationship intact."

Dick Schilffarth developed a training program for brokers who were interested in learning the consulting process, and in May 1974, the first training workshop was held. At the time, Hutton clients had to meet $100,000 minimums, and each broker was assigned 12 to 15 accounts. "The brokers in the top decile earned 12 to 15 percent commission on their accounts, while the brokers in the lower deciles earned only 1 to 2 percent," Schilffarth recalls. "Initially, the training program was aimed at the brokers in the lower deciles, because they were not successful in the transaction business. We were trying to sell them on a new way of dealing with clients, a more holistic approach that offered them the opportunity to capture more assets and earn higher commissions."

A fee was considered an asset-based commission; the fee schedule was 3 percent on the first $500,000 of an account, 2.5 percent on the next $500,000, and 2 percent on accounts in excess of $1 million. "It was necessary for the broker who wasn't an avid stock trader to make money in the markets of 1973 and 1974," Schilffarth says. Much to everyone's surprise, the program did not appeal to brokers in the lowest decile, but rather those in the middle. "The top brokers were very transaction-oriented. They were active traders. They had no hesitation about calling clients because they had the ego that said, 'I know I'm right.' The lowest-decile brokers did not have a lot of turnover; they were very reluctant to call clients. The middle producers did not have the egos of the top producers, nor did they have the reluctance of the others. They took a more thoughtful approach, and that was perfectly suited to the consultative services we were looking to sell."

With the then-recent passage of ERISA, Lockwood's group aggressively pursued the employee benefits market. "Most brokers did not get into employee benefit plans, and for the guy running a small to midsize pension plan—one with less than $1 million in assets—ERISA really boggled his mind," Schilffarth says. "We would go to these pension fund managers and say, 'Look, for one fee you can have access to top money managers. The fee will cover the cost of the manager, the cost of all trades, the cost of consulting services, and the cost of outside review to make sure the plan complies with the new regulations.' The concept caught on very quickly."

In retrospect, the reason is obvious, even if few saw it at the time. "There needed to be something for people with serious money who didn't want to play the market," he says. "People who inherited money, or sold a business, or received a settlement in a divorce, or retirees with pension plans—people with a large, one-time pool of money had different needs and different issues than active traders, but no product existed to address those needs. And there was no one there to advise them."

On May 1, 1975—"May Day"—the New York Stock Exchange abolished its fixed-rate commissions, believing that competitive rates would ultimately result in more efficient capital markets. On the plus side, money management firms could attract new business by offering lower commissions; but on the minus side, as rates declined profit margins were pinched. Competition intensified, as firms that wouldn't—or couldn't—compete on price were compelled to compete on performance.

Lockwood saw this as an opportunity for money managers to join the ranks of other fee-based professionals like attorneys and certified public accounts and introduced the concept of charging a fee for services in lieu of commissions.

"That's when separate accounts really took off," says Muratore. "It was very interesting to the client, because now the broker had absolutely no benefit in trading or not trading, and as a result brokers didn't want to see a lot of trades. Also, with the investment managers all charging the same fee, there was no reason for the consultant to not pick the best manager for the client, and no hidden ways for the broker to be biased."

The Trend Spreads

E.F. Hutton had the separately managed account (SMA) market all to itself for nearly a decade. "After we got out of the down market of 1974, there was a period of great inflation from 1975 to the 1980s," Schilffarth says. "People were selling certificates of deposit (CDs), oil wells, tax shelters—but not a lot of equities. Firms would not embrace the concept of consultative selling and would not spend the money to create the infrastructure you had to have to support the program." In 1987, after the stock market crashed and reform legislation eliminating many tax shelters sent high-end investors scrambling for other ways to protect their assets, other firms started to take a second look at separately managed accounts. Merrill Lynch Consults was launched as a head-to-head rival to E.F. Hutton Suggests. Soon after, both Prudential and PaineWebber added managed account programs to their client offerings.

Until the mid-1980s, money managers in brokerage firm programs set their own fees and account minimums, handled their own accounting, and dealt directly with clients, while the firms introduced the managers and handled the custody and trades. In 1987, the Hutton team again changed the landscape by introducing Hutton Select Managers, a program that took over the fiduciary duties of accounting, performance reporting, and client interaction. This helped lower minimums and fees and freed up the managers to do what they did best—manage the portfolios.

If technology was the engine driving the new phase of separately managed accounts, then the volatile market of 1987 provided the gas. April 1987's precipitous drop in bonds was followed in October by the historic 508-point plummet in the Dow Jones Industrial Average. Investors and brokers alike flocked to managed accounts and the stability of professional advisory firms.

Of course, each firm brought a slightly different spin to the managed account phenomenon. In 1986, Shearson Lehman Brothers began to offer fee-based brokerage through guided portfolios where trades were run by company analysts. Two years later, Shearson acquired Hutton and marketed the Hutton Select program through brokers of both firms. Shearson brought product and technology structure to the Hutton programs, further empowering their growth. Advest and Wheat First pioneered fee-based brokerage for nondiscretionary accounts in 1989–1990, making the industry truly comprehensive—any client and advisor could participate. In the roaring bull market of the 1990s, as investors acquired wealth at a faster rate than ever before in American history, more and more of the newly wealthy turned to separately managed accounts in search of customized investment, risk management, and tax efficiency.

In 1990, Shearson Lehman Hutton conducted the first-ever comparison of managed account fees versus costs associated with traditional commission-based accounts, concluding that managed account fees were not higher—and often were lower—than the commissions. The study had a dramatic impact on the firm's stockbrokers; by the end of the year, more than a quarter of them had opened at least one managed account. That same year, mutual funds weighed in with the first wrap accounts, which are similar to managed accounts but differ in the sense that investors do not own individual securities, as they do in managed accounts, but rather own shares of the underlying funds. Wrap accounts offer a comparable account consolidation benefit and services such as asset allocation and rebalancing, but do not provide the same level of customization as a managed account.

Insurers followed in the footsteps of the mutual funds. In 1992, the Equitable Life Assurance Society became the first insurance company to offer a managed account program.

The fee-based approach to money management received a major boost in 1995 when the Securities and Exchange Commission (SEC) released the Tully Commission report, which concluded that asset-based fees were a preferable form of compensation to trade-based commissions. The report was based on the findings of a group of regulators, financial services executives, and consumer advocates led by former Merrill Lynch chairman Daniel Tully, who had been charged by the SEC with studying broker compensation trends and their impact on the investing public. The report stated that investors would benefit from asset-based fees because brokers would be less likely to recommend sales just to boost commissions.

The Tully Commission report not only validated the work that fee-based financial consultants had been doing for years, but also informed the investing public of the benefits of fee-based financial planning and management. Consumers began initiating conversations about fee-based programs with consultants rather than the other way around. (See Figure 1.2.)

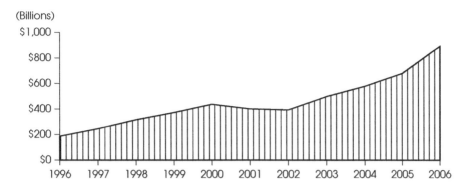

Figure 1.2 Separately Managed Account Asset Growth, 1996–2006
Sources: Money Management Institute; Dover Financial Research.

"Years ago we sold commissions and gave away advice," Schilffarth says. "Now we sell advice and give away the commissions. It's a better way."

Recognizing the rapidly growing interest in fee-based programs and the various products that had been introduced to address that interest, top executives at investment banks, money management firms, financial services technology companies, and other leaders met in 1997 and formed a national organization, the Money Management Institute (MMI). The MMI dedicated itself to addressing common concerns, discussing industry developments, and representing the interests of members on regulatory and legislative issues, with membership open to firms offering comprehensive financial consulting services to individual investors, foundations, retirement plans, and trusts; related portfolio management firms; and firms providing long-term service and support to both sponsor and manager firms.

Later that year, Citigroup unveiled a new concept in separately managed accounts that it called the multidiscipline account (MDA) or multistyle portfolio. Where a traditional separately managed account corresponded to a single investment strategy, an MDA offered investors access to a variety of management styles within the same account, thus allowing them to more easily diversify their portfolios. Within a few years, other firms would be offering their own versions of MDAs, and the multidiscipline approach quickly became the fastest-growing segment of the fast-growing managed accounts industry.

Technology companies serving financial services firms began appearing on the scene with sophisticated programs that helped expand the offerings of managed account solutions. In 1999, Placemark Investments of Dallas was formed to help managed account program sponsors deliver technology-driven products and services to advisors with managed account clients, and Boston-based Vestmark followed two years later with its Managed

Accounts Platform. In 2002, CheckFree Investment Services introduced its multistrategy portfolio functionality, which allowed the sponsor firm to offer clients single-account access to money managers both inside and outside the firm.

As the technology evolved, so did managed account solutions. In 2002, AdvisorPort introduced what is now recognized as the industry's first unified managed account (UMA), and other firms quickly followed suit. "The UMA is an open-architecture platform that can incorporate model portfolios, custom allocations, traditional and alternative investments, client-specific tax management, and other features into a single, consolidated custodial account. To enable these sophisticated features, UMAs employ high-tech overlay portfolio management systems to monitor each account and make adjustments as necessary," explains Lee Chertavian, chairman and CEO of Placemark, one of the industry's largest independent providers of overlay management services. "UMAs offer clients better diversification and therefore better risk management, and also allow them to combine different investments in a single account. Advisors benefit by being able to keep all of a client's investments in one integrated account, rather than having various pieces managed outside the account."

Where We Are Today

Increasing client demand for a wider array of investment products and services, coupled with advances in technology that automate processes once painstakingly performed by hand, have led to a dramatic shift in the way money is managed in the new millennium. As of mid-2007, managed account solutions (MAS) comprise a number of different programs, all of which have been defined by the MMI:

- *Traditional separately managed account (SMA) program*—a single account that corresponds to a single investment strategy. To hold multiple strategies, a client must open multiple accounts. These programs include all of the attributes of managed account solutions: a client profiling and assessment process; a single proposal system; fee-based pricing; investment research; rebalancing, tax management, and customization; and consolidated performance reporting.
- *Multidiscipline account (MDA) program*—a separate account program that houses multiple investment strategies in a single client account. The program allows a client to more easily diversify a portfolio via a single account.
- *Unified managed account (UMA) platform*—a single account that houses multiple investment products such as separately managed accounts, mutual funds, and exchange-traded funds (ETFs). The account leverages a platform that provides the ability to manage an investor's portfolio in a comprehensive fashion.

- *Mutual fund advisory program*—a mutual fund program that allows investors to allocate their assets across multiple mutual funds. The program includes capabilities such as client profiling, fee-based pricing, and rebalancing.
- *Exchange-traded fund advisory program*—a managed account program that utilizes ETFs. The program and its components are similar to those defined for the mutual fund advisory program.
- *Rep as portfolio manager program*—a fee-based, managed program that allows the financial services representative to act as the portfolio manager. Many of the attributes that define managed account solutions apply to this type of program.

These managed account solutions vary in popularity, but all of them are enjoying robust growth. As of the fourth quarter of 2006, MAS assets topped $1.2 trillion, and the MMI expects that figure to double by the year 2010. This growth reflects not only the growth of investments currently held in managed accounts, but also new account inflows. (See Figure 1.3.)

Industry experts expect that growth to continue, particularly as investors become educated about the benefits of unified managed accounts. Indeed, the separately managed account business is evolving into the unified managed account business, according to Leonard A. Reinhart, president of Lockwood Financial (named for managed account pioneer Jim Lockwood), an affiliate of Pershing LLC. "No other product offers so many options and can be customized to meet the needs of so many different types of investors," says Reinhart, whose firm manages more than $1 billion in UMAs and invests those assets in mutual funds, exchange-traded funds, hedge-type funds, real estate investment trusts (REITs), and commodities. "By offering

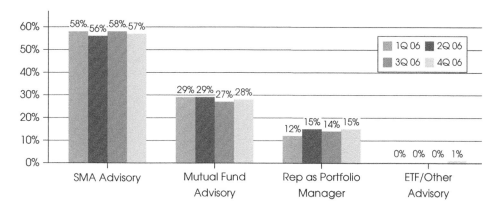

Figure 1.3   Market Share by Major Managed Account Solutions Component
Sources: Money Management Institute; Dover Financial Research.

clients a multi-asset-class, multi-investment platform, we are able to address a wide variety of investment needs with a single product. UMAs may very well represent the future of the managed money industry. In the very near term, I expect the UMA structure will evolve to include leveraged investment vehicles as well as guaranteed lifetime payments to provide retirement income solutions for the baby boomers."

Unified managed accounts have revolutionized the managed account industry in the past five years. In the next chapter, we examine what they are, how they work, and how they can help transform your practice.

The Revolution of Unified Managed Accounts

Unified managed accounts have evolved as investors sought greater coordination among their investments and more diversified portfolios.

"Unified managed accounts (UMAs) are changing the world of managed accounts!" proclaims Frank Campanale, president of Campanale Consulting Group. Many money management experts agree.

"Unified managed accounts, which implement investment strategies through a mix of separately managed accounts (SMAs), mutual funds, exchange-traded funds (ETFs), and alternative investments, are altering the managed account marketplace," says Charles Widger, chairman and CEO of Brinker Capital. UMAs combine the most significant benefits of SMAs, such as greater diversification and ease of administration (clients receive only one Form 1099), and mutual fund advisory accounts, such as lower minimums. "UMAs provide the best of both worlds."

This sentiment is echoed by Larry Sinsimer, managing director of managed accounts at Eaton Vance. "A UMA is more advantageous than a traditional separately managed account in that it allows greater diversification with a lower minimum investment," he says. "For example, a client with $400,000 to invest could hire four separate money managers, each requiring a minimum of $100,000. But in most instances, that would not be the proper allocation," because those four money managers would be investing independently of one another, greatly increasing the likelihood of overlap and thus overexposure to a particular company or sector.

"The right solution might be 50 percent to large-cap domestic, 20 percent international, 5 percent emerging markets, 10 percent market-neutral, and 15 percent in a state-specific municipal bond portfolio," Sinsimer says. "The domestic large-cap can be invested in an SMA or two, the muni in a bond fund, the market-neutral in a fund of funds, and the rest in either a mutual fund or an ETF—in other words, a unified managed account."

An extension of the multidiscipline account, which incorporates multiple investment *strategies* in a single account, a UMA is defined by the Money Management Institute (MMI) as a single account that supports the aggregated delivery of multiple (three or more) investment *products*. The UMA platform enables financial advisors to manage a client's portfolio in a comprehensive, product-neutral fashion. Since being introduced in 2002, UMAs have enjoyed phenomenal growth. As of fourth-quarter 2006, UMA assets accounted for 29 percent of total assets in multidiscipline and unified managed accounts. (See Figure 2.1.)

Investors like UMAs because they offer greater diversification and risk management, tax efficiency, and consolidated statements, among other benefits. Advisors like UMAs because, as Widger explains, "delegation of the investment management function and significantly reduced administrative responsibilities

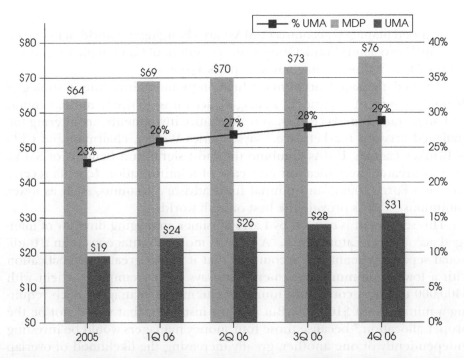

Figure 2.1   Percent of UMA Assets to Total MDA and UMA Assets ($ billions)
Sources: Money Management Institute; Dover Financial Research.

mean more time for client service and acquisition and offer the potential of better client retention. And, because there are fewer manual administrative responsibilities for advisors with a UMA offering, advisors experience greater ease of use than with separately managed accounts."

Len Reinhart, president of Lockwood Financial, says change is being spurred by the mass of baby boomers moving into retirement. Pension plans are nowhere near as common as they were a generation ago; most of today's retirees have to manage their own money. They need help—and options.

Chip Walker, managing director at Wachovia Securities, agrees. "The demographics of this business over the next seven to 10 years are incredible," he says. "So many people will be retiring and making some of the biggest financial decisions of their lives—and as you start to make those decisions, you realize it's not about beating the S&P 500 or the Russell 2000 or some other index. This is about benchmarking your life goals. It's vitally important that financial advisors have the tools they need to help their clients reach those goals."

A UMA is one of the most effective tools advisors can use. Campanale was president and CEO when Smith Barney's Consulting Group introduced one of the industry's first UMAs back in 2002, and he said the idea came from a desire to create a master account that could look at all of a client's holdings at once. "We were trying to come up with something that would simplify the separately managed account process," he explains. "Let's say you had a $1 million client and you wanted to put him in four separately managed accounts at $250,000 each. That necessitated opening four different accounts with four different account numbers generating four different monthly statements, and you had to profile the client four different times. It wasn't an efficient process."

In addition, Campanale says, many clients needed more diversification than SMAs alone could provide. "We recognized that in order to do the job right, we needed to use mutual funds or index funds for a portion of the portfolio. But you couldn't find a separate account manager to do that for small account sizes—and even if you could, the technology didn't exist to tie everything together."

Now it does.

Overlay Portfolio Management

Coordination of the various portfolio components in a UMA is achieved through the use of overlay portfolio management (OPM), and the degree of coordination ranges from rebalancing and cash flow management to tax-loss harvesting and wash-sale prevention. The OPM function can be handled internally, outsourced to a third-party provider, or overseen by the underlying investment manager. (See Figure 2.2.)

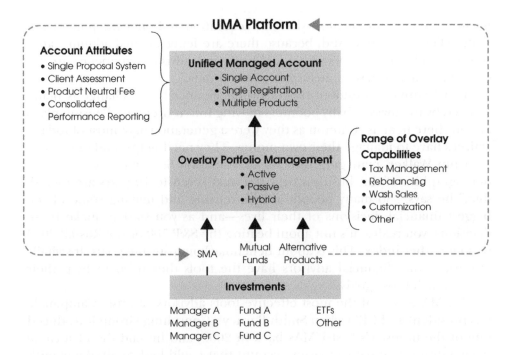

Figure 2.2   UMA Platform Schematic
Sources: Money Management Institute; Dover Financial Research.

There are three types of OPM:

1. *Active.* An overlay manager acts as investment manager and handles trade execution, tax management, customization, and rebalancing.
2. *Passive.* Each investment manager within the same UMA executes its own trades and retains control over its own investment model; the sponsor firm is responsible for basic functions such as asset class rebalancing but leaves most other functions to the participating managers.
3. *Hybrid.* As the name suggests, a hybrid approach combines elements of active and passive OPM. The sponsor firm executes trades related to individual accounts such as wash sales and short-term gain deferrals, and the underlying investment manager executes model-level trades that affect all accounts. Sponsor firms that use this approach must develop rules-based technology that will allow them to initiate and monitor account-level transactions.

Placemark Investments of Dallas was one of the first firms to provide overlay portfolio capabilities and, with more than $6 billion in assets under management, is one of the industry's largest independent providers of overlay management services. Chairman and CEO Lee Chertavian says the concept benefits both clients and advisors. "The advantages of UMAs center on coordination and customization," says Chertavian. "Combining different separate accounts, mutual funds, exchange-traded funds, and so on in a single custodial account and employing an active overlay manager improves coordination among the different investments. This makes it easier and more cost efficient for the sponsor firm and the advisor to manage portfolios while enhancing the client experience by consolidating all of their investments in a single performance report and custodial statement."

Chertavian notes that separately managed accounts, which hold individual securities, were originally touted for their tax efficiency on the grounds that investors weren't buying into embedded gains, as they were with mutual funds. "What little tax management took place centered on either client-generated tax-loss harvesting or the selection of low-turnover managers," he says. "By and large, firms tried to do as little as possible to customize individual portfolios because such efforts required costly manual intervention." OPM technology automates that process.

"Overlay management is a breakthrough that is transforming the managed account industry," says Chertavian. "Advisors have a platform to consolidate all of a client's assets in one place, rather than holding some in a separately managed account and some outside the account, with little or no active strategic correlation between the various components. Overlay managers can look across all the asset classes that a client has and make investment decisions tailored to that individual's unique money management needs. As clients accumulate wealth and seek greater diversification and risk management, I believe more and more advisors will recommend UMAs."

Unified managed accounts vary widely according to investment minimums, the number of investment managers, and the types of investment products. There is also a wide degree of difference in the flexibility offered to financial advisors wishing to customize their client accounts. Some firms provide prepackaged asset allocation models, while others allow advisors to fully customize their client portfolios. According to studies conducted by the MMI and Dover Financial Research, about half of UMA platforms require advisors to use asset allocation models developed by the sponsor firm, 30 percent allow the advisor flexibility within certain parameters, and the remaining 20 percent allow advisors to have complete control over the asset allocation model.

How can a customized investment solution come prepackaged? This is an issue the industry is working to resolve. "Anytime you are in a business that is trying to build customized investment solutions and build scale, that's an oxymoron," says Mark Pennington, a partner at Lord Abbett. "You are trying to accomplish two conflicting goals. One minute brokerage firms are saying, 'We are trying to build scale and trying to price it as a commodity,' and the next minute they're saying, 'We're giving you alpha-generating managers.' The challenge on the horizon is in trying to build both customized investment solutions and economies of scale."

Asset Allocation and Diversification

One of the key benefits of a UMA is that it enables a financial advisor to incorporate a wider range of investments in a consolidated account and thus more effectively diversify a client's holdings. "Diversification is more important than ever," asserts James Patrick, managing director of Allianz Global Investors. "With a portfolio focused on absolute return, avoiding the downdraft is more important than catching the updraft."

That's right, says Wachovia's Chip Walker. "It's not just about creating alpha in a portfolio," he asserts. "It's about risk control—avoiding the potholes while getting the client from point A to point B."

There are plenty of potholes to avoid. Based on the experience of advisors who deal with individual investors, the most compelling reason for portfolio diversification is human nature: We seem to instinctively chase performance and overly concentrate our holdings in particular investments or asset classes. Institutional investors, in contrast, do better. (See Figure 2.3.) They're only human, too, but institutional investors have several inherent (albeit subtle) advantages over individuals. First, as we mentioned in the previous chapter, pension funds are required as fiduciary investors governed by the Employee Retirement Income Security Act (ERISA) to have written guidelines in place to govern investments. By contrast, the 2007 Phoenix Wealth Survey found that only about a third of affluent households (defined

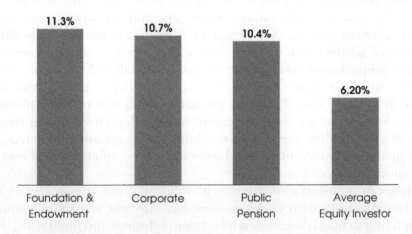

Figure 2.3   Follow the Leaders: Ten-Year Average Annual Returns for Institutions versus Individual Investors

Sources: Mercer Investment Consulting (figures shown are median rank of funds in universe); "Average Equity Investor: Quantitative Analysis of Investor Behavior" Report, 2005 Update, Dalbar, Inc. As of 12/31/04.

as having net worth in excess of $1 million, exclusive of debt and primary residence) have a written investment or financial plan.

Legendary investor Warren Buffett, chairman of Berkshire Hathaway, may have summed up the individual investor's problem best in his quip, "Investing is simple, but it's not easy." By that he meant that diversification and long-term time horizons—simple concepts both—drive returns, but human emotion weakens and heightens the pressures presented by falling security prices and other disturbing macro issues. A long-term investment strategy and truly diversified account can help override those understandable human weaknesses.

What does true diversification look like? Consider the allocation to domestic equity in all three pie charts in Figure 2.4. Public pension funds had a 45 percent exposure to domestic equity, while corporate pension funds allocated 38 percent to the class, and endowments/foundations were at 50 percent. Two of the three institutional approaches allocated less than the 50 percent allocation recommended by many financial advisors based on guidance from most large brokerage firms' research departments.

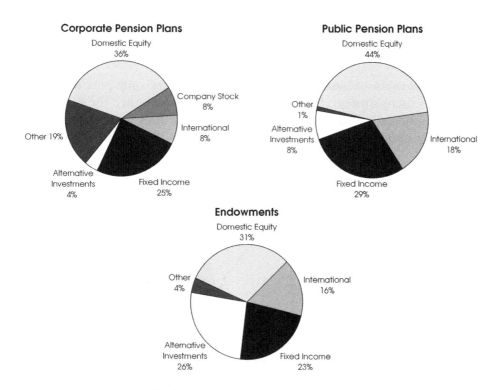

What does your portfolio look like?

Figure 2.4 Institutional Asset Allocation

Source: 2007 Money Market Directory of Pension Funds and Their Investment Managers. Copyright 2007.

In addition to being less dominated by domestic equities, institutional portfolios are more exposed to international equities and alternative investments than individual portfolios. (See Figure 2.5.) At Harvard and Yale, in fact, alternatives comprise nearly half the endowments' holdings. Alternative investments have grown to become mainstream components of a fully diversified institutional solution. Slightly modified, they can be important additions to individual investor portfolios as well.

Surveys have shown that most institutional investors have a commitment of 8 to 14 percent of their portfolios in foreign stocks, but only 11 percent of the clients of a major national brokerage firm had *any* foreign equities in their accounts. If the ownership of international stocks is any guide, individuals have some catching up to do if they want to follow the path forged by institutional investors.

What is the benefit of having exposure to multiple asset classes, including equities, fixed income, real estate investment trusts (REITs), international stocks, and various alternative investments? Peace of mind. Modern portfolio theory posits that exposure to multiple asset classes whose correlations are less than perfect or even negative should in theory increase the return of a portfolio for a given level of risk or maintain the expected return level of a portfolio with less risk.

Here are four strategies for constructing a more diversified portfolio:

1. *Use alternative investments.* Stocks and bonds are only part of a total investment strategy. Other types of assets can enhance the long-term risk-adjusted return of a portfolio because they tend to perform at different times. For example, more than 10 percent of Harvard

What's your international allocation?

Figure 2.5   Average 401(k) Investor versus Institutional Investors in International Equities
Sources: Greenwich Associates, "Asset Allocation Strategies Target Incremental Alpha," February 2005; Profit Sharing/401(k) Council of America, as cited in "Case for International Investing," MFS, August 2004.

University's successful endowment fund has been invested in real estate, much of it acquired while the stock market was going down. Specific strategies that have use as diversifiers include hedge funds, natural resources like gold and timber, as well as specialized areas of the markets, such as global utility stocks; we discuss these in greater detail in Chapter 4.

2. *Increase international exposure.* There is considerable potential in international stocks, but few long-term individual investors have allocated sufficient funds to this asset class. By comparison, institutional investors have much higher participation in foreign markets.

   The growth of the global economy has fueled rising stock prices around the world. Despite the tremendous bull market in U.S. stocks, during the 20-year period ending December 31, 2004, U.S. equity markets lagged those of 13 other established countries, including the United Kingdom, Germany, France, and Italy. (See Figure 2.6.)

3. *Buy growth stocks.* Owning multiple investment styles, most commonly those of growth or value, is an important aspect of diversification. Like other asset classes, investment manager styles rotate over time, moving in and out of favor. Growth investing produced terrific gains in the years 1994–1999, but has underperformed value since that time. Is growth due for a rebound?

4. *Upgrade portfolio quality.* Another measure of investment value is quality. Some companies are more successful than others, resulting in stronger growth and earnings over time. These companies are generally accorded greater value over the long term.

   In the short run, however, lesser-quality companies can attract the attention of aggressive speculators and outperform better-quality firms. Opportunities for investing in quality companies follow periods

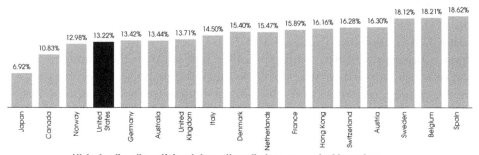

Historically, diversifying internationally has rewarded investors.

Average annual returns for 20 years ended 12/31/04. Returns are based on the countries' respective Morgan Stanley Capital International (MSCI) indexes that had a 20-year record. Market capitalization is the total dollar value of a company's outstanding shares.

Figure 2.6   Global Markets Return
Sources: International Stock Investing MLIM; ZephyrStyle ADVISOR; Phoenix Investment Partners.

when high quality has underperformed. We are currently at the lowest point in the relative performance of high-quality securities versus low-quality stocks, and high-quality investing has been out of favor for three years. Is quality investing due for a comeback? There are early signs of improved performance in the quality sector.

Because UMAs allow multiple strategies and multiple products to be included in a single account, financial advisors have greater flexibility than ever in the choice of the products they use for meeting clients' investment needs. You don't have to discriminate among separately managed accounts, mutual fund managed accounts, and mutual fund marketplaces, because as long as you obtain the investment solution for your client, the methodology or products are irrelevant.

John McCormack, senior vice president/investment consultant at Phoenix Investment Partners, recommends using separately managed accounts in conjunction with mutual funds if it makes sense for the client. "Managed money comes in many different flavors," he says. "For the masses, the definition of professional management is mutual funds. For those with high net worth, it's separately managed accounts. In some instances, the best customization is both. Let's say a client has $300,000 to invest. He or she might consider $100,000 in a large-cap growth SMA, $100,000 in a large-cap value SMA, and the rest allocated among four or five funds with other styles to ensure diversification. It's not all or none and it's not either-or. An effective solution can really be a blend of products."

Once the advisor determines the appropriate mix of products for the client, the next step is to find the right investment manager.

Manager Selection

The MMI/Dover research found that about half of the firms currently sponsoring UMAs allow the financial advisor to select the investment manager (from a preapproved list), while the other half controls the manager selection or relies on third-party research to make the manager determination.

Evaluating, selecting, and monitoring managers involves sound judgment and significant due diligence. The search is complicated and technical, as risk patterns, return history, and turnover rates need to be analyzed to best match a client's performance, tax, and long-term financial plans. Most consulting firms do the research on managers and, when approved, include them on an internal list to help you decide which managers might be best suited for your clients.

"Financial advisors need to make sure the asset managers they choose are as transparent as possible," says Chip Walker. "Money management firms want to make sure they're not giving away their magic elixir, but access to information is key. You need to understand what is unique about that money manager and how that manager can help investors meet their life goals. Financial advisors are the conduits of information, so they must make sure they are full and correct stewards of the story."

Many advisors and high-end consultants prefer to do their own manager search and selection. Even if you don't, it still is important to understand the process so you can relate it to your clients when explaining why you offer certain managers.

Donald B. Trone, president of the Pittsburgh-based Foundation for Fiduciary Studies and co-author of *Procedural Prudence* and *The Management of Investment Decisions*, emphasizes that advisors need tools and information to assess their manager choices. "Objective and quantifiable criteria should be used," he says. He recommends asking five critical questions of any manager you are considering for your clients:

1. *What are your performance figures?* If a manager shows you returns for his or her retail managed accounts, ask for the performance numbers for the institutional managed accounts. Get both—and if the numbers are different, ask why.

   Performance reports should comply with the Level II standards set by the CFA Institute (formerly the Association for Investment Management and Research) and should reflect the following:
   - Time- and asset-weighted returns.
   - Actual performance (no model portfolios, unless specifically identified).
   - Reported performance—gross and net of fees.
   - Quarterly and annual results as well as cumulative results for three, five, and ten years.
   - Risk-adjusted returns.
   - Audits by an independent third party, such as an accounting or investment consulting firm.

2. *Which portfolio manager will handle my accounts?* For any track record you're shown, ask who created the record. Is it the same person or team who will be handling your clients' accounts? In many cases, one team handles retail clients, while another handles institutional clients.

3. *Will my clients' trades be included with those of the manager's institutional clients?* Ask how the manager allocates offerings (IPOs) of stocks and/or bonds among clients. Are there limits in the investment process to percentage ownership of a company's shares?

4. *When will my clients be fully invested?* Find out how long it will take for the money manager to fully invest your clients' funds into the market. Determine whether this strategy meets your clients' expectations.

5. *What tax-advantaged strategies are used?* Many managers say they offer tax-sensitive trading strategies, but you need to ask for specifics. Tax-advantaged strategies may include purchase of low-dividend-paying

stocks, year-end harvesting of losses, low portfolio turnover, and selling highest-basis shares first. Remember, of course, that the best after-tax returns can begin with the best pretax returns!

Finally, Trone says, make sure that any manager selection is done within the guidelines of the Employee Retirement Income Security Act (ERISA):

- All investment decisions must be made by prudent experts, such as registered investment advisors.
- A duc-diligence procedure is followed when selecting money managers.
- General investment direction is provided to money managers.
- Money managers must acknowledge their fiduciary status in writing or by signing a copy of the investment policy statement.
- The managers' activities must be monitored.

It's important to review costs, too, since expenses can have a significant impact on portfolio returns. This is a key fiduciary responsibility and something you need to be aware of. The four categories of costs are:

1. Money manager fees.
2. Trading costs.
3. Custodial charges.
4. Consulting and administrative costs.

Use your clients' investment policy statements as guides to find the money managers to implement the strategy you have in mind for them. Trone says that many times advisors doing their own searches put too much emphasis on manager selection and not enough on the overall investment structure.

Let's take a look at how a few industry analysts evaluate and choose managers for their approved lists. You'll see a number of similarities in the due-diligence process and have a better understanding of the intensive work the analysts perform.

"First, we use industry databases to evaluate managers," says an analyst at a leading brokerage firm. "For separately managed accounts we look at the manager's track record; for large-cap growth or large-cap value, we prefer five years' performance. For small-cap or other specialty, we'll look at fewer than five years, but the managers must have great numbers.

"Next, we have a preliminary meeting with the managers. Our key investment officers assess the managers' investment processes. We talk one-on-one with the portfolio managers, the management team, and the research people. We have a concise, but thorough, list of questions.

"When we monitor the managers, the same individuals who handle the up-front analysis also do the monitoring. This creates consistency in our process," this analyst explains. "We conduct performance-attribution analysis to communicate how the managers are doing and look for a match between what we expected and what actually transpired. For example, if a manager espoused a research-intensive, bottom-up approach to stock selection and we determined that the manager was making sector bets, that would be an area of concern."

Attributes this firm reviews when evaluating managers for its preferred list include:

- Block trade reports for the portfolios.
- Samples of individual accounts.
- Quarterly analysis regime for performance attribution (this can be done on a day-to-day basis, too).

In addition, the analyst says, "we visit with the managers at least once a year in their offices, so we can touch base with all of the key players, and once in our offices, to give the entire research group the ability to evaluate the investment manager."

Managers have to undergo complete scrutiny by large numbers of highly trained individuals at the sponsoring firms. The process is similar in most due-diligence cases for most firms. For example, one wirehouse has a committee of 25 specialists to pay attention to the smallest details.

"If we have an interest in a particular manager," says the wirehouse's managing director, "the first step is to have them send in some basic information on the firm in preparation for a formal presentation to the research committee. Our committee will look at such things as the size of the manager's firm, its age, number of portfolio managers and staff, performance—the customary items. Next, the manager meets members of the due-diligence committee. This is an extremely rigorous process that focuses on the infrastructure of the firm." The group then follows up with the manager in his or her office to substantiate the information they have received.

The firm's ongoing review of managers is a complex process. The monthly analysis includes reviewing the performance of all accounts; assessing dispersion, asset allocation, investment policy breaks, and performance of securities; and conducting a peer review of each asset class. "The quarterly reviews include the same process, but we add a questionnaire on organizational structure, a review of any changes in the portfolio team, a review of the model portfolio, and a review of our accounts versus the manager composite," the managing director says.

A yearly meeting is held in the manager's office, where the due-diligence team reviews Form ADV and then has a roundup of all managers from a sector and asset allocation perspective. They also completely revisit the investment process at the meeting.

What happens when the firm fires a manager? "The termination of managers is not common, but it does happen," says the managing director. "We don't like to terminate a manager just because his or her asset class is out of favor. What may cause us to let a manager go is a combination of the following items: poor performance relative to the peer group, style drift, process changes, cap creep, and capacity issues. Unfortunately, some financial advisors are too fast in asking us to fire a manager because they just got a beating from a big client. That's a really bad idea. What we may be looking at is just a short-term losing record, so we have to be careful before we consider pulling the plug."

Advisor Tip

Slow to Hire, Slow to Fire

Keats, a successful advisor, agrees with the managing director of the brokerage firm on the measures to consider before letting a manager out of the stable. "You fire managers when there is a breakdown in the people and the process," he says. "Did key people leave? Was there a sudden shift in staff? You can't fire on performance reasons alone. One big mistake that a financial consultant can make is a quick decision on hiring and firing managers. Be patient and evaluate before you act. Remember, the client is the least talented in this process, and the financial consultant is only the second most talented. The portfolio manager is the top dog."

Industry data indicate that more than 30 percent of all accounts offered by managed account sponsor firms have only one manager. One wirehouse sponsor reports that more than 50 percent of its clients in managed account programs have only one advisor. That is simply not a good idea. Here is a good way to explain the risk to your client: "You may believe you're diversified, but you're not. We need to make sure you recognize the problems you may have from being too concentrated with a single manager."

When explaining the benefits of diversification to clients, it helps to become familiar with industry standards for calculating risk, return, and money manager performance. While you may not do this yourself, you need to understand the process so you can converse with your clients. That's your value.

Don Berryman, formerly national sales director for Phoenix Investment Partners' Private Client Group and a certified investment management analyst, offers this assessment (and a few lively analogies) of the most common measures of performance evaluation:

Return on Investment

Return on investment (ROI) measurement has two aspects, time-weighted measurement and dollar-weighted measurement. Time-weighted measurement is important in measuring manager effectiveness and disregards the effect of the timing of cash contributions or withdrawals from the portfolio. Time-weighted measurement takes into consideration the time value of money over an accumulation, or specified, period.

Dollar-weighted measurement focuses more on the client's goals. It uses simple dollars, in and out, without consideration for the time value of money. The timing of cash flows, in or out, does make a difference in dollar-weighted measurement.

Standard Deviation and a San Diego Snowstorm

Simply put, standard deviation is the measurement of how far the price of a market or security or portfolio is expected to deviate from normal.

$$\sigma = \sqrt{\sigma^2} = \sqrt{\frac{\sum_{i=1}^{n}(x_i - \bar{x})^2}{n}}$$

σ = Standard deviation
Σ = Summation graphic
x_i = Sample return
$\bar{x}$ = Sample average return
n = Number of observations

The standard bell curve shows the relationship of this measurement to the normal expected range of the entity. (See Figure 2.7.) Statistically, approximately 66 percent of all events are within one standard deviation

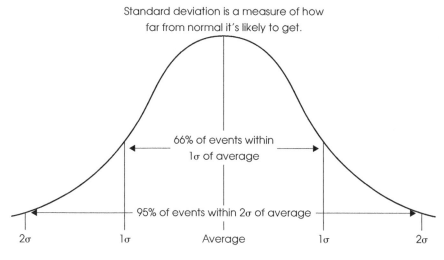

Figure 2.7   Standard Deviation

of average. Approximately 95 percent of all events are within two standard deviations of average.

For example, let's compare the temperatures in Dallas and San Diego. Assume the average temperature for both cities is 65 degrees, but the standard deviation in Dallas is 20 degrees and the standard deviation in San Diego is 10 degrees. My Mom can't tolerate temperatures above 100 degrees or below 40 degrees. Some cities experience extremes—snow in the winter and 100-degree heat in the summer—so this parameter would exclude Phoenix and Chicago, say, but include both Dallas and San Diego. Which city would Mom prefer? Using our new knowledge of standard deviation, we might determine that:

- There is a 66 percent chance of temperatures staying between 45 and 85 degrees in Dallas (average of 65 degrees plus or minus 20 degrees standard deviation).
- There is a 66 percent chance of temperatures staying between 55 and 75 degrees in San Diego (average of 65 degrees plus or minus 10 degrees standard deviation).
- There is a 95 percent chance of temperatures staying between 45 and 85 degrees in San Diego.
- There is a 95 percent chance of temperatures staying between 25 and 105 degrees in Dallas.

So, where do we want to send Mom? Figure 2.8 illustrates why Mom would be happier in San Diego.

Beta and Alpha and a Sailboat Race

Beta is a measurement of a portfolio's (or security's) volatility relative to a benchmark, such as the S&P 500 index, and it tells you how the portfolio is expected to perform given the movements in that benchmark. A beta of 1.0 means the portfolio should have a return similar to that of the benchmark. If the beta is greater than 1.0, expect more volatility; if it's less than 1.0, expect less.

For example, if the beta on your client's portfolio is 1.2 and the benchmark gains 10 percent, the portfolio should rise about 12 percent (1.2 × 10 percent). If the index falls 8 percent, your client will probably lose about 9.6 percent (1.2 × –8 percent). A beta that's higher than the benchmark means more volatility in both directions.

Think of two portfolios as sailboats. Given the same wind conditions (the market), the boat with the bigger sail (beta) will move the most.

Knowing the beta will help you evaluate a portfolio's performance, but there is more to it, especially when returns deviate from the expected beta

San Diego Temperatures

- Average temperature is 65°.
- Standard deviation (σ) in San Diego is 10°.
- Mom can't stand it above 100° or below 40°.

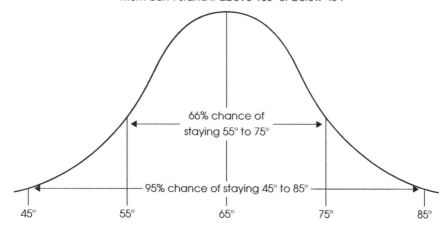

Dallas Temperatures

- Average temperature is 65°.
- Standard deviation (σ) in Dallas is 20°.
- Mom can't stand it above 100° or below 40°.

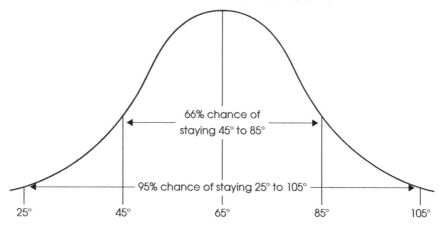

Figure 2.8   San Diego and Dallas Temperature Charts

values. This is where alpha comes in. Alpha is the difference between the return expected, given the beta, and the portfolio's actual return.

Alpha can be positive or negative. For example, assume the benchmark returned 12 percent and the beta on your client's portfolio is 1.1. The expected return of the portfolio is 13.2 percent (12 × 1.1).

Let's take the two scenarios and calculate the alpha.

Actual Return	Expected Return	Alpha
15.0%	13.2%	1.8 (15.0 − 13.2 = 1.8)
9.5%	13.2%	−3.7 (9.5 − 13.2 = −3.7)

So, what does the alpha tell you? It's the value added (or value sub-tracted!) by the manager. In the first scenario, the manager's actual return exceeded the expected return by almost 2 percent. In the second case, the portfolio underperformed by 3.7 percent.

R-Squared—Ice Cream and Shoes

The relevance of all this depends on how well the data fit the assumption and how closely the portfolio imitates the index; the quality of the fit is known as R-squared.

Consider a scenario in which you are trying to conduct business at the beach. The temperature at the beach will have an effect on ice cream sales, but it probably will not have an effect on shoe sales. Put another way, the predictability of ice cream sales in relation to temperature is high, while the predictability of shoe sales is low. (See Figure 2.9.) That, in essence, is R-squared, which quantifies how closely the movement of a portfolio's return relates to its benchmark.

R-squared is a measure of correlation. Over time, if the returns of a port-folio and benchmark behave in a similar manner, they are positively corre-lated. If they move in opposite directions, they are negatively correlated.

Risk-Adjusted Return

The risk-adjusted return of a portfolio is the measure of how much an investment returned in relation to the amount of risk it took. It compares a high-risk, potentially high-return investment with a low-risk, lower-return investment. Three formulas allow us to compare disparate portfolios on an apples-to-apples basis:

1. The Sharpe ratio, named after Dr. William Sharpe, adjusts the return of the portfolio based on the amount of risk taken to achieve it. It indicates how much excess return was achieved per unit of total risk, as measured by standard deviation.
2. The Sortino ratio, named after Dr. Frank Sortino, measures return earned per unit of downside risk.
3. The Treynor ratio, named after Jack Treynor, measures return earned per unit of beta, or market risk.

Formulas for these ratios can be found in Appendix B.

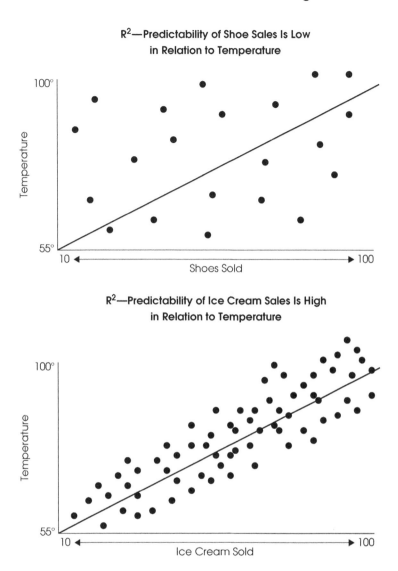

Figure 2.9   Predictability of Shoe Sales and Ice Cream Sales in Relation to Temperature

A risk/return graph is a useful tool to illustrate the performance of a portfolio and its risk level as measured by standard deviation. Also known as a scattergram, the graph is divided into four quadrants, the best being the northwest, which reflects returns that exceed the benchmark and have less risk. (See Figure 2.10.)

These ratios, as well as the other measures we've discussed, are useful in evaluating portfolio performance. While no single risk/return statistic is a perfect performance measurement tool, together they offer a relatively clear picture of how well a portfolio performed. Figure 2.11 compares a hypothetical portfolio and its characteristics to the S&P 500 index.

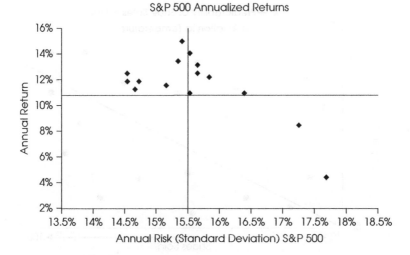

Figure 2.10   Risk/Return Scattergram

Hypothetical Equity Portfolio over Five Years					
	Standard			Alpha (Risk-	Deviation
Annualized Return	Deviation (Total Risk)	Beta (Market Risk)	R-Squared (Diversification)	Adjusted Return)	("Bad" Risk)
Portfolio 10%	10.8%	0.9	96.8%	1.6%	6.5%
S&P 500 Index 8.7%	11.6%	1.0	100.0%	0.0	7.0%

Portfolio Sharpe Ratio: 0.5%; Sortino Ratio: 0.8%; Treynor Ratio: 5.5%

Conclusions

- The portfolio earned 1.3% more return than the market index.
- The portfolio took less total risk than the index to achieve that return (10.8% vs. 11.6% standard deviation).
- The portfolio took only 90% of the market risk represented by the index (0.9 vs. 1.0 beta).
- The portfolio was well diversified, or highly correlated to the market (96.8% R-squared.)
- The portfolio earned 1.6% more return (alpha) than expected, based on its market risk.
- On a risk-adjusted basis, the portfolio earned 0.5% (Sharpe ratio) for every unit of total risk taken, 0.8% (Sortino ratio) for every unit of downside risk, and 5.5% (Treynor ratio) for every unit of market risk taken.

Figure 2.11   Performance and Risk Analysis

Note: Numbers taken from Mobius M-Search database.

Source: "Performance Measurement and Evaluation," © 2001 Investment Management Consultants Association.

The process of monitoring and supervising the portfolio goes beyond accounting for returns. "You also have to determine whether the investment policy statement is meeting its goals," says Trone. "Effective monitoring gives the investor sufficient information to evaluate the program's strengths and weaknesses and keeps the program on track."

And that's the real value of providing managed account solutions. "It's all about the client being able to have a better investment experience," says Lord Abbett's Pennington. "Investors are looking for individualized solutions, rather than a one-size-fits-all approach, to enable them to reach their goals."

Eaton Vance's Sinsimer agrees. "The UMA is the best choice for any client looking for a total solution that coordinates their assets in a goal-oriented manner," he says. "The UMA may also help those advisors who have only a portion of their clients' assets capture the balance based on a fully coordinated solution."

With so many benefits for both clients and advisors, it's not surprising that UMAs are among the fastest-growing managed account solutions. In the next chapter we look at another fast-growing managed account solution, the mutual fund advisory account. Not long ago these accounts, more frequently referred to as mutual fund wraps, appeared to be headed toward extinction. Today, they're on their way to becoming more popular than ever.

CHAPTER

3

Mutual Fund Advisory Accounts

Financial advisors can leverage the potential of multiple mutual funds in a single client account by using a mutual fund advisory account.

If you thought mutual fund wrap accounts were a thing of the past, think again. "Wrap accounts are enjoying a second life," says Mark Fetting, president of Legg Mason Funds. "They are alive and well."

Indeed they are. According to studies conducted by the Money Management Institute and Dover Financial Research, roughly 30 percent of managed account assets are in mutual fund advisory accounts—a new name for an established product—and these accounts are growing at a rate that is roughly 50 percent faster than that of separately managed accounts (SMAs). (See Figure 3.1.)

"In the last couple of years there has been a resurgence of interest in mutual fund wrap programs," says Fetting. "There has been, and there will continue to be, a lot of growth. People are starting to realize that separately managed accounts are not the only answer. Clients can get exposure to the same asset classes in other ways. For example, it's easier to include a top-ranked international fund in a wrap program than to try to set up the same allocation through a separately managed account."

James Patrick, managing director at Allianz Global Investors, supports that assessment. "In the old days, separately managed accounts were all the rage, and inevitably were well adopted in the wirehouses," says Patrick. "They were sold against mutual funds, but there are some asset classes—emerging market bond funds being one example—that are impossible to include in an SMA."

There's another reason why mutual fund advisory accounts are again on the rise. "It's the advice component," says James Tracy, executive vice president

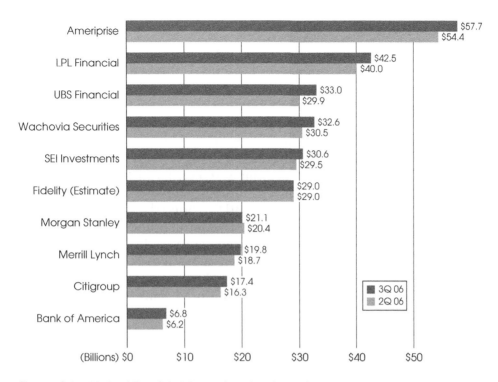

Figure 3.1   Mutual Fund Advisory Assets—Top 10 Firms
Sources: Money Management Institute; Dover Financial Research.

at Smith Barney Consulting Group. "Mutual fund advisory accounts have experienced phenomenal growth in the past three years or so, and this tremendous growth is primarily because most programs include some embedded asset allocation advice. Advisors can develop a consolidated strategy for their clients utilizing mutual funds, and investors know that proper asset allocation produces better results."

A study conducted by the Investment Company Institute (ICI), a Washington-based research organization, quantifies Tracy's view. A report titled "Why Do Mutual Fund Investors Use Professional Financial Advisors?" found that "most shareholders with ongoing advisory relationships cite the need for guidance in understanding their total financial picture and allocating their assets across a range of investments," and 80 percent of shareholders who delegate investment decision making to their advisors cite asset allocation as their top priority. "Fund investors who choose to work with advisors indicate that the relationship improves their chances of growing their money and gives them peace of mind about their investments," the ICI report noted.

"The advice game has been won," explains Mark Pennington, partner at Lord Abbett. "There are still plenty of do-it-yourselfers out there, but if you are looking for a customized investment solution, the advice component is incredibly important—and investors know it."

What's Changed . . . and Why

Ten years ago, when SMAs were marketed as the platform of choice for high-net-worth investors, there were far fewer U.S.-based mutual funds in existence than there are today—about 3,000 fewer, according to the ICI, and that figure excludes funds of funds and exchange-traded funds. Investors have more choices than ever, but to many that's a mixed blessing. While there are more offerings, the sheer number of choices can be overwhelming. Investors need help navigating this very crowded marketplace.

Mutual funds were the first investment vehicle for many baby boomers, who were introduced to the concept through employer-sponsored retirement plans. Those plans, primarily the 401(k), offered a limited number of investment selections to investors, many of whom allocated their investments heavily toward equity growth stocks to accumulate wealth. They are comfortable with mutual funds. As these boomers move into retirement, they're confronted with three challenges: shifting their focus away from growth, shifting their assets away from employer-sponsored plans, and ensuring that they don't run out of money.

"The client is changing," says Tracy. "The boomer cycle rotation is already taking effect. Clients today are less focused on performance and more focused on the ultimate goal: ensuring they have significant assets to maintain a comfortable retirement."

That's where you, the financial advisor, come in. "With the help of their advisors, clients are taking a longer-term view of what they want to accomplish and are less concerned with the performance of a single fund," Tracy adds. "They want to develop a cohesive and complementary strategy, and they look to advisors to help them do that."

The mutual fund advisory account will be the managed account solution of choice for some of your clients. Let's take a look at how they work. There are two types:

1. *Discretionary.* After reviewing the client's financial objectives, the advisor chooses the appropriate asset allocation model from among the offerings of the program sponsor. As with a multidiscipline account, a mutual fund advisory account includes a range of investment strategies to ensure sufficient diversification; professional money management; ongoing due diligence; and regular, automatic rebalancing to maintain the original allocation. The sponsor may adjust its asset allocation model when it deems changes are necessary and can add or remove funds without authorization from the investor.

2. *Nondiscretionary.* This account is similar in structure and approach to the discretionary account, with the primary difference being that investors must approve any changes to the portfolio, including rebalancing.

At one time, mutual fund advisory accounts were most sought after by investors who wanted professional money management but couldn't meet SMA minimums. That's not true anymore. "Multimillionaires are just as interested in mutual fund advisory accounts as in SMAs," says Tracy. "And because of lower minimums, SMAs are available to larger numbers of investors than they were in the past."

And even larger numbers in the future. "Billions of dollars are being rolled over from 401(k)s every year," says Michael Evans of Financial Research Corp. "Many of these rollover opportunities will be ideal candidates for mutual fund advisory programs—and since it is qualified money, the tax implications are typically going to be far less complicated, which may make the mutual fund the ideal candidate."

Key Benefits

Like all managed account solutions, mutual fund advisory accounts offer many benefits to clients. Here are the main ones:

- *Lower minimum investments.* While it's true that mutual fund advisory accounts can serve the needs of a wide range of investors at all asset levels, they still tend to have lower account minimums than separately managed accounts; the average is $25,000 versus $100,000 for an SMA.
- *Fee-based approach.* Clients pay a single fee based on assets under management, with no commissions on trading.
- *Diversification.* Mutual fund advisory accounts provide clients with diversified portfolios and can include some asset classes that can't be included in an SMA (or whose inclusion in an SMA would be at a level inappropriate to the client's needs).
- *Professional money management.* Investors have access to top-performing fund managers.
- *Consolidated reporting.* Whether the account is discretionary or nondiscretionary, clients receive a single statement showing all of their holdings, making it easier to track the progress of their portfolios.
- *Multiple layers of professional oversight.* With a mutual fund advisory account, the fund managers are responsible for the performance of their funds, program sponsors are responsible for the performance of their fund managers, and financial advisors are responsible for the performance of the account in relation to the client's investment objectives. Clients get three levels of oversight for the price of one asset-based fee.

"With a mutual fund advisory account, investors receive significant diversification but far fewer administrative burdens and much less paperwork," says Brinker Capital's Charles Widger, adding that these accounts are probably the easiest of the three managed account offerings for a sponsor to deliver, with SMAs being the most burdensome and unified managed accounts (UMAs) being somewhere in the middle. "However, with mutual fund advisory accounts there are fewer opportunities for personalization and tax management."

There are other drawbacks as well. "A lot of great money managers don't want to get into the wrap account business because they feel too many clients expect them to chase the hot dot," says Chip Walker, managing director at Wachovia Securities. "They want long-term investors, because it's easier to run the money when you don't have funds flowing in and out."

That's what Legg Mason wants, too. "We emphasize the increasing importance of saving and investing for retirement, and plans should be put in place around that goal," says Fetting. "It's less of a benchmark-driven strategy than determining how far the client is along in meeting his or her goals. Clients are not unmindful of performance—that's how you get where you want to be—but there is more of an appreciation of long-term investing."

Perhaps the biggest drawback to mutual fund advisory accounts is the fact that clients buy into the embedded gains of shareholders who got there before them; they own shares of the fund, not the underlying securities, and so have very few opportunities for effective tax management. If a fund manager is forced to sell underlying securities because of mass redemptions, clients could be punished with a capital gains tax bill for sticking with their investment strategy when others fled. However, advisors can minimize this risk by carefully selecting mutual fund managers.

The ICI found that about 80 percent of investors who own mutual funds outside of a retirement plan purchased those funds through a financial advisor. Eighty percent! And while people of all ages and incomes turn to advisors for mutual fund selection and management, the ICI identifies four groups more likely to work with advisors.

1. Investors with household assets of $250,000 or more.
2. Female investors who are in charge of household investment decision making.
3. Older investors.
4. Investors who do not go online for investment information.

How can an advisor determine which managed account solution is right for which client? Generally speaking, by the amount of his or her assets. "With assets of $100,000 to $500,000, a mutual fund advisory account is usually best," says Widger. "When investor assets are between $500,000 and $1.5 million, a UMA should be given serious consideration. When assets exceed $1.5 million, SMAs begin to make sense, although UMAs can be attractive up to $5 million because of diversification and ease of administration."

While the three approaches are very different, they all have one thing in common: helping clients achieve their financial goals. "Because of changes in the marketplace, SMAs, mutual funds, exchange-traded funds, and alternative investments are all becoming more readily available at every asset level," says Tracy. "What was once thought of as a solution for high-net-worth investors only is now available to the mass population of investors. If you wanted to have a diversified portfolio, you needed to have a significant amount of assets to achieve that goal. That's not the case anymore. You have the ability to highly diversify at much lower minimums than in the past."

Greater diversification of client portfolios can be achieved through the use of alternative investments. In the next chapter we look at some of the most popular types of alternative investments, including exchange-traded funds, real estate investment trusts, and hedge funds, and explain how they work and why each can be a meaningful addition to the managed account solutions you provide to clients.

The Debate over Small Accounts

Nearly every securities firm has implored its advisors to seek larger accounts. The Securities Industry and Financial Markets Association reports that the average brokerage book contains 538 accounts, and the average account value is $107,000. Consider the 80/20 rule, and it's not inconceivable that most accounts are much smaller than $100,000.

However, many desirable clients lurk in these smaller accounts, and it's safe to assume that a good number of them have spread their assets across multiple relationships and may be in search of a single advisory home. Your goal should be to develop strategies that encourage them to consolidate their assets and, in the process, bump off at least some of your competitors. So what can you offer?

- Asset allocation funds, especially those with automatic rebalancing.
- Multidiscipline accounts, which offer several investment strategies within a single client account. Many have lower account minimums and better diversification than SMAs, and also typically offer rebalancing.
- Mutual fund advisory accounts, which offer multiple funds across a variety of asset classes and manager styles with a single client account. These, too, have lower account minimums and better diversification, and discretionary accounts include automatic rebalancing. Plus, performance reporting and tax-lot record keeping are time-saving client service bonuses.

One advisor we know has begun to use a fund of funds for his accounts under $250,000. "I get the diversification the clients need without the headaches of too many statements and too much fund oversight," he says, "and rebalancing is automatic, which is helpful because even the best clients balk at rebalancing in the heat of the moment." This advisor's team has raised more than $40 million with this approach and is actively prospecting smaller accounts—with very limited competition.

Alternative Investments

Alternative investments offer greater diversification and risk management than ever before, and many clients are asking that alternatives be included in their portfolios.

Chances are, if your clients haven't already asked about alternative investments, they will. Alternative investments are all the rage, even among investors who don't know what they are. "People are talking about alternative investments now the way they were talking about dot-coms in the 1990s, and the way they were talking about separately managed accounts before that," says one wirehouse manager we know. "It's the cocktail party phenomenon all over again. One guy mentions that his advisor put him in alternative investments, and now the other guy feels he should be in alternative investments, too. No one wants to feel like they're missing out on the next big thing."

Make no mistake: Alternative investments *are* the next big thing for affluent clients.

Unlike dot-coms or even separately managed accounts, however, alternative investments cover such a wide range of options that clients can't simply be "put" into alternative investments; much consideration must be given as to the type of alternative investment and what function it will play in the portfolio.

So, what are alternative investments? An alternative investment can be described as any asset purchased with an eye toward appreciation, diversification, and risk management. Examples include exchange-traded funds (ETFs), although some would argue that ETFs, which are indexed mutual funds that trade like stocks, do not qualify; real estate investment trusts (REITs); as well as commodities, hedge funds, futures, options, foreign currencies, and credit derivatives—even fine art and collectibles. They are assets whose performance is not correlated to the movement of capital markets, but investor interest in them is often directly correlated to the movement of capital markets. (See Figure 4.1.)

Case in point: In 2001, in response to the meltdown of the U.S. equity markets and the political and socioeconomic events that followed, the Federal Reserve Board embarked on a strategy of slashing its federal funds rate in an effort to stimulate economic growth. The funds rate was cut 13 times between January 2001, when it stood at 6.5 percent, and June 2004, when it reached a low of 1.0 percent. The low interest rates that soon prevailed contributed to a rebound in equities, but income-oriented investors were adversely affected as most fixed-income vehicles failed to provide the desired level of portfolio yield. They needed to look for income-generating investment opportunities elsewhere.

Similarly, international investments have often been included in client portfolios to minimize the effect of a domestic downturn, but the increase in globalization and symbiotic relationships between the economies of the world have systematically increased the correlation between the performance of the world economies and markets. Increased volatility in U.S. markets in late 2000 spread to other markets around the world, and the inclusion of global allocations failed to reduce the overall portfolio volatility of most investors during the start of the new century.

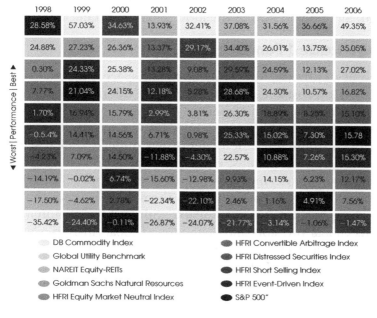

Figure 4.1   Elements of Diversification—Alternative Investments
Source: Phoenix Investment Partners.

The search for alternatives that would not move in lockstep with U.S. equities and fixed-income markets began in earnest.

Firms that offer managed account solutions (MAS) are developing ways to incorporate alternative investments within their MAS platforms, and some sponsors are further along than others. "We offer hedge funds, private equity, and public and private REITs through both our separately managed account platform and our mutual fund wrap platform," says Lidiette Ratiani, director of investment consulting solutions for Wells Fargo Private Client Group. Given the inherent contradiction in that hedge fund managers are notoriously secretive about the investments they're holding, whereas transparency is one of the key attributes of a managed account solution, Ratiani acknowledges that offering hedge funds through an MAS platform is challenging. "Right now we do everything manually," she explains. "The managers submit to us on a monthly basis the asset values of their hedge funds, and each quarter they report performance, and then we update everything. It's time-consuming, but worth the effort."

Ratiani says Wells Fargo's decision to include hedge funds and other alternative investments—the firm also offers a pure-play commodities option in metals—was driven by two primary concerns. "First, our larger clients were asking for these types of investments," she says. "The second reason is that as we build out our asset allocation guidelines, we needed to find a way to offer greater diversification."

Diversification to minimize risk is often the key incentive for adding alternative investments to a portfolio. Here is an overview of these instruments, with an in-depth look at the most popular of them all: hedge funds.

Exchange-Traded Funds

A relatively new entrant in the passive investing space is the exchange-traded fund (ETF), a low-cost and tax-efficient vehicle offering the ability to invest in significant markets like the Standard & Poor's 500 or Japan's Nikkei 225, as well as narrow slivers like certain fixed-income maturities, commodities, or drug stocks. Combining the benefits of a publicly traded security with those of index or sector funds, ETFs represent a breakthrough for investors seeking a convenient method of participating in specific markets. Their status as a publicly traded security gives them tax efficiency through their internal management that is not available with traditional mutual funds.

Barclays Global Investors and State Street Global Advisors are two of the largest players in the ETF space; together, they accounted for nearly 80 percent of ETF assets in 2007. "ETFs have changed the landscape by offering financial advisors a new way to diversify their clients' portfolios," says Valerie Petrone Corradini, national sales manager for Barclays Global Investors. "Before, advisors who gravitated toward separate accounts were limited by the sponsor's platform and manager minimums. For example, many clients didn't meet a manager's minimum investment requirement, so their advisor couldn't fully diversify across all asset classes. With ETFs, they can, and they can do so in a way that gives them precise exposure to the asset classes they want."

"Much of the growth in the ETF industry occurred during one of the country's worst bear markets, in 2001 and 2002," notes Anthony R. Rochte, director of sales for State Street Global Advisors. "This period saw fee-based advisors gravitate toward ETFs given they were transparent daily, low-cost, and, most important, tax-efficient." Exchange-traded funds permit advisors and clients to create portfolios at low cost with the built-in advantage of always representing the market. Beating the benchmark is not the objective of the passive strategy that ETFs offer; gains are achieved through the time-honored method of asset allocation. The passive strategy is designed to avoid surprises, such as manager style drift or other underperformance. "Implementing ETFs in a portfolio to complement active strategies puts control back in the hands of the advisor," explains Rochte. "While alpha does exist, once found it does not always persist. With ETFs alongside active managers, you can control expenses, taxes, and ultimately the allocation at the portfolio level."

In addition, ETFs allow clients to participate in very limited segments of the market, even individual industries, without the added risk of investment manager stock selection. And they are becoming increasingly popular. According to the Investment Company Institute:

- U.S. assets in ETFs rose by roughly 40 percent in 2006, from $300 billion at the start of the year to more than $420 billion by the end.
- The number of ETF offerings doubled in 2006, from 200 at the start of the year to more than 400 by the end.
- ETFs experienced a net issuance of $74 billion in 2006.
- ETF assets have grown by approximately 350 percent since 2000, while mutual fund assets have climbed by about 27 percent.

The growing popularity of ETFs can be attributed to five key factors:

1. *Tax efficiency.* Mass redemptions can force a mutual fund manager to sell underlying securities to raise cash, thereby triggering capital gains distributions for which the individual shareholder is responsible (unless the fund is in a tax-deferred account). This can't happen with ETFs. Investors sell to other investors at the current market price, so the underlying securities are not affected when individual shares are bought and sold. ETFs can make capital gains distributions if they must buy or sell securities to keep pace with the corresponding index, but such distributions are rare. Although Barclays offers more than 120 ETFs, "we've had only two capital gains distributions in the past five years (to 2006)," says Corradini. Adding to tax efficiency: "By taking advantage of in-kind delivery, the portfolio manager of an ETF can always deliver out the

low-cost-basis stocks," she explains, keeping the higher-cost-basis stocks within the fund. "We're always cleansing the low-cost-basis stock out of our portfolios, minimizing the investor's exposure to distributions."

2. *Lower fees.* In general, ETFs have lower annual fees than traditional mutual funds, and ETFs do not carry a redemption fee.
3. *Lower minimums.* Most mutual funds require an initial investment ranging from $1,000 to $2,500 on up, which can put limitations on a client's diversification and asset allocation capabilities. ETFs have no minimum investment except for the share price on the day the client is investing.
4. *Liquidity.* Clients can liquidate their ETF positions at any time, whereas mutual fund liquidations take place at the close of the trading day. Also, ETFs allow clients to set limit orders, something they cannot do with traditional mutual funds.
5. *Pricing.* Because ETF shares trade like stocks, their prices are updated throughout the day and reflect current market pricing, whereas the net asset values of mutual fund shares are determined at the close of each trading day.

Including index funds in general, and ETFs in particular, a managed account solution provides two key benefits to investment advisors:

1. *Time savings.* Index investing all but eliminates the final two steps of the four-step investment process: manager selection and ongoing review.
2. *Easier diversification.* "ETFs enhance how broadly an advisor can diversify a client's portfolio and makes it easier to perform fine-tuning," Corradini says. "For example, if the consultant feels that an international fund manager is not concentrated enough in Europe, then he or she can fine-tune the portfolio by putting a European ETF alongside that manager. You've deepened the breadth of the allocation without having to reconstruct the entire portfolio."

Given the fact that ETFs are available for virtually every segment of the market, it's possible to build an entire portfolio using just exchange-traded funds, a strategy that might be appropriate for some clients. Most, however, require at least some degree of active management, and Corradini says her firm has worked with advisors to develop sophisticated strategies using ETFs as a component in an overall managed account solution.

"As advisors become more savvy about understanding alpha and beta, they are realizing that ETFs are a very cost-efficient way to increase beta exposure while allowing a portfolio's active managers more flexibility in pursuing alpha," she says. "For example, because clients can be so broadly diversified with ETFs, tactical advisors might recommend shorting them on a downtick to mitigate risk. Also, because investors are extremely benchmark sensitive—the financial services industry created that monster—by increasing the ETF allocation you allow active managers to be active: They can stray from their benchmark while the overall portfolio moves in line with the market and remains tax efficient. Institutions tend to allocate upward of 60 percent of their portfolios to index funds. That strategy is very new to the private client world but very familiar to institutional investors, who demand more benchmark purity."

Real Estate

Alternative investments are not entirely new to most investors; most have had an investment in real estate through their primary residences. The benefits of a real estate allocation and its low correlation to the equity markets became apparent when real estate prices in many areas of the United States exploded through 2005, and investors were able to earn double- and sometimes triple-digit returns on properties whose appreciation was fueled by a low-interest-rate environment fueling attractive mortgage rates.

What is new to investors in real estate, at least, is the ability to allocate to the asset class at lower minimums and in a more cost-efficient manner. Clients can invest in publicly traded real estate investment trusts (REITs), which pool their investors' capital and invest in income-producing properties, such as office buildings, shopping centers, and apartment houses. In order to qualify as a pass-through entity that avoids taxation at the corporate level, a REIT must meet certain criteria, including distributing 90 percent of its taxable income in the form of dividends. At least 75 percent of a REIT's investment assets must be in real estate.

By generally paying dividends in the range of 6 to 10 percent owing to the required 90 percent distribution of taxable income, REITs provide income-seeking investors an option other than the meager dividends typically paid by common stocks. REITs also allow investors to diversify their income-producing securities beyond corporate and municipal bonds, bond funds, and agency securities. Finally, REITs are much more liquid than a direct investment in real estate.

As of year-end 2006, there were more than 180 publicly traded REITs in the United States, with a total market capitalization in excess of $438 billion, according to the National Association of Real Estate Investment Trusts (see Figure 4.2). In addition, there are mutual funds, closed-end funds, and exchange-traded funds that provide professional management of the asset class. These can offer broad exposure or a concentration on a segment of the REIT market, such as commercial or residential real estate. There are even funds that specialize in subsectors such as movie theaters or medical offices.

Including REITs in a diversified portfolio improves its risk/return trade-off and historically has provided greater portfolio returns with less volatility due to

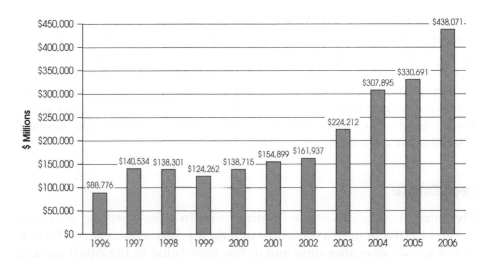

Figure 4.2   Growth of REITs by Market Capitalization, 1996–2006
Source: National Association of Real Estate Investment Trusts.

the low correlation of REITs to the equity and bond markets. Besides providing the opportunity for long-term capital appreciation and current income, REITs are an effective inflation hedge because they have the ability to increase rent payments, either contractually or by attracting new tenants.

When analyzing a REIT it is important to review not only the dividend paid, but also the underlying company's fundamentals, because the success of the business aspect of the REIT will allow it to sustain and grow its dividends over time. Investors should take a total return approach to REITs and calculate dividend yield as well as share price appreciation when investing.

REITs do have two significant drawbacks. One is that their relatively high dividends are considered nonqualified and thus are taxed at a higher rate. The other is that in a rising interest rate environment, many REITs perform poorly because they employ floating rate debt in their capital structures.

Commodities

Commodities are raw materials that are used in the manufacture of finished goods ultimately purchased by consumers and corporations. The commodity asset class consists of energy (oils and gases); industrial metals (aluminum, zinc, lead, nickel, and copper); precious metals (gold and silver); livestock (cattle and hogs); and agriculture (wheat, timber, soybeans, corn, sugar, coffee, and cocoa).

In "Facts and Fantasies about Commodity Futures," a 2004 report that analyzed almost 50 years of commodities prices, K. Geert Rouwenhorst, a professor at the Yale School of Management, and Gary Gorton, a professor at the University of Pennsylvania's Wharton School of Business, determined that fully collateralized commodities futures offered the same returns and Sharpe ratios as equities while being negatively correlated with equity and bond returns. Rouwenhorst and Gorton attributed this negative correlation to different behavior over the business cycle and also found that commodities futures are positively correlated with inflation.

The groundbreaking paper supports the benefits of including commodity investments in a portfolio to increase returns and lower volatility through the negative correlation with equities and the effective hedge against inflation.

There are several ways to add commodities to a portfolio. The traditional method is to purchase the underlying commodity, such as a herd of cattle or bushels of wheat. This approach suffers from obvious drawbacks such as the need for physical storage and care of the asset. An investor also could purchase the publicly traded stock of a commodity producer, but there can be basis risk where the underlying commodity increases in value but the stock performs poorly because of company mismanagement. Investors can trade commodities on the futures exchanges, but this can be logistically difficult due to complicated margin requirements and the variability of trader skills. Managed futures funds, which have been in existence for several decades, are overseen by experienced Commodity Trading Advisors (CTAs) who manage money for institutions, pensions, and endowments. The capital is invested on a discretionary basis, and a managed futures fund is just as likely to be short commodities as it is to be long, which may add volatility to the asset class. If an investor is looking for long-only exposure, this may not be the ideal instrument to use to add the commodities asset class to a diversified portfolio.

The simplest way for an investor to gain either broad or subsector commodity exposure is to purchase one of the many actively traded commodity mutual funds or exchange-traded funds. Mutual funds may use commodity futures/swap contracts to gain their exposure, while commodity ETFs are a simple way to gain passive exposure to the asset class. (They trade the same way as other ETFs.) Commodity mutual funds and ETFs have lowered the minimums required for investment and eliminated the custody and transaction issues associated with other methods of acquiring commodity exposure. Also, investors do not have to contend with the issues of margin calls and rolling positions that coincide with purchasing and administering a futures position.

Hedge Funds

The most dramatic development in alternative investments over the past five years has been the explosive growth of hedge funds. (See Figure 4.3.) Before we discuss the role hedge funds play in a diversified portfolio, it is important

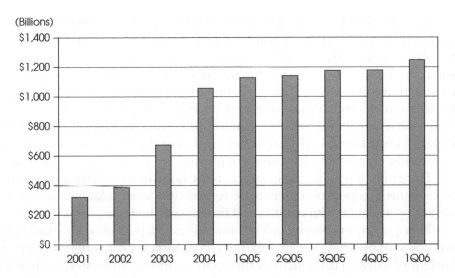

Figure 4.3   Hedge Fund Industry Assets under Management
Source: Barclays Hedge LLC (www.barclaygrp.com).

to understand how a hedge fund is structured and the minimum requirements an investor must meet to make a contribution.

A hedge fund is a private investment company created and operated
under certain exemptions from registration under the Securities Act of 1933
and the Investment Company Act of 1940. Most hedge funds are structured
as limited partnerships whose suppliers of capital are "accredited investors"
or "qualified purchasers." Under Securities and Exchange Commission Rule
501 of Regulation D, an accredited investor may be someone who has individual net worth (or joint net worth with a spouse) that exceeds $1 million
at the time of the purchase; someone with income exceeding $200,000 in
each of the two most recent years (or joint income with a spouse exceeding
$300,000) and a reasonable expectation of the same income level in the cur-
rent year; or a trust with assets in excess of $5 million that was not formed to
acquire the securities offered.

A qualified purchaser must be a financially sophisticated investor not
in need of the protection of state registration when securities are offered
or sold. A qualified purchaser must own not less than $5 million in invest-
ments; and those who own and invest on a discretionary basis for others
must control not less than $25 million in investments.

In order to avoid registering under the 1933 act, a hedge fund must
make its offering available only to accredited investors and qualified purchasers, and it is not permitted to market directly to the public, among
other requirements. Hedge fund managers must rely exclusively on
referrals.

The capital supplied to a hedge fund by its limited partners (the qualified purchasers and accredited investors) is invested at the manager's discretion. An investor's liability is limited to the capital supplied, an important factor considering the use of leverage in many hedge funds. Typically an investor can participate in either a funds-based account, where everyone has identical exposures, or a managed account, where each investor's exposure can be adjusted according to his or her appetite for risk.

Hedge fund capital is managed either by an individual (usually the general partner) or a team of financial experts. In order to limit their personal liability, most hedge fund managers create a corporation or limited liability company to serve as general partner. The portfolio managers design, implement, and monitor a particular investment thesis or strategy as defined in the fund's Private Placement Memorandum. It is not uncommon for a hedge fund's manager to be one of its largest capital providers.

Unlike mutual funds, whose managers are required by federal law to abide by their fiduciary duty to investors and by National Association of Securities Dealers regulations limiting sales charges and distribution fees, hedge funds are not subject to any limitations on the fees a manager can charge. The fund will charge an annual asset management fee (usually 2 percent) and a performance fee based on a percentage of the fund's income and profits (typically 20 percent).

$$\text{(Beginning Assets} \times \text{Asset Management Fee)} + [\text{(Portfolio Return} \times \text{Beginning Portfolio Value)} \times \text{Performance Fee}] = \text{Total Compensation}$$

$$(\$100 \text{ million} \times 2\%) + [(10\% \times \$100 \text{ million}) \times 20\%] = \$4 \text{ million}$$

A hedge fund can incorporate certain benchmarks, known as hurdle rates and high-water marks, to make the fund more attractive to prospective investors. A hurdle rate restricts a manager's ability to take a performance fee to periods where the fund's return is in excess of a benchmark such as the Standard & Poor's 500 index.

$$\text{(Beginning Assets} \times \text{Asset Management Fee)} + \{[\text{(Portfolio Return} - \text{S\&P Return)} \times \text{Beginning Portfolio Value]} \times \text{Performance Fee}\}$$
$$= \text{Total Compensation}$$

$$(\$100 \text{ million} \times 2\%) + \{[(10\% - 5\%) \times \$100 \text{ million}] \times 20\%\} = \$3 \text{ million}$$

A high-water mark requires a manager to recover any previous losses (specific to each investor) before a performance fee can be assessed. High-water marks must be tracked for each individual due to the fact that investors enter the fund at different times.

Before investing, investors should review the hedge fund's lockup period, the time during which their assets may not be removed from the portfolio.

Two-year lockups allow a fund to avoid registration, but longer time periods are possible. Lockups allow portfolio managers to implement a strategy without fear of mass redemptions if the fund is down over the short run.

Leverage

Hedge fund managers often incorporate the use of leverage—that is, borrowing against the portfolio's assets or buying securities on margin. The use of leverage provides a portfolio manager with far greater purchasing power than the pooled capital of investors. In recent years, prime brokers, the broker-dealers who engage in the highly lucrative business of providing various services to hedge funds, have been very willing to offer margin loans to hedge fund managers. Moreover, historically low interest rates have made managers more willing to borrow and have increased the amount of leverage used by many funds.

The degree to which leverage is used in a hedge fund can provide substantial outsized returns. But leverage also adds risk and can lead to the sudden loss of an investor's entire fund contribution. Suppose, for example, that investors put $10 into a fund, which then borrows $90 and invests the $100 total. If the total investment grows by 10 percent, to $110, investors would earn 100 percent on their initial $10. But let's say the $100 pool loses 10 percent and becomes worth only $90. In that case, the investors' original $10 investment would be wiped out. (For the sake of simplicity, the analysis in Table 4.1 ignores the impact of borrowing costs.)

The story of Long-Term Capital Management is a cautionary tale. The Greenwich, Connecticut–based hedge fund boasted a board of directors that included some of the brightest financial minds of the twentieth century, such as Robert Merton and Myron Scholes, co-winners of the 1997 Nobel Prize in Economics. The team developed complex financial models to take advantage of the perceived fixed-income arbitrage available in the sovereign debt marketplace. The fund had a tremendous track record in its early years. Starting in 1994 and ending in 1997, its annual returns were 28 percent, 58 percent, 57 percent, and 21 percent, respectively. New and existing investors were making large contributions of capital into the fund, and eventually the fund stopped accepting new investors. At the beginning of 1998, the fund had $4.7 billion of equity, and its managers had leveraged the portfolio to north of $120 billion.

When the Russian government unexpectedly defaulted on its bonds in September 1998, the portfolio sustained massive losses as loan providers

Table 4.1 Leverage Effects

Initial Investment	Loan Amount	Total Investment	Return	Ending Investment
$10	$90	$100	10%	$110
$10	$90	$100	−10%	$90

demanded liquidation of the fund's positions. The ensuing downward spiral in the fund's value prompted the Federal Reserve to take action in order to avoid a disaster in the financial markets. The banking industry has taken steps with the major lending institutions to avoid a recurrence, but most hedge funds still incorporate some degree of leverage.

Investors can invest in hedge funds directly (if they qualify) or through a fund of funds, structured notes, or hedge-like mutual funds. The tax implications of investing in each vehicle differ, so advisors are wise to suggest that an investor discuss alternatives with a tax expert before considering a hedge fund investment. Advisors making hedge fund recommendations should know something of the many strategies available. Here are a few of the most popular approaches.

Equity Long/Short

This is the original hedge fund strategy, created by Alfred Winslow Jones, an associate editor at *Forbes*, in 1949. Jones called his technique a "hedged strategy," giving rise to this asset class, which seeks absolute returns, often by taking advantage of arbitrage opportunities among different markets and investment vehicles.

The equity long/short approach is the one employed by the greatest number of managers and has the most assets under management. It relies on superior stock selection and usually uses little leverage. The portfolio manager buys (goes long on) securities that are estimated to be undervalued and shorts (or purchases a put on) securities or indexes that are overvalued. The manager is free to select any security for both sides of the portfolio and can be long or short to any degree.

Long/short is the ultimate stock picker's strategy and provides a superior manager the ideal strategy to add portfolio alpha. The strategy has a somewhat higher correlation to the overall market than a market-neutral strategy, but still can provide absolute returns. The risks are in the many ways the portfolio manager may err in security selection or market timing, which can lead to large losses in short periods.

Equity Market-Neutral

This is a variation of the equity long/short strategy. Here, the portfolio manager attempts to use his or her superior security selection while neutralizing the effect of the macro environment on the portfolio. The manager assembles a portfolio based on a method known as "pairs trading"; he or she goes long one security and shorts an equal dollar amount of another security in the same sector, industry, market capitalization, or country. Stocks in the same sector tend to have returns that correlate with the performance of the overall sector, but superior companies should appreciate faster than weaker companies when the sector is advancing and decline more slowly than their peers during a sector downturn. The strategy derives most of its return from the manager's ability to select both the stocks that will outperform and those that will underperform. The biggest risk is that the manager will pick the wrong stocks for either or both legs of the strategy.

Relative Value Strategies

A perfect arbitrage is one in which a manager can buy a security and simultaneously sell it in another market at a profit without taking on any risk. Perfect arbitrages theoretically do not exist in an efficient market where securities are properly priced. In a relative value strategy, the portfolio manager attempts to lock in the price difference between two securities by purchasing an undervalued security and selling (short) an overvalued security while taking on some degree of risk. The manager attempts to reduce the position's market exposure through various hedging techniques (short sales, derivatives) and take advantage of the perceived arbitrage opportunities in the market. These strategies usually require the use of leverage, as spreads are relatively small.

The problem with relative value strategies is that a successful manager's trading strategy is usually copied, and as more managers implement the strategy the price inefficiencies can shrink or evaporate entirely. Also, the manager's long position can fall and his short position can move against him, resulting in investor losses on both positions simultaneously.

Opportunistic Strategies

Opportunistic hedge fund strategies seek out undervalued securities while actively looking to short securities that are overvalued. Unlike a relative value fund, the manager does not try to hedge market exposure or attempt to attain excess returns on both long and short positions. An opportunistic fund can produce tremendous returns if the portfolio manager is able to select undervalued positions for the long positions and overvalued securities for the short positions. The risk is in making the wrong choices.

Convertible Arbitrage

Convertible arbitrage is a market-neutral investment strategy that involves the simultaneous purchase of convertible securities and the short sale of the same issuer's common stock. The premise of the strategy is that psychology and illiquidity sometimes lead to pricing anomalies between convertibles and underlying common shares. In this strategy, the portfolio manager buys a convertible bond and shorts the issuer's common shares to hedge the long position and remove the effect of any stock-price movement through a process known as delta hedging. During times when there are only small movements in the stock price, the short position hedges those movements (making the position market-neutral), and the investor collects the coupon payments. In addition, as a result of the short sale, the investor earns a Treasury bill–like return from the short-sale rebate paid by the lender of the stock. If the stock price drops dramatically, however, the delta hedge breaks down and the short position will increase at a greater rate than the loss on the long bond position (when the short is covered, the manager must return the same number of shares that were borrowed, but profits if the stock price is lower). In such cases, the investor captures the spread. If the stock price rises dramatically, the increase in the convertible bond will be greater than the loss on the short position in the stock because the convertible bond will trade at the greater of the straight bond value or its conversion value (when the stock rises, the conversion value increases as well).

The risk of the strategy is that the two securities may move independently of each other and the stock price may increase as the bond's price decreases. Such a scenario was rumored to have happened in early 2006 to a large hedge fund that shorted General Motors (GM) stock and took a long position in GM bonds (although the bonds were not convertible). The bonds were downgraded during a rally in the stock's share price. Another risk is that a large number of managers may use the same strategy, so that a convertible bond's price may be bid up along with the underlying stock price, and the spread that provides the return for the strategy may diminish or disappear.

Fixed-Income Arbitrage

Here, the fixed-income portfolio manager attempts to profit from pricing inefficiencies by going long and short on various fixed-income instruments while limiting interest rate exposure caused by changes in the yield curve (remaining interest rate neutral). The manager will incorporate a high degree of leverage to magnify the results of the captured widening or narrowing spread between the two securities. The manager may try to exploit pricing inefficiencies between Treasuries and corporate bonds, various government fixed-income securities, and municipal bonds through complex trading techniques and instruments (swaps, forwards, futures). The strategy has the ability to perform in all market environments, assuming the manager is correct in his or her security selection; the strategy also has a low correlation to the overall market. Risks? The strategy has been described as "picking up nickels in front of a steamroller" for its propensity to provide consistent nonstellar returns with periodic, full-blown meltdowns. It tends to perform best in low-volatility environments.

Event-Driven

An event-driven hedge fund strategy is predictive in nature. The portfolio manager purchases a security that he believes is undervalued due to an expected special situation or announcement. The returns are not dependent on the direction of the market, and the strategy has the ability to provide absolute returns in all environments.

There are many different event-driven strategies. One is merger arbitrage, in which a portfolio manager typically takes a long position in a company that is the subject of a stock tender offer and shorts the company making the acquisition. The target company will normally be trading at a discount to the offer price, and the portfolio manager attempts to lock in the spread (or deal risk premium) between the offer price and the current market price of the target and thus profit as the market price converges to the offer price (as the deal nears completion). The manager hedges exposure by shorting the buyer and earns a short-sale rebate on the proceeds. A manager may also use leverage to increase returns. The strategy requires a buoyant mergers and acquisitions market, and the key risk involves the possibility that a deal will fall apart.

Another event-driven strategy involves distressed securities. Here, a hedge fund manager takes a long position in equity, bank debt, and the high-yield bonds of companies that are under duress, in default or bankruptcy, or near bankruptcy. These securities often trade at a large discount to their intrinsic value due to market sentiment, fear of the entity no longer functioning as a going concern, and the fact that many institutions are restricted from owning distressed securities. The fund manager is looking for a turnaround story that can lead to large trading profits if he or she is correct. If not, the entire investment can be lost.

Global Macro

Global macro portfolio hedge fund managers have fewer restrictions than other hedge fund managers. They can scour the globe to capture gains through leverage and the tactical use of derivatives when making investments in stocks, bonds, currencies, commodities, futures, real estate, and an endless list of other liquid and illiquid investments. Managers can market time the economies of any countries they choose and use fundamental or technical analysis to make decisions. One of the more famous global macro managers is George Soros, whose Quantum Group fund made $1 billion by betting against the British pound. Needless to say, this strategy, with its many moving parts and enormous information flows, is very risky, and most experienced successful global macro managers do not accept new investors.

Fund of Funds

For hedge fund investors who want to hedge their bets, a fund of hedge funds provides a diversified choice. Generally a limited partnership, a fund of funds pools investor capital and purchases a portfolio or basket of individual hedge funds. Portfolio managers add value through their expertise, their ability to perform the necessary due diligence, and their ability to select the best managers for inclusion. Value also comes from tactically allocating the pooled capital into the various hedge fund strategies based on the fund-of-funds manager's perspective on the market environment.

The ability to correctly time the investment into the next best-performing manager and remove a poorly performing manager is what leads to long-term results. For the difficult and time-consuming process of analyzing the macro environment, knowing the strategies of various hedge funds, and selecting 10 to 25 managers from among more than 9,000 individual hedge funds, the fund-of-funds manager receives a fee, usually 1 percent on assets, and a 10 percent performance fee.

Ricardo Cortez, president of the institutional and private client group of Torrey Associates LLC, a billion-dollar fund of funds in New York, points out that while there are some star managers who are able to attract enough money on their opening day so as to need no more clients, this is rare. "Most hedge funds start out small and gather assets as they gain experience and establish a track record," he says. One technique a fund-of-funds manager can employ, Cortez says, is to be an early stage investor with a new hedge fund, which enables the fund of funds to participate so that even if the hedge fund manager closes to all new business, the fund of funds can place money with that manager until the capacity allocation limit is reached.

Early stage investing also may allow the fund of funds to gain more transparency into the security holdings and strategies within the portfolio. In addition, a number of academic studies have shown that hedge funds often demonstrate better performance in their first few years of existence.

The main drawback to fund-of-funds investing is the extra fee layer on top of the already hefty fees charged by the hedge funds themselves. Moreover, some of the top hedge funds do not permit fund-of-funds investments, and the more assets a fund of funds has under management, the more difficult it may be to enter and exit from investments in small and emerging hedge funds. Finally, investing in a fund of funds may unknowingly result in overexposure to certain securities held by the investor outside of the fund of funds. (See Figure 4.4.)

Multistrategy Funds

A multistrategy fund can be thought of as a hybrid between a hedge fund and a fund of funds. An investment in a multistrategy fund is a direct investment by an investor managed by one investment team (similar to a hedge fund), but the pooled capital is invested in a variety of strategies (similar to a fund of funds). A multistrategy fund provides the diversification benefits of exposing a client to more than one strategy with the same level of investment that a direct investment in a single-strategy hedge fund would require. The biggest advantage a multistrategy fund has over a fund-of-funds approach is that the multistrategy fund eliminates the second layer of fees. Although multistrategy funds usually have lockup periods, portfolio managers have the flexibility to quickly reallocate if a profitable opportunity can be exploited by one of the fund strategies.

The main drawback of a multistrategy fund is manager risk. Simply put, the manager can make investment decisions and/or timing choices that lead

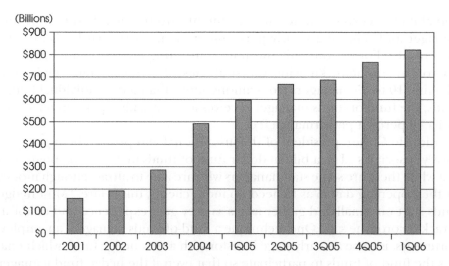

Figure 4.4   Fund of Funds Industry Assets under Management
Source: Barclays Hedge LLC (www.barclaygrp.com).

to inferior performance. Funds employing a multistrategy approach also may have high asset management fees, with some approaching 4 percent, and performance fees as high as 40 percent.

Other Ways to Implement Hedge-Fund-Like Strategies

Retail investors who are neither accredited investors nor qualified purchasers can gain exposure to hedge-fund-type returns through mutual funds, investable indexes, and structured notes.

Hedge-Fund-Type Mutual Funds

The first and probably most important advantage of the mutual fund approach is the low minimum investment. Several hedge-type mutual funds have investment minimums of $25,000, and some are as low as $5,000. Mutual fund fees also are lower than hedge fund fees. Prohibited from charging a performance fee, hedge-fund-like mutual funds often charge asset management fees slightly higher than those of a standard mutual fund to compensate for extra trading. Even so, these are typically lower than the standard 2 percent rate charged by a hedge fund manager. Expenses for a mutual fund that shorts stocks may appear higher than the actual expense rate due to short dividends being considered part of the expense calculation.

Another advantage is that a mutual fund provides daily liquidity, and the daily pricing of mutual funds provides a greater level of transparency than that offered by hedge funds. Moreover, mutual funds are registered and provide lots of disclosure.

The drawbacks to the mutual fund approach are the limited strategies that are available. Most of the mutual funds that offer hedge-fund-type strategies are structured as long/short portfolios; few offer merger arbitrage, convertible arbitrage, covered call writing, distressed debt, or fixed-income arbitrage strategies. With the limited number of funds available, it may not be possible to create a diversified basket of hedge-fund-type mutual funds.

Structured Notes

These instruments pay a return linked to the performance of an underlying benchmark or index and can be based on a variety of asset classes, including equities, commodities, corporate credits, and foreign exchange. With hedge fund linked notes, investors are paid a return linked to the performance of a portfolio of hedge funds. On the maturity date, the note pays the principal amount plus return (if any) based on the percentage change in the underlying hedge funds.

Since a structured note typically requires only a minimum investment of $50,000, its barrier to entry is much lower than that of a fund of funds. Because it is based on an index of many hedge funds, a structured note also greatly minimizes an investor's fund-specific risk. Most structured notes are continuously offered by a dealer, allowing the investor to purchase additional units at any time; they have weekly liquidity (although there may be a redemption fee), and do not have lockup periods. Structured notes can be used in a core-satellite approach to hedge fund investing in which an investor makes a passive, low-cost investment in an S&P 500 ETF to capture market return while seeking alpha through a structured note.

One drawback to this approach is that some top-tier managers may be excluded from an index's database because the manager either opted not to be included or failed to meet the criteria necessary for inclusion (such as minimum asset levels, being open to new investors, or having a favorable portfolio track record). Such restrictions may exclude top-performing funds that are closed to new investors and emerging fund managers who do not have the necessary track record or minimum asset levels.

Evolution Is Under Way

It's early yet, insofar as the inclusion of alternative investments in managed account platforms is concerned, even if a lot of investors are suddenly asking about them. "There has been so much written and spoken about them in the financial media that alternative investments are hardly foreign concepts anymore," notes Larry Sinsimer, managing director at Eaton Vance. "What's been lacking is a vehicle to show the investor and the advisor how these asset classes can be used to increase the probability of successfully meeting one's investment goals while decreasing risk."

Lee Chertavian, chairman and CEO of Placemark, agrees. "By and large in today's market, very few sponsors offer any significant level of alternative assets within unified managed accounts," he says. "We have only one client that uses a fund of hedge funds, none that offer commodities, and only a few that offer REITs."

But that is likely to change in the coming years, says Wells Fargo's Lidiette Ratiani. "As more and more of the population moves into retirement, they are going to be looking at managing their money very differently," she says. "They will have less tolerance for risk, so anything that can be done to lower risk will be welcome. They will be looking to their advisors for ways to further diversify their portfolios, and will be expecting them to bring in additional asset classes and more risk management types of products." Technological innovations will have to occur in order to accommodate all of these investments within an MAS framework, but they will happen—and probably sooner rather than later.

Now that we've surveyed the evolution of managed accounts and the recent revolutions in new products and services available, let's take a look at what managed account solutions can offer your clients, your practice, and you.

Key Benefits of Managed Accounts and Recurring Revenues

Managed account solutions allow for a more efficient use of the advisor's time, access to a more affluent clientele, a consistent revenue stream leveraged by the market's growth, and a more valuable business entity; plus, clients prefer fees over commissions.

Managed account solutions (MAS) offer multiple benefits to investors: access to top money managers, greater diversification, better risk management, account integration, and so on. There is a huge benefit to advisors, too: the opportunity to establish a recurring revenue stream that will enable them to build and expand their practices, offer a wider array of services, and deal with a select group of clients.

Under the old commission-based model, an advisor's focus was always on the sale. Under a fee-based approach, an advisor's focus is always on the client relationship. The difference between the two distinguishes the advisor as a seller of products from the advisor as a supplier of solutions. That's not meant to denigrate commission-based consultants; the financial consulting industry was originally built on a commission basis, and over the years there have been many fine practices whose revenues came primarily if not exclusively from commissions. In fact, as we saw in the first chapter, prior to the introduction of the managed account concept, there simply was no alternative to commissions—and at the time, few people were looking for an alternative.

In the early days of managed accounts, the concept wasn't well understood by brokers and branch managers, many of whom were not immediate fans of managed accounts because they couldn't understand why a broker should forgo a commission in order to receive what appeared to be a smaller fee. Furthermore, the idea of giving control of an account to a money manager was anathema. The two primary objections first heard from advisors were:

"You've got to be kidding! If I can't earn more than 3 percent on an account in a year, I shouldn't be in the business!" That line came from an experienced New York City broker. Advisors like him weren't calculating their return on assets and the annuity that would be accumulating.

"I'll lose control of my best clients!" The advisors who feared this result didn't realize the advantage of leveraging the time they would spend gathering assets and servicing clients. This would be time to do bigger and better business.

That attitude was understandable for its time. In the mid-1980s, the industry offered 8.5 percent front-end-loaded equity funds—themselves fairly new on the scene—and because of these attractive loads, mutual funds were early competition for managed account business. However, mutual fund sales had obvious limitations: Once the sale was completed, the client had no further use for the broker (and vice versa) until it was time for another sale.

Separately managed accounts became popular with consultative advisors because they offer a more significant long-term revenue stream. Managed accounts and mutual funds each offer professional investment management, but only the managed account option truly offers the potential for a long-term relationship with the client. Farsighted advisors realized they could make more money over time providing managed account solutions than they could by selling funds.

Managed accounts have other advantages over mutual funds, as Figure 5.1 illustrates.

The perception that managed accounts led to reduced income was easy to counter. In 1988, Steve Gresham managed the consulting group at Advest, a regional broker-dealer based in Connecticut. Advest did a study of its accounts to determine how much revenue per account was being generated per dollar of assets. Excluding mutual funds and annuities held away, Advest found an average return on assets of about 70 basis points, or 0.7 percent—a figure that remains common. By comparison, a typical managed account sported a fee in excess of 2 percent.

Clearly, revenue improvement was possible with managed account fees, while improving results for clients. Top producers could double or triple their income if all accounts were converted to a fee basis. Firms began to preach the gospel of fees to their reps. Shearson put information about return on assets (ROA) on its brokers' desktop systems so they could see not only their commission runs, but also their ROA for any particular client.

Understanding the potential of fee income was critical for advisors and managers. Managed accounts offered leverage—income from assets under management plus participation in the market's growth. Now, branch

	Mutual Funds	Managed Accounts
General Features		
Access to professional money managers	Yes	Yes
Diversified portfolio	Yes	Yes
Ability to customize portfolio	No	Yes, investors can restrict specific securities from their portfolios
Manager independence from the herd instinct	No, if clients want to redeem shares, fund managers must sell to raise the cash to do so	Yes, money managers can buy when the herd is selling and vice versa, customizing the decisions to the client's objectives
Withdrawals/ redemptions	Most funds have restrictions	Unlimited
Typical account minimum	$1,000	$100,000
Liquidity	Typically, next day	Three-day settlement of trades
Access to asset classes	Numerous	Somewhat more limited than funds
Performance Reporting Features		
Performance reporting	Typically semiannual, some more frequent	Quarterly performance rating
Customized performance reporting	Generally no, investors must calculate their own performance, which is problematic, particularly for investors who dollar-cost average	Yes, automatically sent to investors every quarter; includes performance of individual portfolios and of aggregate of multiple portfolios

Figure 5.1   Managed Accounts versus Mutual Funds
Source: The Money Management Institute (MMI).

	Mutual Funds	Managed Accounts
Tax-Related Features		
Separately held securities	No, investor owns one security, the fund, which in turn owns a diversified portfolio	Yes, investor owns securities in an account managed by money managers
Unrealized gains	Yes, average U.S. mutual fund has a 20% embedded, unrealized capital gain[1]	No, cost basis of each security in the portfolio is established at the time of purchase
Customized to control taxes	No, most funds are managed for pretax returns, and investors pay a proportionate share of taxes on capital gains	Yes, investors can instruct money managers to take gains or losses as available to manage their tax liability
Tax-efficient handling of low-cost-basis stocks	No, stocks cannot be held in an investor's mutual fund account, so there is no opportunity to manage low-cost-basis stocks	Yes, the handling of low-cost-basis stocks can be customized to the client's situation, liquidating in concert with offsetting losses, and so on
Gain/loss distribution	Virtually all gains must be distributed; losses cannot be distributed	Realized gains and losses are reported in the year recorded
Cost-Related Features		
Expenses (including brokerage costs)	1.56% average[1]	1.25%[1]
Volume fee discounts	No, all investors pay the same expense ratio	Yes, larger investors enjoy fee discounts
Other costs	12b-1, sales loads, redemption fees, and so on	None

Figure 5.1   (Continued)

[1]Morningstar Principia Plus for Windows, February 2002. Brokerage costs estimated at 0.13% for the 10 largest funds. Costs do not include advisor fee, which will vary.

offices would have a new revenue dimension to look at, not simply the gross commissions of a producer.

Nonetheless, many financial advisors continue to resist managed accounts, arguing that fees are too high and clients can receive an equal benefit from mutual fund investing for a lower cost. Yet mutual fund fees do not include transaction and other costs that are included in managed accounts. Mutual funds also net out fees before they calculate a fund's net asset value. If consulting is included, managed account clients receive valuable services on much smaller asset sizes than previously would have been possible—for about the same fees as a mutual fund.

There is more, outlined in Phoenix Investment Partners Investing Essentials[SM], *Benefits of Managed Accounts.* The all-inclusive managed account fee provides customized investment expertise and gives clients:

- Active account management tailored to their specific investment goals, risk tolerance, and time horizon.
- Access to a personal financial advisor to develop a written statement of their investment objectives.
- Ability to exclude certain investments—for example, stock of companies that make weapons or tobacco products.
- Daily portfolio monitoring as market conditions change.
- Regular performance reporting and record keeping.
- Strategic tax planning.
- Flexibility to offset capital gains and losses.
- Ownership of the actual security, which prevents buying into a shared, historical tax liability of a mutual fund.

Five Key Benefits of Managed Account Solutions

First Benefit: Clients Prefer a Fee-Based Approach

A joint survey performed in 2000 by the Washington, D.C.–based research firm VIP Forum and Chicago-based consulting firm Spectrem Group on U.S. affluent investment preferences and behaviors asked individuals about investment fees. Survey respondents said that commissions were their least favored method of compensation for financial advisors, while fees were the most favored. In addition, the Securities and Exchange Commission (SEC), after an exhaustive review of broker compensation practices, released a report in 1995 concluding that asset-based fees were more likely to result in objective investment advice than trade-based commissions (the Tully Commission report cited in Chapter 1). The SEC has maintained that stance ever since.

Obviously, it's easier to attract and retain clients by offering the compensation structure they prefer. Through high-profile marketing campaigns by the National Association of Personal Financial Advisors and other trade organizations, consumers are aware they have a choice when it comes to how they pay for financial services: fee or commission. Many prospects will ask if you provide services on a fee basis, and that question provides the perfect opportunity for you to educate them on the advantages of a fee-based managed account solution.

Second Benefit: MAS Offer a More Efficient Use of Your Time

Providing managed account solutions allows you to remove yourself from the process of managing money. You eliminate the problem of not having enough time for yourself and your business and delegate this responsibility to a professional money manager.

More efficient use of your time is a benefit that cannot be overstated, because the more time you must spend selling products, the less time you can devote to servicing clients—and poor customer service is the number one reason why clients look for a new financial advisor. According to the 2007 Phoenix Wealth Survey, two-thirds of clients who said they were looking for a new advisor attributed the reason to either "the advisor is not proactive in maintaining contact with me" (44 percent) or "the advisor is difficult to get hold of" (22 percent). Think about that for a moment: If the number one reason that clients leave an advisor is because he or she is not devoting enough time to them, then any strategy that gives the advisor more time to spend with clients is well worth considering, isn't it? (By the way, poor customer service was cited at twice the rate of poor investment performance by clients looking for a new advisor.)

Third Benefit: MAS Allow You to Work with a More Affluent Client Base

Managed account consulting gives you a better opportunity to work with very large clients. Affluent clients, for example, want personalization and customization. They want to control their tax destiny. If you want to work with wealthy individuals, foundations, and endowments, or small to midsize institutions, then you must upgrade your services.

This is where managed account solutions fit in perfectly—you have the time to work on more complex financial issues, not just investments. In the 2007 Phoenix Wealth Survey, 24 percent of clients looking for a new advisor attributed the reason to their current advisor's inability to offer the products and services they felt they needed—services such as tax planning, estate planning, wealth transfer strategies, health care planning, and retirement planning.

Give some thought to the types of prospecting and marketing activities you enjoy that could bring bigger business your way if you focused more on those activities:

- Do you socialize among the affluent?
- Are you visible in your community?
- Are you involved in civic activities? Do you volunteer for charities?
- Do you sit on any boards?

- Do you have exposure to wealth through your country club?
- Do you have good referral relationships with accountants and attorneys?
- Do you think you are equipped to work with affluent investors by offering a broad array of financial services, not just investments? Why?
- Do you seem to naturally attract affluent clients? How?
- Are you in a position to see affluent investors on a regular basis?

If you responded affirmatively to more than half of these questions, you are poised to either begin your transition or continue building your managed account business.

Fourth Benefit: MAS Enable You to Leverage Your Income

Managed accounts allow you to add the market's returns to help boost your income. This leverage is a major advantage for those advisors who sell managed account solutions versus those who sell only commissioned mutual funds. Let us illustrate.

A mutual fund or securities commission is based on the initial deposit, whereas the managed account annual fee is based on the value of the portfolio every quarter. If the markets and your investment managers have positive performance, you will receive a lift in income with no effort. If you believe in the future of capital markets, you're creating built-in raises for yourself with managed accounts. (See Figure 5.2.)

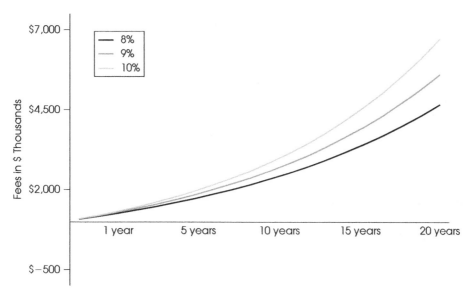

The assumptions are: $1,000,000 production per year, starting at $1,000,000.
Assumes fee of 2.44% with rep payout as 50% of annual fee.

Figure 5.2   Annuitize Your Business

You can attain a far superior long-term income flow from managed accounts—and thus a more valuable practice—than you can by working only with commissions. Indeed, an AIM/Gresham Company, LLC, survey of financial advisors found that the more successful the advisor, the larger the percentage of his or her revenues that came from fees:

- Fully 90 percent of advisors surveyed making $300,000 or more (net) get some fee revenue, and fees account for at least 25 percent of revenues for more than half of those advisors.
- Only 18 percent of advisors earning $75,000 to $300,000 (net) receive more than 25 percent of their revenues from fees.

Assume you open an average of two new fee-based accounts per month at $500,000 each. At the end of the first year, you will have built a business that can generate $90,000 in fees (based on $12 million of assets under management paying 75 basis points). You would have to trade an order of 500 shares of stock about 15 times per month to earn the same amount in commissions (based on a full-service commission rate of $525). The next year, the fee-based assets under management stay on the books, and you don't have to worry about finding new stocks to trade to keep your income steady!

Here is a case in point: In the late 1980s, Steve Gresham welcomed a top producer at a major wirehouse to a regional brokerage firm trying to promote separately managed accounts. The advisor had a large book of separately managed accounts, and at the start of his second full year with the firm, in the first week of January, Steve announced that the advisor was on track to become a member of that year's Advisory Council. Steve's phone rang off the hook with calls from other Advisory Council members demanding to know how this new guy could possibly make the Council in the first week of the year.

How did the new guy qualify? With the projected value of his managed account fees. The announcement caused quite a stir, and soon the concept of projecting annuity income from fees began attracting attention as other advisors entered the business. Those advisors and brokers who looked to the long term and realized the value of advice—for themselves and their clients—were among the first to model their business for assets and fees.

Fifth Benefit: MAS Help You Create a More Valuable Business

A fee-based practice is worth more than a practice fueled primarily by commissions. "The reliability and predictability of a firm's future revenue is critical to its valuation," explains Mark Tibergien, a principal with Moss Adams LLP and the industry's foremost authority on the valuation of financial planning practices, in *How to Value, Buy, or Sell a Financial Advisory Practice*. "Practices that generate revenue from fees charged on assets under management tend to be valued more highly than those that generate revenue from commissions.

That's because the ongoing revenue stream is more predictable in a fee-based practice. Conversely, revenues generated from commission-based practices are less certain because they depend on future transactions."

What is the value of your financial consulting practice? If you don't know, you're not alone. One of the great ironies in our industry is that many advisors don't take the time to create a financial plan for themselves or their businesses, so they have no idea of the true value of the practice they've built. They rarely think through their goals as a business owner, much less the value they will need to realize from the sale or transition of the business in order to fund their own retirement dreams, hopes, and goals. There are many sad stories of advisors selling their firms for the wrong reasons, either because they lacked a plan or because they were forced into selling due to unforeseen circumstances.

There are many ways to calculate and determine the value of a financial practice, with considerable misinformation surrounding the process. Using simple rules of thumb, such as a multiple of revenue, can lead to poor strategic decisions on the part of both buyers and sellers, and even to transactions that ultimately fail and destroy business value and goodwill in the process. Consider, for example, an advisory firm in the South generating $3 million in revenue per year, whose two owners take home less than $75,000 due to the firm's inefficient operation. Using the two-times-revenue multiple typically employed by transition web sites and business brokers, the firm would be valued at about $6 million. But who would want to pay that relatively hefty amount for the opportunity to earn $150,000 and work 60 to 80 hours a week? You'd be better off putting the money in CDs and playing golf!

The value in any transaction resides largely in the down payment, earn-out provisions, tax treatment, and other seemingly ancillary elements, as well as in the negotiated price. Moreover, investment advisory firms—unlike tax preparation or restaurant franchises that have standardized pricing, technology, and service delivery models—often have vastly different economics, service models, and target markets, making them extremely difficult to compare.

Determining the Value of Your Business

Fortunately, there are some simple tools that can serve as a framework for determining underlying business value, such as the capital asset pricing model (CAPM), that old tool from accounting and finance classes. The formula is $V = CF/(r - g)$, where value (V) is equal to cash flow (CF)—also known as operating profit; operating cash flow; earnings before interest, taxes, depreciation, and amortization (EBITDA); or other similar term—divided by risk (r)—a factor that is unique to each firm—minus growth (g), which is the long-term expected growth rate, not necessarily the historical rate at which the firm has grown in the past. Why look at this formula in detail? By exploring each variable, you can translate the implications of what impacts those variables into specific actions you can take to maximize business value.

As its definition indicates, cash flow is determined by the underlying profitability of the firm. This measure can be simplified by taking an income statement approach and classifying expenses into direct and overhead expenses. With regard to income, Mark Tibergien notes that fee-based firms usually produce higher values than commission-based firms. "Trends should be studied carefully," he says. "Are the revenues growing over time? Are they moving in a smooth and consistent fashion, or do they move erratically up and down? Investors value predictability and prefer more consistent movements over large swings." Remember, for the purpose of this exercise, you must put yourself in the place of the potential buyer, not the potential seller, even though it is your firm being scrutinized. Would you buy your firm, based on the results of this equation?

Direct expenses (the cost of goods sold, in the accounting sense) may be defined as the costs incurred in the process of delivering advice to investors. Due to the people-intensive nature and personal touch of the industry, direct expense consists of all advice delivery and business development activities that are the direct compensation for people involved in those roles. Overhead expenses consist of the remaining expense items such as rent, technology, insurance, advertising, and administrative and operational staff. If a managing owner is also an advisor with client and business development responsibilities, his or her compensation as an advisor and manager would be allocated to direct expenses based on the time spent working with clients and developing new business; the remaining compensation would be allocated to overhead expenses, reflecting contributions to managing the firm's operations.

Continuing with the income statement approach, we arrive at cash flow by taking revenue and deducting direct expense. That gives us gross profit, from which we subtract overhead to produce cash flow. Recent studies by the Financial Planning Association and the accounting and consulting firm Moss Adams LLP have yielded industry benchmarks based on the financial performance of several top-performing advisory firms. On average, efficient advisory firms spend roughly 40 percent of revenues on direct expenses and 35 percent on overhead expenses, leaving 25 percent of revenues as the operating cash flow of the business.

The next step in computing value is creating a proxy for the r in the calculation, or risk. In essence, we are trying to determine the rate of return required to compensate the owners for the business risk they are taking by owning a small investment advisory business. Risk is determined by several factors including firm size, concentration of the client base, overall client demographics, dependence on key employees, and types of revenue (recurring fees versus commissions). Clearly, firm size matters. A larger advisory firm with a diverse client base is less dependent on any one client as a percentage of total revenue; simply put, in a large firm there is less risk if any one client, no matter how significant, leaves. Similarly, a larger firm is less dependent on any one employee. If a key employee were to leave, the impact likely would be greater in a small firm than in a larger firm.

Other risk areas involve business operations. Is the firm fully compliant with regulatory procedures? Are there any "ticking time bombs" in the client base in terms of potential litigation or regulatory fines? Even the kind of investing a firm encourages entails risk. If the firm is equities-oriented, for example, its value is more at risk if equity markets were to turn down and the value of client assets were to fall.

So, what is a good proxy for risk in the formula? If we look at other asset classes and the rates of return required to compensate investors for the risks of investing in those, we can see that r for a closely held, illiquid, small business like an investment advisory firm is somewhere between the risk of a small-cap stock traded on NASDAQ (about 15 percent) and that of an investment in venture capital (50+ percent). For most established advisory firms with a history of profitability, industry experts agree that the risk figure usually is in the 20 percent to 35 percent range.

This brings us to the last variable, growth (g). Growth in the CAPM formula is reflective of a long-term growth rate and is therefore theoretical in nature. It is not the historic growth rate of the firm; many advisory firms are less than 25 years old and have a high rate of growth due to their youth and the recent performance of the financial markets. They do not have a track record over a long enough time frame to compare performance over several market cycles. "The number of years that should be analyzed is largely dependent on the cyclicality of the business environment," Tibergien says. "For financial advisory firms, you would ideally analyze a minimum of three years and optimally five."

In other words, g is determined by a number of variables, including the economy, investor demographics, and growth expectations of the specific business. It is therefore likely to be somewhere between 0 percent and 10 percent and can actually be negative in cases where a large portion of the client base would be likely to defect given an ownership transition. A 2005 study commissioned by Fidelity Investments of Boston concluded that up to 40 percent of clients will leave a firm after it is sold.

The demographic makeup of your client base is extremely important. If your firm has a large percentage of older clients receiving distributions from fixed-income investments, for example, growth would be slow (or even negative). Compare that to a client base consisting of young executives and professionals accumulating assets during their prime earning years. The aging of the baby boomers, in fact, will have a powerful impact on advisory firm valuation going forward, as more and more advisors focus on serving the distribution phase of wealth accumulation. Other factors that can influence g are operational efficiency and whether your firm can scale its existing infrastructure, whether it has a systematized sales and marketing capability that is proven to attract assets regardless of market conditions, and the area in which the firm is located; is your region growing and economically vibrant?

Now, let's look at a hypothetical efficient, long-established advisory firm having $1 million in revenue and good growth prospects. What would its value be? Returning to the formula $V = CF/(r - g)$, we find that cash flow is $250,000, risk is 20 percent, and growth is 5 percent, producing a value of $250,000 divided by 15 percent, or $1.7 million. How does your firm compare with this one? If your findings fall short of expectation, what can you do about it?

Build a Better Future

The preceding exercise helped you determine what your practice is worth *today*. The next step is determining what your practice must be worth when you sell it to fund your own retirement and whether your current approach is sufficient to help you achieve your own financial goals.

You can choose between two paths in building your business. One choice is serving clients by selling financial products and earning income from commissions, and the other is advising clients about strategies for their wealth and earning greater control of client assets. Typically, remuneration for this second path is based on fees, primarily by offering managed account solutions. Whichever path you choose, you will need a plan. To help you get started, take a look at the sample business plan included in Appendix A, courtesy of Joe Lukacs at International Performance Group, LLC.

Putting together the physical plan shouldn't take more than 15 to 30 minutes, but give serious thought to the process. You may not have all the data you need in the beginning, but don't get frustrated. It's better to get started and just fill in the blanks with an educated guess than to not complete any of it.

Much like an architectural blueprint that is critical to building a house, a business plan provides the structure and definition needed to build your business. It is important to have solid numeric targets; otherwise, you can get lost in potentially unproductive activities. Often advisors fail to use specific numbers—assets, clients, income—or they target their numbers incorrectly. According to our research (AIM/Gresham Company, LLC, Phoenix Wealth Survey 2000), only 20.3 percent of advisors have a current written business plan; 16.4 percent have a plan, but it is out of date; and a whopping 63.3 percent do not have a plan. The study concluded that 57.6 percent of successful advisors with incomes of $300,000 or more have a business plan. At the other end of the spectrum, 88.5 percent of those advisors whose income is less than $75,000 do not have a business plan.

Let's say an advisor earns $50,000 a year but, after completing the aforementioned exercises, he concludes that his income needs to be $150,000 a year in order for him to realize his personal and professional financial planning goals. If his income is primarily based on commissions, then he will need to sell three times as many products in order to reach his goal. That may or may not be realistic, depending on the level of support he has and the hours he is willing to work. Even if it is, he must ask himself if that is a sustainable workload—next year, five years from now, 10 years from now, and so on until he retires—because his current plan is heavily reliant on ongoing sales.

Now let's look at the same situation for an advisor who decides to offer managed account solutions as a way to boost current income and build a business that will be valuable to a potential buyer. To increase her income by $100,000 a year, she needs to capture $10 million in assets—say, 10 new clients with an account minimum of $500,000 and 20 with an account minimum of $250,000. (For the sake of reference, the average-sized separately managed account in 2007 is $325,000, according to the Money Management Institute.) Her plan, then, is to add 30 new clients over the course of the next year, or one new client approximately every two weeks. Remember, too, that by offering managed account solutions, she is not limited to finding new clients, but capturing more assets from existing clients by offering additional wealth management services such as retirement planning and estate planning.

Assume the advisors in the foregoing examples each achieved their goals in the next year. What about the year after that? The first advisor must keep up the same pace in order to realize the same level of income, and he is building little or no equity in his practice. "You can't build a business on transactions, because when you retire, you ideas go with you," explains managed account pioneer Richard "Dick" Schilffarth. The second advisor will start the year with her goals already met, because she now has $10 million in assets under management and is earning recurring revenue from those assets. "By using a fee-based approach and creating a revenue stream, you are building a business that you can sell or share in the profits when you retire," Schilffarth says. "You don't have to put in a trade every day, because your income is evergreen."

Time that otherwise would have been devoted to sales can now be focused on other pursuits, such as client retention, specialization, or even working fewer hours—and all the while the advisor is building up equity in her practice.

The reason we suggest you distill your income goal this way is because the managed account is a conceptual sale. Unlike the sale of a new issue or a single product offering, it's not a campaign—there is no urgency. You need to take a sale that might extend over months or years and reduce it to daily activities. The successful advisors we know break down their business plan into people and numeric terms to more effectively stay on track to reach their goals. The worksheet in Figure 5.3 is one way to help you go through this exercise.

Take a good look at the business plan you've just completed. Are you on the path to realizing your own financial goals and objectives? Will you be

		Sample
Incremental Income Goal:	_____	$100,000
/ Average Fee to Advisor:	_____	1.00%
= Assets Needed:	_____	10,000,000
/ Average Account Size:	_____	250,000
= Number of New Accounts:	_____	40
/ Months in Selling Period:	_____	12
= New Account Target (Monthly):	_____	$3^{1/3}$

This plan results in a new managed account almost every week.

Figure 5.3   Income Targets Worksheet

able to spend the remainder of your earning years working with the types of clients you prefer and doing the type of work you enjoy? Will you be able to enjoy a financially secure retirement at the time of your own choosing? If so, then obviously you are doing everything right and there is little reason to change. If not—if your advisory practice is not worth what you think it should be, and if your business plan is not putting you on the road to success—then it's time to consider changing the way you do things. More and more advisors are discovering that by providing managed account solutions, they can use their time more efficiently, gain access to more affluent clients, develop a consistent and predictable revenue stream leveraged by the market's growth, and build equity in their businesses. In the next chapter, we will help you determine if managed account solutions are right for you and your practice.

CHAPTER 6

How to Tell If Managed Account Solutions Are Right for Your Practice

Are managed account solutions right for you? Here's how to evaluate your potential for success.

In the preceding chapters we've discussed the various managed account solutions and their benefits to investors, and we've outlined the advantages of recurring revenue in building an advisory business. But one question remains: Are managed account solutions right for *your* practice? You are the only person who can answer that question. Here are some questions to ask yourself and scenarios to consider when determining your response.

First, consider what is most important to you in the way you operate your current practice. Do you love prospecting and selling? Do you enjoy working with clients? Do you enjoy watching the market and making stock picks? Are you personally handling duties in your business that you would prefer to delegate to someone else? We'll explore these issues and more in a search for the direction best matching your natural skills.

The checklist in Figure 6.1 highlights activities associated with both fee- and commission-based business models. Read through each list and mark the ones that most accurately reflect your attitude. Chances are, after you've gone through each list, one side will have more check marks than the other. This will tell you which approach to business suits you better. If you have more check marks on the commission-based side, then transitioning your practice to a fee-based model may not be the appropriate move for you.

Fee-Based Advisor	**Commission-Based Product Advisor**
❑ I prefer to delegate investment responsibility.	❑ I like to be in control of all the details of my accounts.
❑ I don't feel the need to be involved in every detail or day-to-day investment decisions.	❑ Being involved in the day-to-day investment decisions helps me focus on my clients.
❑ I need additional time for servicing the complex needs of clients.	❑ My clients want me to pick their stocks and manage their money and like to call me and talk about it.
❑ I enjoy working with affluent individuals.	❑ I'm not really comfortable with affluent clients; I relate better to mom-and-pop clients.
❑ I have confidence I can improve my business model.	❑ I'm not sure whether I really want to change my business; I'm somewhat hesitant to start over at this point in my career
❑ I would give up a large, short-term payout in favor of a larger income stream over time.	❑ I like the thrill of a large commission check.
❑ I don't particularly enjoy researching or picking stocks.	❑ I like studying and researching the companies behind the stocks.
❑ I like the comfort of using a proven process.	❑ I do not have the patience for involved processes and prefer a faster-paced business.
❑ I am comfortable explaining my added value as an advisor to prospects and clients.	❑ Teaching is not my strong suit; however, I thoroughly enjoy the stock market and working with clients who enjoy it, too.
❑ I obtain most of my clients through referrals.	❑ I obtain most of my clients by cold calling, direct mail and seminars.
❑ I can make a firm commitment to transitioning my business, and have the patience required to do so.	❑ I like getting paid immediately for my sales.
❑ Most of my clients are affluent and require customization.	❑ Most of my clients do not need account customization and are either stock traders or clients who need specific financial products like mutual funds or life insurance.
❑ I am at my best when I use a consultative approach.	❑ I believe my value is in choosing the right stocks and other products for my clients.
❑ I typically think long term and would like to build a valuable business.	❑ I get a lot of satisfaction from picking stock winners.

Your score: Where are your check marks? If you marked five or more in either column, that probably is your comfort zone.

Figure 6.1 Fee/Commission Checklist

Are You a Salesperson or a Solutions Provider?

If you have more check marks on the fee-based side, then it's time to give serious thought to becoming a provider of managed account solutions. If you've been considering making the transition for some time but haven't been able to bring yourself to take action, ask yourself what is holding you back. If you are like most people, the answer is simple: fear of change.

At this point in your career, you have achieved a certain level of success. Embarking on a new venture—even one that holds the potential for greater success—may be intimidating and not seem worth the risk. But don't think of the transition to managed account solutions as a 180-degree move; rather, determine your strengths and make them the foundation upon which you can build. The process will be evolutionary, but the results will be revolutionary.

Of course, there is a more practical concern for many advisors: the short-term loss of income. Most advisors who make the transition from a commission-based practice to a fee-based approach do experience a temporary decline in income—two to three years is the industry average—but this decline is followed by a surge once the transition is complete.

It's human nature to focus on short-term negative consequences rather than long-term positive results and thus to postpone taking action. If you find yourself slipping into that mode of thinking, consider this: If you've been an advisor for any length of time at all, then you have seen your income fluctuate and decline. Think back to the tech wreck and the market turbulence of 2000–2001. How did your income in those years compare with your income in 1999? If you were a commission-based advisor at that time, then odds are those years were pretty rough—but you got through them, even though at the time you did not know how many lean years there would be or how long it would take the markets (and your business) to recover.

In making the move to managed accounts, you have a rough idea of how long it will take, based on the experiences of other advisors who've already made the transition. In addition, there are variables that affect the transition time, such as:

- The number of clients you currently have who would make viable candidates for managed account solutions.
- The number of new clients you will have to find in order to achieve the income level you desire.
- The tools available from the service providers you partner with.
- The pace at which you are able to implement the transition.

At this point you may be thinking, "I know that providing managed account solutions would be better for me and my clients and I will change my business model one day, but why should I do it today? The market is doing better than it has in years. I can't afford to take time right now and restructure my business, because I will miss out on a lot of income opportunities, and who knows what the market will be like in two to three years?" While it's true that the stock market and the financial advisory industry are both enjoying robust growth, many advisors are not enjoying the full benefits of this environment because they are not properly positioned to do so.

According to the 2006 Financial Performance Study of Advisory Firms by Moss Adams LLP, firms are growing at the fastest rate in 20 years, with top-line revenues rising from an average of $777,927 in 2000 to $1.36 million in 2005. During that same period, however, advisors' yearly take-home pay inched up from an average of $253,000 to an average of $273,000. Think about that for a moment. If you're an average advisor, you've enjoyed only an 8 percent increase in pay—over five years!—while your revenues shot up 74 percent. Your practice has enjoyed a lot of motion, but very little forward momentum. (See Figure 6.2.)

The report highlighted another development: From 2003 through the end of 2006, the average firm increased its client base by nearly 30 percent. To keep up with the increased client load, firms have had to hire more advisors and support staff—direct expenses, as explained in the

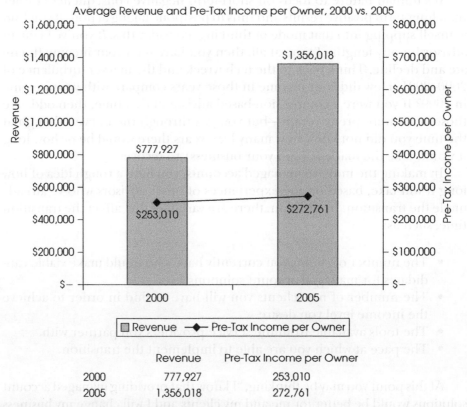

	Revenue	Pre-Tax Income per Owner
2000	777,927	253,010
2005	1,356,018	272,761

Figure 6.2   Revenue Outpaces Income

Source: Moss Adams LLP. *2006 Moss Adams Financial Performance Study of Advisory Firms.* Sponsored by JPMorgan Asset Management and SEI Advisor Network. Seattle: Moss Adams LLP, 2006.

preceding chapter—and this has put pressure on profit margins. Many advisors are paying a high price for their current success.

If you completed the exercises in the previous chapter to determine how much your practice is worth and your current income as determined by your business plan, then you have a good idea if your practice is experiencing the same challenges as the firms in the Moss Adams study, with revenue far outpacing income. Despite being in the throes of a successful market, many advisors have a difficult choice to make. As the study's authors pointed out, "Advisors will need to place even greater emphasis on new client acquisitions or evaluate their pricing and service offerings."

You can work harder and achieve modest results. Or you can work smarter and enjoy substantial gains. If the latter sounds like a preferred course of action for you, then you're ready to become a provider of managed account solutions.

Are Your Clients Good Managed Account Candidates?

If you are a veteran advisor and further along in your career, consider the types of clients you have. How many of them have the requisite account size to make a fee-based approach a cost-effective strategy? Since your greatest asset is your existing clientele, reflect on why they hired you. What were their financial needs? What services do you offer them? Where are the opportunities? Take an inventory of your business and analyze your top clients, using the worksheets in Figure 6.3.

Check off the services and products you now provide to each of your clients, such as securities, mutual funds, retirement planning, and estate planning. Profile at least 10 clients—better yet, 20—and then aggregate the answers. Run the numbers on your clients' assets and see where they are invested. Look for assets that can be better managed. A perfect managed account candidate is a client who owns a number of mutual funds and securities who now claims substantial assets. How many of your current clients fit this profile?

Gerry, an experienced advisor, transitioned a large client from mutual funds to managed accounts. "The client is a married 47-year-old surgeon who has no time to spend on his finances," says Gerry. "He responded to a mail campaign I conducted to physicians. The mailer discussed the high-end services that our firm provides and the importance of having a professional manage your assets. I met him for lunch and we completed an extensive planning profile that included an asset allocation proposal. He also gave us a one-inch pile of statements from his online brokerage account. His account was essentially full of mutual funds and was a classic study of overlapping investments. It wasn't a pretty picture.

"I had no additional contact with the client until several months later, when he sent me a letter stating that he remembered our meeting and the valuable assistance. He wanted to visit with us again. This visit included his

Evaluation of Current Client Base

Who do you work for? What would your clients say you do?

Client's Name _____

Complete one sheet for each client.

Products/Services

	Check all that apply	Assets
Cash Management Account		
Securities		
Mutual Funds		
Mutual Fund Managed Accounts		
Separately Managed Accounts		
Variable Annuities		
Life Insurance		

Financial Strategies

	Check all that apply	Date Completed or of Last Review
Asset Allocation		
Retirement Planning		
College Funding		
Estate Planning		
Charitable Giving		
Disability Protection		
Asset Protection Planning		
Long-Term Care		

Figure 6.3   Evaluation of Current Client Base, Top Client Analysis, and Productivity Analysis

Source: Attract and Retain the Affluent Investor, Dearborn Trade, 2001.

Top Client Analysis

What products and services do you offer? Where can you gain productivity and net assets?

Products/Services *(Check all that apply)*

Client's Name:														Total number of clients with product/service
Cash Management Account														
Securities														
Mutual Funds														
Mutual Fund Managed Account														
Separately Managed Account														
Variable Annuities														
Life Insurance														

Financial Strategies *(Check all that apply)*

Client's Name:														Total number of clients with product/service
Asset Allocation														
Retirement Planning														
College Funding														
Estate Planning														
Charitable Giving														
Disability Protection														
Asset Protection Planning														
Long-Term Care														

Figure 6.3   (Continued)
Source: Attract and Retain the Affluent Investor, Dearborn Trade, 2001.

Top Client Analysis

What products and services do you offer? Where can you gain productivity and net assets?

Products/Services *(Check all that apply)*

Client's Name:	B. Johnson	T. Smith	J. Shapiro	R. Kelly	M. Lynch	C. Edwards	W. Brown	K. Woodward	A. Nelson	N. Murry	R. Harris	C. Jones	T. Davis	S. Miller	Total number of clients with product/service
Cash Management Account		√	√	√		√			√		√	√	√		8
Securities	√		√	√	√	√	√			√	√		√	√	10
Mutual Funds		√	√			√		√		√		√	√		7
Mutual Fund Managed Account		√	√		√		√		√		√		√		7
Separately Managed Account	√			√		√		√			√		√		6
Variable Annuities		√							√				√		3
Life Insurance					√										1

Financial Strategies *(Check all that apply)*

Client's Name:	B. Johnson	T. Smith	J. Shapiro	R. Kelly	M. Lynch	C. Edwards	W. Brown	K. Woodward	A. Nelson	N. Murry	R. Harris	C. Jones	T. Davis	S. Miller	Total number of clients with product/service
Asset Allocation	√	√	√	√	√		√	√	√		√	√	√		11
Retirement Planning		√	√	√		√	√		√	√	√	√		√	10
College Funding	√		√		√		√	√	√			√	√		8
Estate Planning	√			√	√		√			√		√		√	7
Charitable Giving				√		√				√					3
Disability Protection															0
Asset Protection Planning	√		√												2
Long-Term Care					√										1

Figure 6.3 (Continued)

Source: Attract and Retain the Affluent Investor, Dearborn Trade, 2001.

Productivity Analysis

What do you do? What would your clients say you do? Where are your new sales opportunities?

Products/Services *(Check the number of clients you provide with these products/services)*

	0 clients	1–5 clients	6–10 clients	11–14 clients	15 or more clients
Cash Management Account					
Securities					
Mutual Funds					
Mutual Fund Managed Account					
Separately Managed Account					
Variable Annuities					
Life Insurance					

What new products/services do you want to offer?

_____

_____

_____

_____

_____

To whom?

_____

_____

_____

_____

Financial Strategies *(Check the number of clients you provide with these strategies)*

	0 clients	1–5 clients	6–10 clients	11–14 clients	15 or more clients
Asset Allocation					
Retirement Planning					
College Funding					
Securities					
Estate Planning					
Charitable Giving					
Disability Protection					
Asset Protection Planning					
Long-Term Care					

What new financial services do you want to offer?

_____

_____

_____

_____

_____

To whom?

_____

_____

_____

_____

Figure 6.3 (Continued)

Source: Attract and Retain the Affluent Investor, Dearborn Trade, 2001.

Productivity Analysis

What do you do? What would your clients say you do? Where are your new sales opportunities?

Products/Services *(Check the number of clients you provide with these products/services)*

	0 clients	1–5 clients	6–10 clients	11–14 clients	15 or more clients
Cash Management Account					√
Securities					√
Mutual Funds				√	
Mutual Fund Managed Account		√			
Separately Managed Account		√			
Variable Annuities		√			
Life Insurance		√			

What new products/services do you want to offer?

Separately Managed Accounts

To whom?

J. Shapiro

M. Lynch

Financial Strategies *(Check the number of clients you provide with these strategies)*

	0 clients	1–5 clients	6–10 clients	11–14 clients	15 or more clients
Asset Allocation					
Retirement Planning					
College Funding					
Securities					
Estate Planning					
Charitable Giving					
Disability Protection					
Asset Protection Planning					
Long-Term Care					

What new financial services do you want to offer?

Charitable Giving

Asset Protection Planning

To whom?

T. Davis

H. Mullen

B. Taylor

Figure 6.3   (Continued)
Source: Attract and Retain the Affluent Investor, Dearborn Trade, 2001.

wife to get her onboard with the process and benefits of using managed accounts. The meeting was a big success! The client has recently transferred approximately $7 million to us, mostly from a major mutual fund company. We are transitioning him slowly out of the funds because most of the account is taxable. One thing I believe gnawed on the client was the big tax check he had to write last year for the gains on his growth funds. More importantly, though, the client was convinced of the advantages of using a managed account for a portfolio of this magnitude."

The 2007 Phoenix Wealth Survey looked at more than 1,800 high-net-worth individuals (defined as those with more than $1 million exclusive of any debts and the value of their primary residence). Nearly three-quarters of the individuals surveyed said they owned stocks, 59 percent owned mutual funds outside of a tax-deferred retirement plan, and 48 percent owned bonds—but only 19 percent owned a separately managed account. If the clients in your practice are similar to the participants in this survey, then many of them are in need of managed account solutions.

You can be the provider of that solution, or another advisor can. The competitive reality is that affluent clients may be happy with what you do, but if you are not able to offer all of the services they require, eventually many of them will find an advisor who can. The Phoenix Wealth Survey found that 24 percent of high-net-worth clients who plan to change advisors in the coming year will do so because their current advisor does not provide the products and services they need. In other words, many affluent clients *want* to do more with their advisors, and presumably most advisors want to do more with their affluent clients, but in many cases this isn't happening. By becoming a provider of managed account solutions, you can make sure that you don't lose your affluent clients to another advisor who is able to offer services that you can't.

If you are doing the majority of your work in financial and estate planning but are not capturing assets for investment management, you are leaving money on the table. This is especially true for advisors who focus more on the life insurance needs of clients. Accustomed to solving estate planning and business succession issues using insurance, these advisors often leave the investable assets for other advisors. You have an opportunity to complete the relationship with your clients and make the move away from protection and transition services (like insurance) and into asset management.

Conduct an inventory of clients who have additional assets elsewhere. Through improved client service, you have the potential of earning additional assets from a certain percentage of your existing client base. Make an educated guess about how much you think you could capture—20 clients at $100,000 each? Or 15 clients who each have $500,000 with another advisor or institution? Use the Prospecting Model Worksheet in Figure 6.4 to make a list with actual client names and actual numbers to give you some sense of what the financial reward might be if you provide enhanced client service to these individuals.

		Sample
ANNUAL INCOME GOAL:		**$100,000**
ANNUAL ASSET GOAL:		**$10,000,000**

EXISTING CLIENTS:		
B. TAYLOR		**$50,000**
H. MULLEN		**$100,000**
A. NELSON		**$250,000**
J. SHAPIRO		**$500,000**
B. JOHNSON		**$50,000**
R. HARRIS		**$50,000**
TOTAL EXPECTED FROM EXISTING CLIENTS:		**$1,000,000**

NEW CLIENTS:		**$10,000,000**
		–1,000,000
Assets from New Clients		**$9,000,000**
/ Average Account Size:		**$250,000**
= Number of New Accounts		**36**
/ Months in Selling Period		**12**
= New Account Target (Monthly)		**3**
ASSET GOAL:		**$9,000,000**
ACCOUNTS:		**36**
MONTHLY GOAL NEW ACCOUNTS:		**3**
FORMULA FOR CLOSING RATIO:		
Number of Qualified Prospects		
per New Account		**5**
× Monthly New Account Goal		**3**
= Total Monthly Prospects		
per Seminar		**15**
FORMULA FOR PROSPECT RATIO:		
Number of Invitees per Prospect		
Mailing Lists:		**30**
× Monthly Prospects		**15**
= Total Invitees per Month:		**450**

Figure 6.4 Prospecting Model Worksheet
This plan calls for sending 450 seminar invitations and closing 3 of the 450 prospects each month.

If you are like most advisors, your clients range from modest to wealthy, with a substantial number in-between. Even though you may have more than 500 accounts, when you go beyond the top 20 households, it's difficult to provide a full range of services. Our research indicates that even the most successful advisors are able to provide a full solution set to only a small number of clients.

George, an advisor in the Midwest, made the transition to managed account solutions and narrowed his focus to a smaller number of families. He eventually converted all of those accounts and stripped his book from 600 accounts to just over 100. He was rewarded with 30 percent more assets and 25 percent more income within nine months of making his transition.

"After my assistant and I began to sort through my book of clients, I realized that many individuals were not really clients; they were buyers," says George. "It soon became clear to us that we'd collected a lot of accounts over the years, but relatively few of them had developed into relationships. This was troubling because we wanted to be advisors to our affluent clients, not just brokers peddling stocks to anyone who called."

Does this scenario sound familiar to you? It's safe to say that most veteran advisors have long-term clients who suit their temperament and fit well with the services they provide. But, due to the sales nature of the business, some advisors may have accumulated a few clients who don't fit. Some advisors and brokers never say no to a prospect and, consequently, have clients on the books who don't match their desired profile. They may be clients who are potential referral sources or those with few assets who are friends of good clients. They may be clients who might come into more money at some point. These clients are all difficult to part with, but many of them just don't materialize into solid, long-term business.

As you consider whether a move to managed accounts is right for you, you must determine if you are willing to limit your practice to the type of client you want to duplicate. They are the ones with whom you will distinguish yourself, which will ultimately lead to more referrals. The exclusivity of your services will draw a certain type of client. These individuals are willing to pay a higher percentage of their income to avail themselves of special and custom services. But in order to establish this reputation and win this business, you must be willing to define your target market—and that means turning away some prospects and transitioning some current clients to another firm.

Most firms are promoting fee-based business, managed accounts, and consulting. One firm in particular has created a specific program to discourage smaller accounts. Every firm has weighed in, in some way, with a wealth management focus. The financial advisory firms of the future are focused on these key areas and, as an advisor today, you will benefit tremendously from the trend toward an upscale clientele.

Fewer Clients, More Opportunities

In many ways, George's experience is typical of that of many advisors—and also reflective of the way the financial services industry has evolved. He began his career in the 1980s trading futures in the Chicago pits. About 10 years later, a friend who worked for a wirehouse told him about the firm's new emphasis on financial planning and consulting. The idea appealed to George because he was ready to move out of the futures and stock business and into a more value-added area of financial consulting. He soon joined his friend and became a broker.

George liked the approach of financial planning, and he began providing clients with 60- to 80-page plans for $175 each. Soon after, he developed an aggressive prospecting campaign and spent a great deal of time networking with other professionals, namely certified public accountants (CPAs) and attorneys. "By the mid-1990s, I was doing more business and—theoretically—lots of planning," George says. "But the reality was that I was out chasing new business rather than implementing what I said I would do in the financial plans we had developed."

George was spending more time selling than he was advising, and he was not comfortable in that mode. "I finished 1997 with $422,000 in production and $48 million in assets," he says. "I had 630 accounts and I had done 211 comprehensive financial plans." He realized that *more* was not *better*. He had reached a plateau and was overwhelmed, exhausted, and worried that he was not delivering to his clients what he had promised.

After careful evaluation of his business, George determined that he could effectively service 100 clients. But he wasn't clear whether he could make a living serving such a small number of individuals. Long hours of calculating and analyzing led him to realize that he was, in fact, operating two separate—and very different—businesses: a brokerage business and an advisory business. It then became clear that the brokerage side was interfering with his responsibilities as a valued advisor. George's assistant helped him confirm that phone calls from small brokerage clients outnumbered calls from larger advisory clients by an overwhelming ratio of 17:1.

Armed with this information, George and his assistant created criteria, or screens, that he used to rank his clients. He developed 11 key screens that helped him cull and manage his current book of clients.

1. *Account by Production*—a report of each account by production for the first eight months of the calendar year.
2. *Value of Assets*—a report of each account evaluated by its assets.
3. *List of Priority Clients*—a list of clients holding assets of at least $250,000 at the firm or contributing $5,000 in production for the year; there were 40 such individuals.
4. *Likability*—a more subjective, but equally important, criterion was whether or not George liked his clients and vice versa.

5. *Investment Approach Acceptance*—a screen that helped George determine which clients believed in his managed account approach.
6. *Financial Qualifications*—a crucial element in establishing which clients had significant assets to implement George's suggestions and/or plans.
7. *Premier Client Capability*—a list of the clients most likely to use more of the firm's services.
8. *Hard-Dollar Profitability*—an analysis of all expenses incurred while traveling or entertaining certain clients.
9. *Soft-Dollar Profitability*—a determination of costs based on how much time each client required.
10. *Price-Value Test*—a crucial element for George (and any advisor) who needs to screen out clients who insist on negotiating fees or receiving discounts.
11. *Future Growth Opportunities*—a screen to determine which clients might assist the advisor in capturing more assets. George discovered referrals, family business opportunities, and other ways to increase business through interaction with certain clients.

Once he analyzed his current client list on the basis of the 11 screens, George was startled by what he discovered. "It took us four months to get to those 11 screens, and when we finally analyzed which clients made it through all of them, we ended up with just 33," he says. "At first, we thought it was impossible: How could 631 accounts yield just 33 good clients [some of whom represented more than one account]? How could we base a business on 33 clients?"

George crunched some numbers to see what would happen to his income if he worked with just those 33 clients, and the results were startling. If he gave up all of his other clients and focused exclusively on the 33 who had cleared his screen test, he would lose only 9 percent of his production!

He decided to rework his approach and focus on "creating, implementing, and monitoring life plans," as he began to describe it. Too often, George says, financial consulting ends up being a one-time event despite the best initial intentions of both advisor and client. His "life plan" is a process that allows George to be involved with his clients on a continuing basis, and it gives him the opportunity to follow the client along the wealth life-cycle process and change the financial plan as the client evolves.

"I met with all 33 clients for two- and three-hour conversations and explained my new plan," he says. "I told them I was making a huge commitment to this new way of doing business and asked them to help me find 45 more clients similar to themselves, which would bring my total client list to 78. If they didn't help me, I explained, I'd be right back scrambling to get clients and not being able to give them [current clients] the attention they deserved. Happily, they went along with me."

George soon discovered that filtering prospects through the entire 11 screens was too time-consuming, so he devised a custom three-part strategy that allowed him to assess prospects in about 30 minutes. Here are the three parameters George eventually chose:

1. It is imperative that I like the client and the client likes me.
2. We must agree on the business and investment philosophy.
3. The client must have the financial solidity to implement the investment plan.

Today, George meets with each of his clients once a month, and all clients receive a biannual portfolio review. In addition, he spends one full day every year with his top 35 to 40 clients—breakfast-through-dinner sessions, not just an afternoon of golf. "I want to spend time at their place of employment, at home, and over meals getting to know them better and truly understanding what is important in their lives," he says.

As a result of his new business model, George was able to develop a client management system that allows him the necessary time to devote to his clients without being rushed or overwhelmed, as he was in the old days. He has regularly scheduled phone appointments and in-person meetings, and each client has a time slot each month "for the rest of their lives," he says.

Most of his clients are not interested in the stock market or any other particular investment. Taxes, estate planning, life insurance, business advice, and other issues are most important to them, he says. George oversees average client assets of $1.6 million and a return on assets of about 1 percent.

His advice to other advisors who want to change their business model? "Pick your own business objective and live it passionately," he says. "You have to believe—and act on the belief—that more is not better, and you have to change your outlook accordingly."

Are You Ready to Change *Your* Outlook?

George's business transformation is startling, but not unique. Many advisors report similar dramatic changes when they adopt managed account solutions and focus their efforts on providing more services to fewer clients. Advisors are happy because they have more time, more money, and greater job satisfaction. Clients are happy because they can turn to one trusted source to handle all of their wealth management needs.

What would happen to your own practice if you followed George's example? As you consider whether being a provider of managed account solutions is the right move for you, ask yourself the same 11 questions about your clients that George asked about his:

1. How much revenue does each of your accounts generate?
2. How many assets are in each account?

3. Which accounts do you or your firm consider premier based on revenue generation, assets, or other important criteria?
4. Do you like your clients? Do your clients like you?
5. Are your clients in sync with your investment style and process?
6. How wealthy are your clients? Rank each one according to their asset size (or what you think it might be, as well as an amount you might possibly capture).
7. How many clients buy more than one service from you?
8. Do you have clients who are expensive to maintain?
9. Do some of your clients demand too much of your time?
10. Do some of your clients constantly ask for discounts or want to negotiate fees?
11. Do your clients have good referral sources; do they represent networking possibilities for you?

By answering these questions honestly and listing all of the pros and cons of maintaining your current client base, you might find—as George did—that by focusing on fewer clients, you will create more opportunities for yourself and for them. (See Figure 6.5.) In the long run, you will increase your income and the quality of your clientele.

Client's Name _____		
Complete one sheet for each client.		
Products/Services		
	Check all that apply	Data
Gross revenue/account		
Assets/account		
Do you like them?		
Do they like you?		
Are you philosophically in line?		
Can they execute?		
"Total wealth" prospect?		
Profitability—hard dollar		
Profitability—soft dollar		
Growth potential		

Figure 6.5   What Makes a Great Client?
Source: Attract and Retain the Affluent Investor, Dearborn Trade, 2001.

My ideal client has the following characteristics:

Revenues: _____

                 _____

                 _____

                 _____

Assets: _____

                 _____

                 _____

                 _____

Growth Potential: _____

                 _____

                 _____

                 _____

Referrals: _____

                 _____

                 _____

                 _____

Compatibility: _____

                 _____

                 _____

                 _____

Figure 6.5   (Continued)
Source: Attract and Retain the Affluent Investor, Dearborn Trade, 2001.

Many advisors who make the transition to managed account solutions decide to focus on a particular type of high-net-worth client—small-business owners, doctors, lawyers, and so on. Think about the top 10 to 20 clients you identified earlier. What, if anything, do they have in common with one another? The answer to this question will not only help you define your niche, but also be the key that drives referrals, which are an essential way of attracting new clients.

Remember, the answer can be quite simple: In George's case, they were all people he liked, and he decided he wanted to work only with people whose company he enjoyed. You may draw the same conclusion; after all, it's a lot more pleasant working with likable people, those with whom you share common interests and values. Doing so provides an emotional payoff that won't appear on any balance sheet or income statement, but is crucial to quality of life.

Finding commonality among current affluent clients is crucial in another way, too. Selling managed account solutions to affluent clients and having the confidence and emotional security to handle the sales—that is, without worrying that you are going to lose control of the client—is a function of personality and temperament. You may be wondering if you are suited to this type of client, and this anxiety may be holding you back from transitioning your business.

But just as thinking back to the tech wreck and tumultuous markets of 2000 and 2001 is a helpful reminder that you have experienced periods of fluctuating or declining income but came through them okay, reminding yourself that your work with some affluent clients (even if they represent only a small percentage of your current client base) will go a long way toward alleviating any concerns you may have about becoming a provider of managed account solutions. You may be further along the road than you realize. In the next chapter, we show you how to step on the gas!

Transforming Your Practice into a Wealth Management Business

Step-by-step instructions for explaining managed account solutions to clients and prospects, gathering information and developing an investment policy statement, and structuring an effective client meeting.

Many years ago, a major life insurance company created a memorable commercial slogan to help brand its services: "Too busy making money to manage it?" This question resounded loudly throughout the financial services industry, and many advisors began asking a similar question of clients and prospects: "Do you have the time necessary to manage your own money effectively?"

The question is even more relevant today. Everyone, it seems, is pressed for time and has difficulty fulfilling all of the obligations expected of them. Many investors will acknowledge that they wish they could devote more time to managing their money, but more urgent concerns always seem to take precedence. This is why time is a key selling point of managed account solutions. By reassuring clients and prospects that their money is safely in the hands of professional money managers, you free up their time to focus on other concerns.

Of course, this does not mean that clients and prospects will automatically hand over their account numbers to you, just to save themselves some time. It does mean that the prospect of saving time while also enjoying peace of mind over their investments will likely open the door to further conversation about the other benefits of managed account solutions.

Explaining Managed Account Solutions

Another major selling point of managed account solutions is access to management expertise. Many of the same investors who say they'd like to devote more time to managing their money will admit (albeit reluctantly, in some cases) that they couldn't do as good a job as a professional money manager. Having sufficient time to manage money is meaningless if the investor lacks the requisite skills to invest effectively—and investors know it.

Market performance has been terribly humbling for many people over the years, who may now be convinced of the value provided by professionals. When managed accounts were popularized in 1987 as a product and process for the affluent market, one of the main reasons they were so quickly embraced was because they were introduced in the aftermath of a market crash and investors were looking for help.

The double whammy of the 1987 stock and bond market crashes sent investors running from their own bull market success—they had enjoyed rising prices since 1982 and were unprepared for a sharp, sudden downturn in the market. When it came, and they realized they did not possess the expertise necessary to manage their assets, they turned to professional money managers. The years 2000 and 2001 provided the same experience for many baby boomers, who now dominate the affluent marketplace. According to a recent Phoenix Wealth Survey, more than 80 percent of affluent baby boomers accumulated their wealth in the 1990s, and nearly half accumulated it in the final five years of that decade. In other words, these investors had never experienced a significant market downturn since accumulating their wealth. The bull market had taught them (or led them to believe, anyway) that they knew how to make money, but the subsequent bear market demonstrated that many didn't know how to manage or protect it.

A similar challenge lies ahead for boomers inching toward retirement. They have amassed significant wealth in defined benefit or defined contribution plans, individual retirement accounts (IRAs), and other vehicles, but the accumulation phase is nearing its end and they have questions and concerns about what to do next. Many will embrace a managed account solution once they become aware of its many benefits.

First Benefit: Time Savings

Businesspeople, private-practice professionals, and pre-retirees who are too busy earning money to manage it are ideal candidates for managed accounts. Typically, they spend so much time at work that they have little time left over to worry about second-guessing a money manager. Remember, the managed account, for the most part, is a fully invested position with someone with whom neither you nor the client will have day-to-day contact. That kind of arm's-length relationship will be attractive to some investors, but not all.

A managed account solution, like all strategic investment approaches, focuses on the long term. Investors likely to get caught up in day-to-day and even moment-to-moment market developments are generally ill suited to managed accounts.

Advisor Tip

The Busier, the Better

Bill, an advisor in the Midwest, believes the busier the prospect, the better the prospect: "The businessperson needs to focus on his or her own company and let us manage the finances. The client must have the mentality of 'I have other things to do and don't have time to focus on managing my assets.'"

If clients have plenty of time to oversee their investments and to call you and discuss them, and they are actively involved and interested in the market, then the time issue of managed accounts is not a benefit to them. They enjoy the process; they like the game. But they're not good prospects. Move on.

Second Benefit: Access to Expertise

Personal experience with poor performance is the most significant factor in teaching many investors they don't have the expertise necessary to manage their own assets. It's the less-than-stellar performance of their account and their inability to take action that usually hit home. More precisely, it's the poor decisions they made—choosing an inappropriate investment, holding on to an investment too long, improper asset allocation, and so on—that will spur them to entrust their assets to others who are able to make more adept investment decisions.

Mike, a financial consultant, points out two other powerful considerations when discussing the viability of managed account solutions with prospects and clients. "No one rebalances their accounts for stock splits and, in some instances, won't even do so for changes in risk tolerance. Plus, there is a tremendous amount of expertise available within an outside manager's firm, and to have that availability is a big advantage. I don't want to be limited to my own firm's research."

Third Benefit: Account Aggregation

It's not uncommon for even financially savvy clients to have investments all over the place—a 401(k) from a former job that was never rolled over, shares of inherited stock that have been held with little or no thought to how this investment coordinates with other client assets, and so on. A managed account solution provides clients with one statement, so they can tell at a glance how their investments are doing—even when those investments are spread across a wide range of instruments.

Some clients may initially view the benefit of account consolidation as a concern and invoke the admonition against putting all of your eggs in one basket. This concern is readily addressed, because of course the eggs are not in one basket; they are in multiple baskets of stocks, bonds, mutual funds, exchange-traded funds, alternative investments—whichever instruments best serve the client's needs. The single statement, which reflects the performance of multiple investments, saves the client time and underscores the benefit of working with multiple managers with high levels of expertise.

Fourth Benefit: Discipline

The primary value added by a managed account solution is the disciplined decision-making investment process. "Investors generally can't get that discipline themselves, and they can't get it from mutual funds," says Chuck, an advisor who runs a large practice in the Southeast. He discusses the advantages of transitioning to this type of program in a letter to clients (outlining the tax advantages, customization, etc.). If new clients focus too much on the fees and what the performance numbers look like, he believes they are embarking on a disastrous, two-dimensional decision. "The process is the key to success," says Chuck. "That is why managed accounts work."

A disciplined investment process helps the client avoid making impulsive decisions that ultimately can hurt performance. By drawing up an investment policy statement that outlines the client's long-term goals and objectives, you help the client develop a personal financial plan, stay focused on the long term, and ignore day-to-day market fluctuations.

It's helpful to make clients aware of the fact that success in the markets is limited to only a handful of days. Edwin Friderici, senior vice president with Phoenix Investment Partners, examined the performance of the Standard & Poor's 500 index from January 1981 through May 2007 and discovered that investors who resisted the temptation to move out of the market in times of crisis (1987 and 2001, for example) enjoyed average annualized returns of 9.5 percent. However, had they missed only the 10 best days during that entire period, their annualized returns would have dropped to 7.4 percent—a decline of nearly 20 percent for missing only 10 days! (See Figure 7.1.)

- Had they missed the 20 best days, their annualized returns would have been 5.7 percent.
- Had they missed the 30 best days, their annualized returns would have been 4.3 percent.
- Had they missed the 50 best days, their annualized returns would have been 1.9 percent.

But let's think about what we are asking of this investor. Since we have no way of knowing when the 10 best days—or even the 50 best days—are

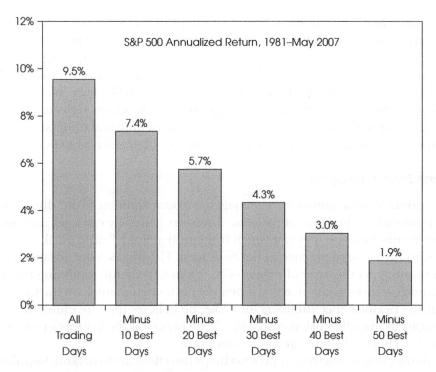

S&P 500 Annualized Return, 1981–May 2007

Figure 7.1 Buy Right and Sit Tight
Sources: Phoenix Investment Partners; Zweig Consulting, LLC.

going to occur, we are asking them to have the patience and the confidence to stay fully invested over decades of volatility. Essentially, we are telling them that to beat cash, they must stay in the market to catch a random collection of banner days. On its face, this is an intellectually offensive statement to make to anyone with any degree of intelligence! The only way to

Advisor Tip

No More Mumbo Jumbo

Says advisor Dan in New York about the process, "We cut through the mumbo jumbo and explain to our clients in plain English how the managed account process works. There is a right way and a wrong way to do managed account presentations. The right way is to position yourself, the advisor, as the cornerstone. Once you explain the process, you describe how your tools differ from others'. Just because your client might have an advisor across the street at a competitor firm who uses the same manager doesn't mean that client will end up with the same results. We explain that important tax issues also can impact overall return. This type of investigative, focused interaction sets us apart with clients and gives us a tremendous edge as a firm."

convince clients to hang in for the long term is to educate them about the benefits of staying in place and to have confidence in the process. As the preceding example illustrates, investors pay a high price for making decisions in the heat of the moment. Having a consistent process and a plan in place shields them from acting in ways contrary to their own best interests.

Fifth Benefit: Objectivity

Managed account solutions offer clients two types of objectivity. First, the individual money managers handling the investments are compensated on their management performance, not on the sale of a particular product or financial instrument. Second, the financial advisor is compensated on the basis of asset management fees, not commissions. The best way to increase your income over the long term is to help your client increase the value of his or her account. You both benefit.

However, advisors should be aware of a potential hidden conflict. With their fortunes linked to asset management fees, an aggressive advisor coupled with an aggressive investor might be tempted to select a manager with the highest returns, not only for the potential benefit of the client, but also for the potential benefit of the advisor. This, unfortunately, unites both investor and advisor in a perilously concentrated run toward a bigger performance number that can compromise the entire process.

Conflict of interest can be more than an advisor putting personal financial gain ahead of a client's interests. It can also mean subjective decision making. Show your prospect or client how working with managed accounts eliminates conflicts of interest in the decision-making process by highlighting the multiple levels of decision making. I like to call this the Hierarchy of Expertise, shown in Figure 7.2.

At the individual securities selection level, a professional advisor employs analysts and portfolio managers. Above them is the consulting group of the sponsoring firm—for example, Smith Barney, Merrill Lynch, Morgan Stanley—another layer of professional analysts who select and provide the ongoing due diligence of the asset management firm. Then there's the expertise of the financial advisor, who helps identify and articulate the client's financial objectives and then matches him or her with an appropriate manager. This is a powerful way to eliminate the conflict of interest that typically occurs from too much reliance on one person or on one firm's research.

Steve, a prominent consultant on the East Coast, manages about $1.2 billion for 350 households. He explains to clients that by using external managers, he avoids conflict of interest; although he works for an investment banking firm, his managers do not. Buy and sell decisions are based on external research, not internal. Objectivity is a key selling point and is met with a receptive ear.

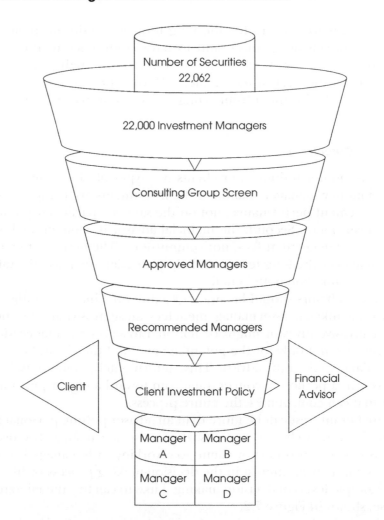

Figure 7.2   Hierarchy of Expertise

Advisor Tip

World Series Advisor

Dan in New York uses his own custom analogy for the Hierarchy of Expertise. "A good discussion of the advisor as the cornerstone in the client/advisor/ manager relationship centers around the structure of the New York Yankees," he says. "Here's what I tell clients: 'You, Mr. Client, are George Steinbrenner. You hire me, Joe Torre, as your advisor. I don't play the game (manage the money), but I have Alex Rodriguez and Derek Jeter do so. With you, Mr. Client, I can bench people, hire new people, and, if need be, fire them.' As New Yorkers, prospects like this comparison, even if it is a simplified way of explaining the process and its benefits."

Sixth Benefit: Customization

Does your client buy off-the-rack or tailor-made clothing? One of the great benefits of a managed account solution is the ability to tailor, within reason, a portfolio to the needs of your client. The customization process begins with the investment policy statement (specific needs and objectives). While it is true that the individual money managers may not do anything different for your client than they would for any other client, it is important to know which manager (or combination of managers) will create the correct mix for each of your clients.

Customization comes in a second form: the ability to eliminate from consideration certain stocks your client might find objectionable or unnecessary (again, within reason and without compromising the manager's mandate for managing clients at the brokerage firm). For example, if your client worked for IBM for 20 years, he or she might want that stock eliminated from the portfolio, since he or she already owns a considerable amount. If your client is concerned about the environment, he or she might want to eliminate managers who would not screen out companies deemed environmentally unfriendly, such as automobile manufacturers or paper mills. If your client is a pacifist, he or she might not want managers invested heavily in defense industries.

A third form of customization is in the area of taxation. If your client has a taxable account, you can help him or her harvest tax losses and shelter gains in some other area. You may also be able to protect your client from wash sales.

Mike is among the many consultants who believe the tax-advantaged benefits of managed accounts can be the real value added for clients. "We control the tax ramifications and capital gains. With mutual funds, the account is not within your control. Think back to 1987, when valuable stocks were sold in fund portfolios to meet redemptions by panicking shareholders. We didn't know what they were selling. With managed money, we do."

Mike also warns that with funds, a client's redeployment options can be limited: Investors can't control their gains in funds, take losses, and have a truly effective personalized strategy. "Mutual funds are really a starter investment strategy," he says. "The sophisticated investor not only needs managed accounts, but also should consider having 5 to 10 percent of the portfolio in hedge funds. This type of mix will become more common in the next few years as investors and advisors become better educated about alternative asset classes."

How to Address Client Concerns

With prospects, you are embarking on a new relationship, and the benefits of managed account solutions outlined earlier should be sufficient to sell them on the concept. However, established clients may have a few questions. These are the people you've worked with for years, who are accustomed to viewing you in a certain light, and you are asking them to change their relationship with you. Prospects come to you because they are ready for something new. Current clients may have to get used to the idea.

Why Change?

Some clients might say something like this: "I am perfectly comfortable working with you the way we have been for years. Why should it change?" State your reasons with conviction, and most clients will understand the benefits. Advisors who have difficulty moving clients to managed accounts or fee-based business typically don't believe in the benefits of the move, and that lack of conviction comes across in their presentation. They toss it out as one idea among many. Clients detect the lack of commitment and believe their advisor was not truly invested in the concept.

Why Fees?

Some clients may wonder why they should pay a fee for a service rather than a commission on a product, and in so doing they've more or less answered their own question. The fee is for the services that the managed account solution provides on an ongoing basis: portfolio optimization, asset allocation, diversification, tax efficiency, management expertise, and so on.

They're still getting the products—and a lot more—for about the same price. "Once clients understand that the total fees can be similar to mutual funds, they generally are sold," says Gerry. "If you take the performance and fees out of managed accounts and focus on the process, it becomes much easier for clients to understand the concept. Stay away from the alphas and betas! Our fee for a $1 million account is about 150 basis points, which is similar to an equity mutual fund, so they can relate to that."

Chip Walker, managing director of Wachovia Securities, says that if clients get caught up in compensation issues, it's because they may not fully understand the new definition of investment success that you're offering them. "This is an issue of perception versus reality in a lot of ways," he says, adding that clients who are accustomed to being sold the latest benchmark-beating stock or fund need to redirect their focus. "Financial advisors need to be able to help clients articulate what exactly they are trying to achieve, and it's not about benchmarking their portfolios against the S&P 500 or some other index, but rather benchmarking against their own individual goals— the beach house, their children's college educations, and so on. Bill Miller had 15 straight years of beating the S&P. No one else has been able to touch that record, but unless as an investor you achieve your goals, then what is the value? You can beat a benchmark and still fail to meet your life goals, so it's important to change the client's assumptions and have a radically different conversation. It's about helping clients figure out what they want to achieve in their lives, what is their time frame, and what investment strategy will enable them to succeed."

Erik is firmly committed to the value of managed accounts and likes to educate his clients. "When migrating clients to managed money, we tell them that this is how real money is managed—institutions do it this way," he explains. "We take them through the process and explain the discipline and philosophy behind the concept. One question we ask when we get resistance is, 'What is your sell discipline?' This is particularly relevant to the investor who likes to be in control. Of course, most investors don't have a sell discipline, which is one reason they do so poorly. As a compromise to the control issue, we suggest those clients keep a small piece that they can manage with us on a small scale in addition to the externally managed account. This can be used in special situations with certain clients."

Where to Meet and What to Ask

You're now prepared to explain the benefits of managed account solutions and address any concerns that clients might have. Where will that meeting take place? The setting is crucial, because when an individual is comfortable in the environment, it's usually easier for him or her to talk openly. A Boston advisor we know couldn't get his prospects to open up in face-to-face meetings; he said he had better luck gathering information over the phone. If you stepped into this advisor's office, you would understand why people were not comfortable: It was stacked with dozens of notebooks holding client statements.

When the prospective clients looked around the room and saw huge books titled A, B, and C—all the way down to Z—they felt intimidated by the sheer number of clients competing for the advisor's time. Another reason: The office itself was a mess and there was activity everywhere, with staff and other advisors running around. Think about that: Would you want to sit down with your banker in a lobby with no walls or doors and discuss personal information while applying for a home mortgage? The most successful private banks provide confidential discussion areas for their best clients.

What can you do to help make potential clients feel more at ease? Always ask prospects where they would feel most comfortable talking, and make sure your environment doesn't work against you. Consider the following:

- Where do you usually meet with prospective clients? Why? If you usually meet in your office, is that because it's convenient for you or convenient for them?
- Is your office quiet?
- Is your office private?
- Do you not have evidence of client records and books lying around?
- Is your computer screen away from your line of sight?
- Do you listen only to your prospect or client, not take phone calls or allow yourself to be pulled away by other distractions?

Try sitting where your prospects sit during a meeting with you. What do you see, and what does it say about you? Be objective. Have a good friend, spouse, or manager view your office and express an opinion about what the setting says about you. Remember: Your prospects are creating an impression of you, and that's why you want to keep the focus on them. Think about how your office reflects you and your personality, work habits, and values. You don't want an excessive amount of decoration or luxury that would distract your prospects.

Advisor Tip

Banking on Success

David in the Fort Lauderdale area sent his decorator to several private banks and asked her to duplicate that feel for his office in a wirehouse branch. The result is an effective blend of rich furnishings and high technology that represents confidence and achievement. Family photos are mixed with interesting trinkets, all inviting a view of the advisor that makes prospective clients feel he has already shared something personal about himself.

The next step is to draw up an investment policy statement (IPS). There is no more valuable tool in the client communication process than the IPS, which helps drive the investment solution. A much-overlooked sales tool, the IPS is the foundation of client communication and, when used correctly, the process of information gathering allows the bonding between you and your prospect to begin.

An effective investment policy statement breaks out all the key issues necessary to guide the parties responsible for executing the investment solution. (See Appendix C for a sample investment policy statement.) These include:

- *Income or total return goals.*
- *Time horizon.* This is the length of time until future liquidity events such as retirement or college education. This is one of the most important determinants in asset allocation and risk tolerance profiling.
- *Risk tolerance.* Delineated in arithmetic form, typically as a percentage volatility tolerance, this is an absolute determination based on real-life requirements.
- *Asset allocation guidelines.* In addition to objective, numeric criteria, special considerations also are included, such as preferences for certain asset classes.
- *Social, environmental, ethical issues.* Some investors may wish to avoid securities of companies that, for example, produce greenhouse gases or supply arms.
- *Roles and responsibilities.* This is an outline of the duties of the investment advisor, investment managers, and custodian.
- *Investment manager selection criteria.*
- *Control procedures*, specifically review criteria, timing, and rebalancing.

To obtain the information you need, it is not necessary to work through a complex questionnaire. Many of the best advisors we know work with simple yellow pads in the beginning. Our belief is that all of the support documents and questionnaires that traditionally are used in this initial information-gathering stage can be minimized. Keep them as valuable tools to pull out of your toolbox when you need them.

It's important to keep this first meeting as human as possible for as long as possible. Remember, some prospects will come to you as a result of a bad experience with someone else, and if that's the case, then you need to know quickly. Try a very simple dialogue: "Mr. Montgomery, have you worked with a financial advisor before? How would you describe your experience with him or her? What were the reasons that prompted you to seek a different advisor?"

Finding out why a prospect has decided to change advisors can be very helpful in determining his or her values and expectations. Was the prospect dissatisfied with the former advisor's availability (or lack thereof)? Was he or she disappointed with portfolio performance? Was he or she looking for products and services that the former advisor could not provide?

This conversation is essential for both advisor and prospect. For the former, it's an opportunity to gain insight into what the prospect expects from an advisor; for the latter, it is a first step on the road to recovery. The prospect has been through a bad experience and needs to speak openly about his or her investing past, and your ability to empathize is one way you can distinguish yourself from other advisors. These types of conversations are not dependent upon questionnaires or financial planning documents, but rather on simple human interaction.

While some prospects are delighted to come forward and discuss their personal affairs, others are more discreet and perhaps less forthcoming about confidential information. Before launching into a series of questions that may strike some prospects as too personal, think about ways in which you can make them more comfortable with the process. The most successful advisors start out by determining (with the client) whether they are a good fit for each other, and that begins with the initial interview.

What is your goal for an initial interview? It's not so important that you get your points across—you can do that later, after you establish a bond with the prospect. Expect to talk about yourself and do a lot of explaining about your background. Keep in mind that you need to spend a significant chunk of time with your prospect during that initial interview just establishing that bond and getting to know him or her better.

Chuck tells us he always spends at least two hours with a prospect in the first meeting. Keats, in Virginia, agrees with Chuck about spending as much time as necessary to get to know your prospect. "The process of uncovering if the client will, in fact, delegate really begins at the profiling stage in the first meeting," he says. "This should be the longest meeting you have. Many advisors take 40 minutes profiling and two hours offering solutions. We do the reverse—two hours profiling, and then we offer solutions. The concept is to get beyond the data gathering to the core attitudes. Can this person delegate philosophically? Ask the client, 'Do you like this idea/concept?' Find out how he or she delegates in his or her own business. Ask, 'Is there a dollar amount that will allow you maintain your lifestyle? What help do your children need to reach their goals? Here is your life as it is today; what do you want it to look like in 30 years?' Those are the kinds of questions that need to be asked. Get the big picture first, dig into the details, and talk about who will manage the money later. A logical, disciplined approach to uncovering core values in the client generates trust; only then will he or she delegate. This is not an easy process, but it works."

Uncovering your clients' goals is crucial. Ask what their investment objectives are, and determine a specific dollar amount that would make them feel secure financially. The top financial goals of affluent investors (those with net worth of $1 million, exclusive of debt and primary residence) who participated in the 2007 Phoenix Wealth Survey are:

- Not run out of money in retirement (56 percent).
- Minimize income and capital gains tax (51 percent).
- Assure a comfortable standard of living during retirement (51 percent).

Many of your clients will express the same goals. To help you determine the products and services they will need, take a look at the Wealth Management Picture in Figure 7.3. Review all of the areas and discuss those that are of

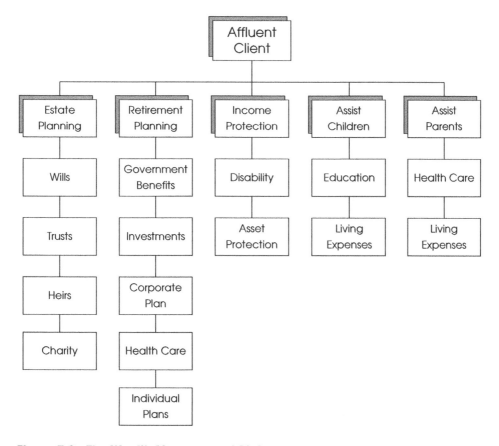

Figure 7.3   The Wealth Management Picture

greatest concern to clients right now, and explain how you can provide solutions to those issues. Here are some suggested questions to ask:

Retirement Planning

- What is your retirement package worth?
- How much of your net worth is tied up in retirement assets?
- Who are the designated beneficiaries of your retirement package?
- Did you know that you could stretch the tax-deferral benefits of your
  IRA over a number of generations?
- Did you know that you could convert some of your excess retirement
  funds to an income-tax-free asset?
- Do you think your current asset allocation matches your investment
  needs? When did you last look it over? When did you last make
  changes?
- What is your plan for retirement? When? Where? What do you hope
  to do?

- What kind of retirement plans do you have? What are the assets? How are they invested? How much do you think you will need for retirement?
- Do you control the asset allocation and investment decisions for your retirement assets? If not, who helps you? Do you need more help? What kind of help would be the most beneficial?
- Do you own long-term care insurance? Do you think you need it?
- Do you know when you're eligible to draw money from your retirement plans? From which account would you first draw income? Which would be last? Do you own any annuities?
- How much does your employer or your company contribute to your retirement plan? Are you vested?
- Have you calculated your expected income from Social Security? How about your benefits from Medicare?

Income Protection

- How will your family survive if your income is cut off by an untimely death?
- How would a disability affect your income? Do you have disability insurance of any kind? How much? When do the benefits begin after a disability occurs? What is the maximum monthly check, and how long would you be eligible?
- Do you own personal liability coverage? Are you confident you have adequate coverage for yourself, your family, and your business? Have you ever been sued?
- Does your business have adequate protection against lawsuits for sexual harassment, product liability, and workers' compensation claims?

Assisting Children

- Do you have children? How many? Ages? Names? Plans for more? Are any of the children from other marriages?
- What are the schooling plans for the kids? How much will it cost? How have you provided financially for those needs?
- Do your children participate in saving or investing? Do they have accounts of their own? Roth IRAs? Uniform Gifts to Minors Act (UGMA) accounts? Do they have 529 plans?
- What about living expenses for the kids? If your kids are grown, do you provide any financial assistance? How? Do you expect that support to grow/stay the same/decline?
- Do you have any grandchildren? How are you assisting them today? In the future?
- Do your children have special needs, either physical or mental? Did you know that without adequate planning they could lose all of their federal and state assistance?

Assisting Parents

- Are your parents living? Your grandparents? Ages? How is the health of each? Where do they live? Any medical history to be concerned about? What kind? Are you providing any care?
- How will your parents provide for their expenses in retirement? How about medical care? Do they own long-term care insurance?
- Are you providing care for any older relatives or friends? How long have you been doing so?
- Are there any other relatives or friends for whom you might one day be responsible? When? In what way(s)? How will you manage those responsibilities?
- Do your parents have a will? Have they completed their estate plan?
- How will their estate plan impact your plan?

Estate Planning

- Do you have a will? When was it last updated?
- What's the primary goal of your estate plan? Avoiding taxes? Providing for your family? Charitable giving?
- Do you have a living will?
- Do you have a durable power of attorney in the event you can't be reached or can't make decisions?
- Who are the principal beneficiaries of your estate?
- Do you have guardians for your children? Trustees for the estate?
- Do you own life insurance? What kind? How much? Who are the beneficiaries?
- Do you own life insurance directly or is it in a trust?
- Do you have enough life insurance? Why do you think so?
- Do you have a business? What is the business worth? Are your key employees adequately provided for? Would you consider adding executive benefits to their packages?
- What kind of succession plan do you have for your business?
- How would you fund the succession plan?
- Do you have any kind of buy/sell agreement for your business with partners or potential successors? Is it up to date? Is it adequate?

If this seems like a lot of questions, it is. Remember, there are three primary objectives for this first meeting: (1) to learn as much about the prospect as possible, (2) to position yourself as the provider of multiple services, and (3) to determine the location of the prospect's assets and show how a managed account solution can provide the prospect with a single, consolidated account that meets all of the person's investment needs. This last point can be a bit tricky, but to do the best possible job for your client it's important to uncover where additional assets are held. Ask whether the prospect has other advisors, and explain that you need to know so you don't duplicate their work.

"The first part of this process involves capturing as much information about the client as possible," says Gary, a veteran advisor. "We need to know exactly what he or she has with another advisor. If the client brings us $5 million and the overall portfolio is worth $20 million, we need to know all of the other holdings and who has them; otherwise, we won't accept the account. We want to complement what the other managers are doing."

The most successful advisors simply will not move forward with a prospect or client until they have all of the necessary information from the individual. That posture sends a message to clients that the advisors are not willing to risk exposing themselves in the form of giving bad or incomplete advice. The not-so-subtle message to the investor is, "If you are willing to work with an advisor who won't ask these same questions, then you are not working with a professional."

Top advisors use the following tactics to help get more information from clients and prospects:

- "To do our best job, we need to see your total financial picture. Please provide us with copies of your other account statements."
- "If we were to buy a stock for you that had recently been sold for a tax loss by another of your advisors, did you know you would still be liable for the tax consequences under the wash sale rule?"
- "If we give you advice based on our belief that these are all the assets you have exposed to equities and you actually have more, then we are committing financial malpractice."

The information-gathering process lays the foundation for the formal declaration of account guidelines. Once you understand the overall needs and concerns of the investor, you lock down the parameters used to determine asset allocation and to select managers. If you haven't created your own multimanager solutions, now is the time to do so.

How to Explain the Multimanager Concept

To explain the changing roles of different sectors, styles, and asset classes, there is no better tool than the Elements of Diversification chart. (See Figure 7.4.) Explain to your client that market leadership varies and that you created a multimanager solution for him or her because it's difficult to know exactly which manager is going to outperform whom. No one ever really knows when the party is going to be over. Rather than wait until the music stops and the client has to grab for the best-performing asset class, tell your client that it's best to participate with managers who complement each other. Tell your client, "We are never certain which of the managers will perform

1989	1990	1991	1992	1993	1994	1995	1996	1997	1998	1999	2000	2001	2002	2003	2004	2005	2006
Large Cap Growth 35.92%	Fixed Income 8.96%	Small-Cap Growth 51.19%	Small-Cap Value 29.14%	Int'l 32.94%	Int'l 8.06%	Large-Cap Value 38.35%	REITs 35.25%	Large-Cap Value 35.18%	Large-Cap Growth 38.71%	Mid-Cap Growth 51.29%	REITs 26.36%	Small-Cap Value 14.02%	Fixed Income 10.26%	Small-Cap Growth 48.54%	REITs 31.56%	Int'l 14.02%	REITs 14.73%
Mid-Cap Growth 31.48%	Large-Cap Growth -0.26%	Mid-Cap Growth 47.03%	Mid-Cap Value 21.68%	Small-Cap Value 23.84%	REITs 3.17%	S&P 500 37.51%	S&P 500 23.26%	Mid-Cap Value 34.37%	S&P 500 28.76%	Small-Cap Growth 43.09%	Small-Cap Value 22.83%	REITs 13.93%	REITs 3.81%	Small-Cap Value 46.03%	Mid-Cap Value 23.71%	Mid-Cap Value 12.65%	Small-Cap Growth 14.36%
S&P 500 31.43%	S&P 500 -3.19%	Small-Cap Value 41.70%	REITs 14.52%	REITs 19.67%	Large-Cap Growth 2.66%	Large-Cap Growth 37.19%	Large-Cap Growth 23.12%	S&P 500 33.38%	Int'l 20.33%	Large-Cap Growth 33.16%	Mid-Cap Value 19.18%	Fixed Income 8.44%	Mid-Cap Value -9.64%	Mid-Cap Growth 42.71%	Small-Cap Value 22.25%	REITs 12.17%	Small-Cap Value 13.51%
Large-Cap Value 25.19%	Large-Cap Growth -5.13%	Large-Cap Growth 41.16%	Large-Cap Value 13.81%	Large-Cap Value 18.12%	S&P 500 1.32%	Mid-Cap Value 34.93%	Large-Cap Value 21.64%	Small-Cap Value 31.78%	Mid-Cap Growth 17.86%	Int'l 27.30%	Fixed Income 11.63%	Mid-Cap Value 2.33%	Small-Cap Value -11.43%	Int'l 39.17%	Int'l 20.70%	Mid-Cap Growth 12.10%	Int'l 9.47%
Mid-Cap Value 22.70%	Large-Cap Value -8.08%	Mid-Cap Value 37.92%	Mid-Cap Growth 8.71%	Mid-Cap Value 15.62%	Small-Cap Value -1.55%	Mid-Cap Growth 33.98%	Small-Cap Value 21.37%	Large-Cap Growth 30.49%	Large-Cap Value 15.63%	S&P 500 21.14%	Large-Cap Value 7.01%	Large-Cap Value -5.59%	Large-Cap Value -15.52%	Mid-Cap Value 38.07%	Mid-Cap Growth 16.49%	Large-Cap Value 7.05%	Mid-Cap Value 7.62%
Small-Cap Growth 20.17%	REITs -15.34%	REITs 34.54%	Small-Cap Growth 7.77%	Small-Cap Growth 13.36%	Large-Cap Value -1.99%	Small-Cap Value 31.04%	Mid-Cap Value 20.26%	Mid-Cap Growth 22.54%	Fixed Income 8.69%	Large-Cap Value 7.35%	S&P 500 -9.19%	Small-Cap Growth -9.23%	Int'l -15.66%	REITs 37.14%	Large-Cap Value 15.48%	Large-Cap Growth 5.26%	Mid-Cap Growth 7.61%
Fixed Income 14.53%	Mid-Cap Value -16.09%	S&P 500 30.54%	S&P 500 7.69%	Mid-Cap Growth 11.19%	Mid-Cap Value -2.13%	Small-Cap Growth 25.75%	Mid-Cap Growth 17.48%	REITs 20.29%	Mid-Cap Value 5.08%	Mid-Cap Value -0.11%	Mid-Cap Growth -11.75%	S&P 500 -11.87%	S&P 500 -22.10%	Large-Cap Value 30.03%	Small-Cap Growth 14.31%	S&P 500 4.93%	Large-Cap Value 5.93%
Small-Cap Value 12.43%	Small-Cap Growth -17.41%	Large-Cap Value 24.61%	Fixed Income 7.40%	S&P 500 10.00%	Mid-Cap Growth -2.17%	Fixed Income 18.48%	Small-Cap Growth 11.26%	Small-Cap Growth 12.95%	Small-Cap Growth 1.23%	Fixed Income -0.83%	Int'l -13.96%	Mid-Cap Growth -20.15%	Mid-Cap Growth -27.41%	Large-Cap Growth 29.75%	S&P 500 10.86%	Small-Cap Value 4.71%	S&P 4.19%
Int'l 10.80%	Small-Cap Value -21.77%	Fixed Income 16.00%	Large-Cap Growth 5.00%	Fixed Income 9.75%	Small-Cap Growth -2.43%	REITs 15.25%	Int'l 6.36%	Fixed Income 9.65%	Small-Cap Value -6.45%	Small-Cap Value -1.49%	Large-Cap Growth -22.42%	Large-Cap Growth -20.42%	Large-Cap Growth -27.88%	S&P 500 28.71%	Large-Cap Growth 6.30%	Large-Cap Growth 4.15%	Large-Cap Growth 3.09%
REITs 8.84%	REITs -23.21%	Int'l 12.50%	Int'l -11.85%	Large-Cap Growth 2.90%	Fixed Income -2.92%	Int'l 11.55%	Fixed Income 3.63%	Int'l 2.06%	REITs -17.50%	REITs -4.62%	Small-Cap Growth -22.43%	Int'l -21.21%	Small-Cap Growth -30.26%	Fixed Income 4.10%	Fixed Income 4.34%	Fixed Income 2.43%	Fixed Income -0.65%

◄ Worst | Performance | Best ►

Figure 7.4 Elements of Diversification—Equity Markets
Source: Phoenix Investment Partners.

best, but one will always be in the lead. This manager is leading for now but will be replaced by another in due course. We never know who or when."

Ed Blodgett of Brandes Investment Partners often reminds clients and advisors that true diversification is reached when "you're always upset about something!" Nick Murray offers another epigram: "Diversification is the conscious choice not to make a killing in exchange for the blessing of never getting killed." A well-constructed portfolio can confound even the savviest investor, because long-term success requires a level of diversification that can seem almost like overkill. Making a few big bets seems to be the nature of many investors, who have a hard time keeping track of many ideas that seem to have little in common. "Aren't we spreading ourselves too thin?" is a common query you may have heard.

David Swensen, the chief investment officer who boosted Yale University's endowment by more than $12 billion in a decade, believes that "diversification demands that each asset class receive a weighting large enough to matter, but small enough not to matter too much. Begin the portfolio structuring process by considering the issue of diversification, using the six core asset classes. The necessity that each asset class matter indicates a 5 or 10 percent allocation. The requirement that no asset class matter too much dictates a maximum of a 25 or 30 percent allocation. The basic math of diversification imposes structural parameters on the portfolio construction process." A diversified portfolio based on a client's specific attributes outlined in the investment policy statement attempts to take away the guesswork and market timing that lead most investors down the wrong path and deny them their long-term goals.

As the Elements of Diversification chart illustrates, the best-performing manager does not often repeat the following year. Given this, you don't want to encourage your client to begin second-guessing a manager's performance. Give them information, but also give them guidance and perspective. Clients need to know they may be expecting too much performance too soon. Your job is to coach and educate your clients about how long it can take for the process to reap results, the order in which this typically occurs, and more about your process for making changes.

For example, if your large-cap manager drifts away from the fund's style, do you take that opportunity to choose another large-cap manager? While the client's account is very important to the manager, that manager has thousands of similar accounts. If you want to keep your clients' best interests at the forefront, then you are going watch this manager closely by monitoring the management and style. It is important for your clients to know that you are focused on protecting their investments.

Also, let your client know that you don't necessarily fire managers because they underperform for a quarter or two, but you must have a good answer for any condition under which you would fire one. The consulting department at your firm should have criteria that outline what they look for in the selection of a manager. Review the criteria for your clients when they get a little nervous. Remember, education is most effective in the moment.

According to advisor Bill, not everything works out in the short term. "One couple invested $2 million with us," he says. "Both were physicians; she worked part-time and cared for their young son. We explained the benefits of managed accounts and invested $800,000 of the $2 million in a managed account program with a growth manager. Last year that account was down 34 percent! How did we handle this? We resold the process of managed accounts, not the performance. We explained the downturn in the markets and the importance of using multiple investment professionals with different investment styles. We explained the failure of market timers and the flexibility of changing managers if the style of the manager drifted. They elected to stay the course."

Sometimes clients might tell you they don't recognize the name of a particular manager you've selected. That can be a benefit. The lack of household names on the manager roster is a reinforcement of the process. Explain that your firm has discovered this manager and that particular manager doesn't manage mutual funds, so he or she is not a big name your client might hear every day. However, the manager does advise some of the largest pension funds at major institutions. You might use the following rationale: "What fits within your comfort level: the brand name of a mutual fund company you've read about in *Money* magazine or the name of a manager gleaned from the due diligence team of a consulting firm that has already invested billions of dollars with that manager?" Depending on the client's level of financial literacy, you may wish to explain the manager evaluation, selection, and monitoring process outlined in Chapter 2.

Once you've found the appropriate managers, talk to your client about each one's style, time horizon, potential downside, and proven principles, and how you're developing an integrated solution for your client's wealth management needs with this manager. Discuss the importance of not being too hasty in judging the manager on too short a time frame. Some top advisors say that the client should focus on a 10-year time horizon, and certainly most would say a client should plan to invest for at least three to five years, which would effectively take into account a market cycle.

Investment manager style—typically growth or value—reveals a personality that can be matched with clients of similar orientation to sustain a relationship through the most difficult market periods. Clients who truly understand their investment managers and appreciate disciplines are able to maintain confidence and commitment during those inevitable times when a style is out of favor. The most resilient clients are able to capture additional gains by rebalancing into an out-of-favor manager or investment style, while the less objective ones are often chasing current winners.

A second aspect of style is the natural fit with a client's psychology. For example, a client whose road to financial success was a function of saving and a restrained lifestyle—same car, same house, same spouse—may be more comfortable with a buy-and-hold manager who is long-term focused with several core holdings, rather than a more aggressive manager trading in and out of positions. The more active trader may not reflect the values and mind-set of the long-term "millionaire next door." For the same investor, a value style of management, buying companies currently out of favor but with good prospects, may be more appealing than a philosophy that pursues the latest and greatest technologies—more a growth style. Compatibility with a manager's style is one of the most important drivers of long-term client relationships, and may be the most basic.

As a rule, the most aggressive management styles have the most volatility—the proverbial trade-off between risk and reward. Blended appropriately with other investments, these more volatile results can actually improve risk-adjusted returns, depending on how the path of returns correlates with other management styles. In other words, volatility is not uniformly bad; it should be applied in appropriate measure and not only reflect your investing approach but also match your clients' emotional fortitude.

A branch manager we know uses a remarkably simple illustration to educate clients about volatility. He uses the quarterly account values for his own account with an investment manager he has used in his asset-allocation solutions for clients. The actual account value, net of additions and withdrawals, is on a spreadsheet (not a graph or mountain chart). He includes not only the account value, but also the amount of appreciation or depreciation for that quarter. Though the long-term history of the account is positive, he pauses when showing the bear market periods to emphasize how difficult it can be to stay the course.

History also plays an important role in a client's investing preferences. Asking for such history is a very important part of determining your compatibility with prospective clients. Learning of a prospect's bad experience with a certain type of aggressive bond fund, for example, would be helpful before recommending its use, even if the interest rate situation is much different today. In other words, your knowledge and perspective are superior to most clients'. Don't mistake a bad impression of an investment for its poor timing. The memory of an investment mistake and the attendant embarrassment and loss of capital can forge an indelible memory that is not easily overcome.

Inevitably, after a few quarters, one of your client's managers will probably be doing better than the others, and it should not surprise you if the client says, "Manager X is doing so much better than Managers Y and Z. Why don't we move all the money to Manager X?" This is the first test of your process, and this is where your explanation of multimanagers—and the Elements of Diversification—fits in nicely. Remind the client that with a managed account solution, the whole is equal to more than the sum of its parts. Yes, one investment might be doing noticeably better than the others at the moment, but that could change at any time. Redirect the client's attention to how well the overall strategy is working.

How to Structure an Effective Client Meeting

The ongoing review of a managed account is a critical process unto itself. To keep your clients on the course you have planned together, you must reinforce the plan. Regular meetings provide the venue for reviewing the account, but you should take special care not to make the account and its performance the sole focus, because by doing so you run the risk of developing short-term expectations that undermine the entire managed account relationship and its long-term benefits. Experienced managed account consultants have learned to review their clients' accounts as part of review meetings that address big-picture wealth issues, such as retirement and estate planning.

Too many advisors have trapped themselves in a cycle of short-term expectations by starting off the managed account relationship with a first meeting based on the quarterly performance review. These well-meaning folks get themselves into trouble by unconsciously subordinating their judgment to that of their clients. "Here's your quarterly managed account review," they say. "What do you think of it?" Instead of discussing the goal of the funds—the estate plan, the retirement plan, the charitable gift—these advisors allow the managed account report to stand alone. Yet any client with online capability can review his or her account at any time. Your meeting should be an opportunity to discuss other issues.

Advisor Tip

Happy Birthday

Chuck, a wirehouse advisor, reminds his clients about meetings in a memorable way. "Our meetings are conducted with clients right after their birthdays," he says. "This customizes the meeting and keeps the focus on the client. We tell them, 'Your birthday is the time you take stock in your life.' Handling meetings this way allows us to focus on long-term planning issues."

The average client has a time horizon of more than 20 years. Why should they worry about one quarter? Many advisors have so many clients, they use the report as a communication vehicle and the excuse for a meeting. Your role is bigger than a quarterly performance report.

Individual clients would benefit from knowing how bigger investors handle their managed accounts. For example, private banks conduct in-depth portfolio reviews for their affluent clients, but these reviews usually take place only once a year. Why? Because the markets don't change that often, and the bank wants to set appropriate client expectations about that lack of change. Consider institutions like state and corporate pension funds. These plans have strict investment policy guidelines that direct their investment managers to specific allocations. When market activity drives the allocations out of balance—from a target of 60 percent equity to, say, 65 percent—the managers know they need to reduce the equity exposure to the client's investment policy of 60 percent. No meetings—and often no calls—are held to discuss the move. It's automatic. The review meetings held with the plan's trustees might revisit the strategy, but these meetings do not typically involve the minutiae of rebalancing the account to the investment policy guidelines. It is quite common, however, for the investment managers to offer insight and even recommendations for a change in asset allocation based on a firm's view of the markets during the annual review meeting.

We recommend you follow the practice of many top advisors and eliminate the quarterly managed account meeting. In its place, create a true client review session that focuses on the client's overall wealth needs. Remember, a good review meeting can be a tremendous opportunity to capture more assets. The meeting also reflects your approach to business—and says a lot about you. Ask yourself the following questions:

What Is the Goal of the Meeting?

What is new with this client? What do you need to know? Consider possible family issues, career or business concerns, community affairs—anything that might affect your client's state of mind. Financial issues are secondary if a client's business is in trouble or a child is doing poorly in school. It is also important to review all pertinent financial information about your client prior to the meeting. Combining this with your perspective on your client's real-life issues will help you to have a more informed discussion with your client—and to prepare an appropriate agenda for your meeting.

Should You Have an Agenda?

The most effective organizations maximize the value of their directors by creating agendas to help guide the meetings. Why not approach your client meetings in the same fashion? A written agenda accomplishes a great deal with very few words. A colleague of mine once said, "He who arrives with an agenda controls the meeting." And that control means ensuring your ability not only to take charge at the outset, but also to guide the conversation toward important issues and lessen the chances of getting sidetracked into areas like discussing the market's recent performance. Robert, a top advisor in Montreal, prepares a written agenda and faxes it to clients in advance of the meetings. This way, he can draw them into the meeting process. He reports greater success in preparing clients both mentally and emotionally for meetings, as well as soliciting from them any additional topics or issues they wish to discuss. "Because we don't meet in-depth more than a few times each year, the clients require some preparation for us to get the maximum value from our meeting."

Who Should Attend?

Ongoing reviews and follow-up calls about portfolio performance should be conducted by *you*, not by an assistant, unless you have a team set up to do this in a way that diversifies the job responsibilities. Some advisors we know, like Geoff in Vancouver, have at least two team members attend every meeting so there is always a backup if the clients need to speak to someone about the managers.

How Long Should the Meeting Last?

Several factors contribute to the length, such as the number of topics to be discussed (which you can determine roughly with the agenda) as well as the complexity of topics. Beware of trying to accomplish too much in a single meeting. Advisors often underestimate how much time to devote to a particular topic, and remember to leave yourself room to discuss an unforeseen issue with the clients. You might learn something new about them.

Three 90-minute meetings a year are perfect for some clients with whom you have frequent conversations, while others might need a half-day to get through some sticky issues. One successful advisor says he gets right down to business and needs only 15 minutes, while George in Indianapolis enjoys spending a full day with each of his top 35 to 40 clients at least once a year. The time frame we hear most often for review meetings is about 90 minutes per session about four times each year—top clients only.

Where Should You Meet?

The location of your meeting is extremely important. As we said earlier, your office should project the image of the professional that you are. However, you should also consider visiting your clients at their offices. They may be pleasantly surprised at the suggestion and will appreciate you taking the time to meet at *their* convenience. Two Boston-area advisors we know operate as a team. They report that meeting on the clients' turf removes potential distractions of their office and allows clients to relax. The pair recently took a day away from the office and visited one of their largest clients at his horse farm in New Hampshire. Not only did they enjoy the time out in the country, but they also allowed their client to show them his passion—a dimension of the client they did not know before that now contributes to their understanding of his goals. Both parties now feel more in sync.

What about the Quarterly Report?

With the aforementioned caveats in mind, the portfolio review is an important part of the client review meeting and warrants special attention. The ongoing review can give your clients insight into how their managers invest. Key members of investment management firms have meetings with clients so they will understand their views on the market, stock selections, and details about their style and philosophy. For example, managers we know at a multibillion-dollar management firm present a story about a company to better illustrate the firm's process. During the client meeting, the portfolio manager gives an overview of the company, its history, management team, product or service, its market, competition, and the success it has had. He or she also reports on the company's track record of earnings growth, as well as the money management firm's earnings and growth estimates for the company and the elements that will drive that growth over a five-year period. Included also is an analysis of how the company fits into the client's portfolio, what the specific weightings should be, and the rationale. Finally, the manager records the valuation of the stock and compares its price-to-earnings ratio to those of its competitors.

By relegating the portfolio review to the role of a committee report—merely one facet of the overall client meeting—you reinforce your objectivity. You and the client hired the investment managers in order to execute an overall plan. You should not be defensive if any managers have not performed the role they were hired to perform, and don't fall victim to the tendency to take blame for a poorly performing manager or credit for an exceptional performance. This is perhaps the most important point in a client review meeting. It reinforces to your client the nature of the investment management process and your role in it as an advisor. You and the client together deal with whatever has happened. Review the facts, make observations, and make recommendations to the client for action. How do you both feel about the manager and what the firm has done since you last met? Is everything on track?

Other reports include any product that your client owns. Look over variable insurance policies, mutual funds, variable annuities—anything that requires periodic review. How are these products performing relative to the role they were supposed to play? It is very important that you review all of this information prior to meeting with the client.

What's the Next Step?

Here's a point that even the most experienced advisors sometimes overlook: Be sure you hear everything your clients have to say before ending the meeting. They might be on the verge of offering you another account when you look at your watch and mention you have another appointment in five minutes. You just lost that opportunity to capture additional assets. Don't rush, and always ask your clients midway through the meeting if they are comfortable with the allotted time you are spending.

As the meeting draws to a close, remember to ask whether your clients have anything more to add to the discussion, determine whether all the issues were covered, and thank them for their time and ongoing business. Also, it's important to formally schedule your next meeting. Set the date before your clients leave and mark it on each of your calendars.

Before the clients leave, however, there is one more issue that must be addressed: referrals. The client review meeting is the number one source of new client referrals, because there is no better time to solicit this information. You've just demonstrated your value by showing clients the progress they've made toward achieving their life goals. Do they know of someone in a similar situation who could benefit from your services? They probably do. In the next chapter, we explain how referrals can help you build your managed account business.

Developing Your Managed Account Solutions Business

Referrals from current clients can bring prospects to your door, but you must know how to ask for them and have materials on hand to promote your practice.

The client review meeting is the number one source of the referrals you need to build your managed account solutions business. Whether you meet with clients once a year, twice a year, four times a year, or more often than that, you have regular opportunities to ask your clients to help you achieve your goals just as you are helping them realize theirs.

When you were considering whether to become a provider of managed account solutions, we asked you to identify ideal candidates and consider what they have in common. These clients formed the foundation on which your managed account practice is built, and they are instrumental in helping you grow your practice. Whether the tie that binds them is work-related (e.g., doctors, attorneys, small-business owners) or lifestyle-related (retirees and preretirees), the odds are very good that they know many people in a similar financial situation to theirs—people who would probably make ideal clients for your practice.

Like attracts like. People in the same profession tend to associate with one another, as do people in the same stage of life. Some will refer a financial advisor so that a friend or colleague can gain access to a particular product or service, such as a hedge fund or help with liquidating a concentrated stock position. To encourage a client or business acquaintance to make a *benevolent referral*—one made solely out of concern for the needs of someone else—is more difficult. Aside from the purely selfish motive that a client may not want you to devote your finite time to someone else's problem, the client making the referral must be absolutely certain that you have the expertise necessary to solve the problem at hand. (To address the former concern, you might discreetly point out that the less time you have to spend interviewing prospects, the more time you will have to devote to the needs of current clients.)

A great way to solicit benevolent referrals is first to congratulate your client for having spent the time, energy, and money necessary to tackle a thorny planning issue, such as estate planning. According to the 2007 Phoenix Wealth Survey, nearly three-fourths of affluent households (those defined as having net worth in excess of $1 million, exclusive of debt and primary residence) do not have a current estate plan. Interestingly, 14 percent of respondents said they were concerned that death could cause an inefficient passing of wealth to the next generation and/or charitable organizations, and 12 percent said they were concerned premature death would cause financial hardship on their successors. It's reasonably safe to conclude that survey participants define "premature death" as meaning "before I'm ready!"

The risks to a millionaire family can be enormous if the primary income earner were to die prematurely without an estate plan, and protecting the family from such a risk, however remote, should be a top priority. But even the very best advisors struggle to bring clients to the estate planning table. Typically, a family addresses the issue after an advisor gets them to establish advance directives to ensure appropriate health care for their aging parents. The advisor then suggests that the clients do the same for themselves. This leads to other estate planning issues and often a full plan.

When this occurs, congratulate your clients for their efforts, noting that only about half of households of similar means have taken comparable steps to protect themselves. Then segue into referral mode by asking the next logical question: Do they have friends or colleagues who have similar good intentions but are in the category of folks who have not yet gotten around to estate planning?

The key to creating the benevolent referral is your ability to confront clients with a point of vulnerability and the need to protect themselves. Once you've shown how you can solve some of their more difficult wealth management problems, they will be more likely to refer their friends and associates to you—*but you have to ask!*

Over the years, consultants and financial practice management experts have been exhorting advisors to ask clients for referrals. Advisors often feel sheepish about asking, fearing their clients will interpret the request as an imposition on the relationship or, worse, turn them down because they don't believe the advisor is worthy of a recommendation. By focusing on your area of expertise and the problems you have solved for clients, you can offer demonstrable proof of your value and a clear example of what you might be able to accomplish for a new client. In this way, referrals can become an organic part of your practice.

Develop a System

Referrals are not complicated, but even top advisors fail to maintain a conscious effort to generate them from their regular activities. Most experienced advisors with average-sized books of business probably have at their fingertips all the relationships they need to drive considerable referral business. The trick with referral generation, as with most business practices, is to make the effort creative and sustainable.

As stated previously, client review meetings are the top source of referrals. When you meet with clients—and especially if you've just helped them solve a troubling problem—ask if there are other people they know suffering or at risk from the same problem, or who could benefit from the services you provide.

Take a proactive approach. Make a list of your top 50 clients and identify the number one concern of each client household. You should confirm the issue with each family, and to do so you may have to ask open-ended questions in some cases. Sort clients by issue type: estate planning, charitable giving, retirement planning, care of aging parents. Consider assembling a batch of clients on each topic and creating a plan to address each topic in an organized way with the assistance of other professionals.

For example, if 12 of your top 50 clients need to complete current estate plans, brainstorm ideas with an attorney about how to help clients take up the challenge of completing an estate plan. Can the two of you create an estate planning workshop for your clients? Offer two choices of location and time: one during the day and one in the evening. Make a list of the issues that will be solved in the seminar and send invitations to each client. Call clients yourself—don't delegate the phoning to an assistant—and follow up the invitation. Explain that the seminar was the result of your concern for the client and your interest in creating a simplified solution and an easy way to get started. (Chapter 10 offers step-by-step instructions for hosting an effective seminar.)

Chances are, at the conclusion of the seminar, you will have some clients who want to learn more and some who want to do more. Follow up with individual meetings to help the clients prepare their estate plans, then ask if they found the seminar helpful. Tell them you will be planning another one in the near future, and ask if they have any friends or associates who would welcome an invitation.

A seminar filled with prospects is more challenging than a seminar filled with clients. After all, your clients know you and are accustomed to working with you (and you with them). Prospects may be interested in the subject of your seminar, but know little else beyond that. Put yourself in their shoes. They seldom know what help they need, what questions to ask, or how much the services should cost. And there is no shortage of financial firms claiming to have wealth management expertise. So, how do you convince a bewildered potential client that you are their best choice?

We suggest being a teacher first, a salesperson second. Selling complex services—and being paid well to provide them—often requires that you first explain the situation faced by the client. Would you let a surgeon dig into you without first making sure you understand exactly what he or she was going to do and how it would help you? Top wealth managers are constantly educating clients about risks and the strategies needed to overcome those risks, and often use the case method to do so.

Advisor Tip

Know Your Comfort Zone

One advisor we know identifies his ideal client as someone who has $400,000 to $1 million in a 401(k), owns a home, and has a net worth of about $1.5 million. "They have substantial assets in their retirement plan, and we help them to efficiently manage it. We don't want the superrich client telling us what to do. Our minimum is $300,000. This is the client we are comfortable with. This is our zone." A typical referral? "This fellow was recommended to us by several clients (which goes to our point that your existing clients are your best resource pool). Here is some of the information we captured about him, which shows the depth and scope of our interviews and data capturing. He is married and has been working for a utility company for 35 years. He and his wife have a combined income of $150,000 and a retirement portfolio that is worth $2 million, and he wants to retire later this year. The couple wants to sell their house and move to Mexico, and they will need an income stream. They also need to set up an emergency fund. We know their hobbies, anniversaries, children's names, pet's name—all of this personal data paints the picture. We use extensive data sheets to capture every iota of information about the client. They want to sell their home for $629,000, but we are suggesting that they lower the price. If the husband needs to go back to work to generate income, he can do that by contracting. We are educating them on inflation, what postponing retirement will mean financially, and the 5 percent rule of withdrawal on retirement plans."

In its simplest form, a case study combines education about a specific financial problem with the solution created by that advisor or team for one of its clients. By clearly illustrating the issues and the steps to tackle the challenge, you enable prospects to get a more complete view of what will be involved should they go down the same financial path. Here's how to build a case:

First, select a client for whom you solved a financial challenge and write down the story. Lay out all of the specific action steps that took place, including the process of discovering the problem and how you explained it to your client. Save the narrative. Properly edited, it can be submitted for publication.

Next, convert the words into pictures. Edit the narrative to bullet points of action steps. Draw boxes around each step in the process. Note points when you reached a crossroad and a key decision had to be made. The resulting graphic is now a flow chart with more powerful visual imagery for both prospects and centers of influence, such as attorneys and certified public accountants, who want a clear view of your process.

Bring on the competition! Show how competing firms might respond at many points in your process. Smart clients talk to other people, so why not shorten the sales cycle by speaking directly to that competitive reality? This approach shows confidence and competence.

Finally, collect your cases. An album of successful case studies is better than a wall of diplomas. It shows that you have helped clients through difficult situations and that you were thorough enough to have chronicled the process. Try asking a prospect how many advisors they've met who can match your attention to detail. And those details matter, whether in surgery or wealth management. Who wouldn't prefer the pro with proven process?

Identify Your Target Market

Surprisingly, a majority of top advisors do not actively prospect for new clients. One reason is that many advisors are too busy taking care of their current clients to look for new ones, a problem solved by providing managed account solutions to a smaller number of more affluent clients. And, since your current clientele already defines much of what you are and what you do, your new clients should be very much like current clients so that your successful work practices can continue. Adding clients unlike your existing ones will crimp your productivity and divert your resources.

Targeting specific types of clients and prospects requires defining and going after a very narrow slice of the broad, overall market. The general advertising done by the wirehouses is aimed at the general affluent market, but specialized advisory practices must focus on something a little more precise. Consider these target markets:

- *Clients of a specific accounting firm, estate attorney, long-term care specialist, or pension accounting company.* Are you the number one provider or just one of several advisors on a list given to clients upon request?
- *Membership of your country club, business club, social club, yacht club, beach club, or skiing group.* We recently attended a dinner party at the invitation of a friend who is an acquaintance of a superb financial advisor, who was also in attendance. By the end of the evening, we realized that everyone at the party was a client of the advisor, who is especially effective at creating a so-called closed community of clients. If you are a friend of a client, he will track you down!

- *Clients who are in the same business.* George, an advisor in Indiana, has been a creative thinker for many years as he built his successful practice. One of his best clients owns a manufacturing company and was impressed that George spent so much time learning about the client's business. He invited George to attend a national trade show for his industry. George took him up on the offer and has earned several significant clients as a result of the initial effort.
- *An extended family.* This niche might not be very lucrative unless the family is very wealthy, but it's another potential group of clients that can be secured from competition if you have a good relationship with the right family member.
- *Members of the same medical or legal group.* Steve in Boston was able to secure the account of a successful orthopedist, which led to the management of the physician's group pension, shared with more than 30 other professionals. Management of both accounts has led to other referrals from within the group.
- *Executives of the same company.* Especially effective for working with concentrated stock, retirement plans, rollovers, and executive benefits, this niche can be very lucrative if you are willing to work on behalf of the company and spend time with the top people.
- *Employees of the same company.* Primarily targeting the rollover market, a relationship with the human resources department or treasurer's office can help you develop an exceptional clientele. A wirehouse advisor in Philadelphia has been the main contact for virtually every new retiree at a major nearby petrochemical plant. Advisors in Cincinnati have worked with a well-known Fortune 500 company, providing countless retirement seminars featuring speakers from established investment management organizations available in their firms' managed account programs.
- *Parents of special needs or handicapped children.* An extremely focused group with strong natural bonds, these families are constantly aware of financial challenges and are used to making difficult decisions. They speak openly and often about their concerns and needs.

Advisor Tip

Rolling in Rollovers

Most of John's business comes from rollovers. Of his $230 million under management, more than 85 percent is from 401(k)s. John gets a good amount of business from a local company and has captured a number of rollover assets from individuals leaving the firm. Some of their money can't be rolled over immediately after they leave, so he encourages those clients to send him quarterly statements of the assets remaining at the previous employer. He reviews these with the clients on an ongoing basis.

These types of prospective clients are unaware that you provide wonderful service to people just like them. In order to persuade potential newcomers that you can truly help them and are worthy of their trust (and trustworthiness is consistently the most desired trait in a primary advisor), you should run through the following checklist:

- Do you have a brochure that summarizes the background, experience, and expertise of you and your team? Do your best clients receive copies of this brochure at least once a year, and in the case of referral sources, at least two or three times a year?
- Do you have a web site that supports your practice with the same information? Do your referral sources and top clients know about the site, and do you use it to inform both groups about developments at your practice?
- Do you have a newsletter or other client bulletin? Do you send it regularly to top clients, referral sources, and prospective clients? Is your mailing ever followed up by an invitation to a seminar or workshop hosted by your practice? Does anyone ever call addressees to see if they have any questions about the content and ideas expressed in the newsletter?
- Do you have a pitch book that presents you and your practice as though you were in a formal competition for the client's account? Does each key professional referral source have a current copy, and are those people mailed a new edition when it is revised?
- Do you have ready-made case studies of important solutions you have created for clients? Do your top clients receive copies when you have solved a problem for another client involving a service that those clients have not addressed? Do you offer a workshop to top clients featuring the topic and invite them to tackle this thorny issue in the company of other folks facing the same issue? Do you invite specialist professionals to assist in the workshop and to work with your best clients? Do those professionals reciprocate with referrals for you?
- The bottom-line requirements of this list of prospecting tools: Do they convey your expertise, experience, and value proposition to your existing clients, affluent prospects, and critical referral sources?

Act, Don't Just React

You probably have a considerable array of target markets right at the edge of your current practice. The secret to determining logical and available target markets is a review of your best clients. What groups do they represent? What relationships do they have? List just your top 20 client households one more time. To this list, add several columns for their affiliations. Look at the table in search of relationships and potential areas of common interest. Your goal is to begin building pods of clients in particular areas that can anchor a broader network of clients. These smaller niches can be protected from competitors because of the natural affinity of the members for each other. By infiltrating the group and becoming the advisor of choice, you can add to the group's sense of community—you are *their* advisor, just as they likely have their insurance agent, bank, accountant, restaurant, and golf course.

Advisor Tip

The One Thing Every Client Needs

During a recent meeting of a major firm's top advisors, Steve Gresham asked the audience to recall if they had ever found a product or service so important and so valuable that they proposed the idea to every single client. The result-ing quiet was deafening. After a few moments, a gentleman raised his hand and declared that he did, in fact, offer one product to every client. In fact, he said that he now insists that every client endure his appeal. The audience was immediately attentive. What could the product be? A mutual fund? Shares of IBM? Writing covered call options? His answer: a long-term care policy. Why long-term care? His explanation was telling: "I had a client who saved for many years to fund his retirement. One day, he became ill. He began to receive treatments for his condition, and the unexpected health-care costs depleted his retirement account. He was financially and emotionally devas-tated. I watched it happen, and I was powerless to do anything about it. I have since told that story to every one of my clients, and I demand they consider the risks of not having protection." Steve asked if, prior to that experi-ence, he had ever sold long-term care insurance. "Never," he answered.

Once you have defined a target market, you must employ a value proposi-tion focused on the unique needs of that affinity group. For groups bonded by economic circumstances, it's a lot easier to create a particular approach based on a specific solution. For example, the retirees of a particular large company will all need to know their choices of retirement income options and will value anyone who can provide that information simply and clearly and with understandable, actionable choices. Likewise, for adults with aging parents, the need for long-term care guidance and the use of advance directives can quickly unify an otherwise diverse group around specific topics addressed by your practice.

But target marketing need not be entirely reactive. You can create a niche if you can find an issue or service that draws people to you. Find an area left open by other advisors, develop a convincing and eye-catching story, and then promote your idea with conviction and consistency for as long as it takes to draw a sustainable client base. A good example of this type of marketing is that used by law firms in the aftermath of specific events causing injury or loss, such as asbestos, securities fraud, and tobacco. Law firms seeking clients appeal directly to the victim's desire for retribution—no dainty or passive approaches here.

With a generation of aging boomers facing new awareness of their risks, you have many niches from which to choose in building affinity groups of clients. What hot buttons can you press to reach members of these groups without being drowned out by other financial providers and general advertising? Get personal and get loud. Not only must your idea strike a distinctive chord with your target, it must be a sustainable idea—one you can use to anchor a campaign among affluent clients. You want people to start talking about your ideas to their friends and colleagues so you can leverage your impact. Don't underestimate how many times a prospective client may have to hear your message before taking action. Working for years with financial advisors, we've adopted the industry adage that any marketing message must be delivered at least seven times to a specific prospect for that person to take action; anything less is ineffective. You have to muster the energy to keep talking.

Millionaire Hot Buttons

Establishing your target markets around key emotional issues is one of the best ways to ensure that your efforts resonate with prospective clients. Here are some hot-button issues and associated marketing strategies to consider.

How Good Is the Advice You're Currently Getting?

As we mentioned in Chapter 5, poor customer service is the number one reason why clients change advisors. The 2007 Phoenix Wealth Survey found that two-thirds of clients who said they were looking for a new advisor attributed the reason to either "the advisor is not proactive in maintaining contact with me" (44 percent) or "the advisor is difficult to get hold of" (22 percent). Since many clients complain that the advisors are insufficiently proactive, step into that breach and offer your own suggestions.

One of the best opportunities to acquire high-net-worth clients today is to offer a second opinion to prospects whose current advisor is inattentive. The goal is to demonstrate true financial consulting (asset allocation, manager selection, and other financial advice) so that disgruntled clients can come to understand that they have outgrown a less-enlightened advisor. Most retirement plan wrecks are the result of violating one of the basic rules of intelligent investing. Don't assume a millionaire household fully understands why they have not succeeded or how they can recover. Offer your experience and perspective via a short, professional note with your card attached.

How Do You Invest Your Bonus (or Other Windfall)?

Few affluent executives or business owners earn their wealth exclusively through salaries. Most capture the bulk of their compensation from performance bonuses or profit sharing. Typically, these prospects and clients use those lump-sum payments to fund their investments. The problem for the recipient is what to do with a tidy lump sum once it is received. Since the vast majority of private and public companies pay bonuses in the first three months of a new year, you can work this idea from January through March with confidence that your message will resonate somewhere.

Advertising, discussions with accountant contacts, and targeted letters to executives suggesting a discussion about what to do now in the markets all make sense because of the likelihood of activity. For your existing clients, do their distributions occur quarterly or annually? What are the formulas that determine the payouts? Important issue to note: Is business good enough to warrant a payout? Most payouts are made after the books are sorted out at year-end, providing insight into the current status of the business. Be alert to dips; reversals or slumps can impact the mental health of your clients.

What Is Your Financial Plan after the Divorce?

Although a divorce may have been a long time coming and its specifics well known in advance, the full impact of the event usually is underestimated. Your empathy and compassion are required, as well as a "let's consider your options" discussion. Handled appropriately, this meeting is a listening session, prodded by the occasional simple question and followed by more listening. These are highly charged emotional events, and early actions are typically regretted later. Facilitated often by referral from accountants and attorneys, these cases can make you a valued ally of these important sources if you can provide a view of your strategy and approach to aiding such clients. For divorce cases, an affliction of more than half of married couples, you can prepare. Do you have relationships with matrimonial attorneys? Ask around for the best. In many cases, one of the two parties in the divorce might not be entirely familiar with investments and finance. Prove to the centers of influence that you know the divorce-related issues and are sensitive to their needs. And understand that as an advocate—like the attorney—you will have to pick a side.

What Happens If You Become Disabled?

Disability is more common than accidental death, but most affluent households do not carry adequate protection to maintain their lifestyle or a business should the chief breadwinner no longer be able to work. Even if an executive were covered through a policy at work, it is unlikely that the group policy would provide the income most affluent families require to meet current living expenses. And the likelihood of coverage for a nonworking spouse is negligible, although the lost mobility of that person could be devastating to the household. To address the need, conduct a risk prevention/minimization audit: Where are the family's primary risks? What are the areas of each household's greatest economic vulnerability? What might happen if the household's income producer(s) could not work?

What Happens If You Become Incapacitated?

Surveys of baby boomers reveal that their primary concerns—a major illness, inability to afford health insurance, having to live in a nursing home—center around the fear of losing their independence. This is such a personal and emotional issue that pressing this hot button could traumatize a client. The trick is to turn the emotion into positive energy so that the problem can be addressed without getting wrapped up in a family's angst.

Remind clients that nursing home care and other long-term care needs can be funded with long-term care insurance and perhaps early purchase of arrangements at a continuous care retirement facility. In addition to reminding clients about long-term care options, make certain there are extensive advance directives in place to ensure that the client's wishes are carried out. This phase of your involvement is the most immediate and has the greatest impact. An old therapist's trick to help children address their fears is to have them write out a story or make a picture. Having clients complete a booklet about how they want to live in their older years—and the provisions they have made for the life they envision—can be very calming. Offer a workshop about preparing such a booklet to clients and prospects.

Who Will Provide for Your Aging Parents?

Baby boomers, on average, have more parents than children. This demographic reversal has shifted the economic burden of aging disproportionately to the boomers. Your target clients may be caught off guard by the need to provide care, both economic and emotional, to parents who may have underestimated their own longevity. Your strategy could be to provide a survival package of late-stage liquidity and expense-mitigating ideas. These include long-term care insurance, immediate annuities for longevity protection, and information about how to buy medical insurance and reverse mortgages. Consider sponsoring a discussion group of clients who have parental care challenges.

Who Will Provide for Your Family in the Event of Your Untimely Death?

Appealing to a prospect's fear of premature death is always risky, especially among a boomer generation convinced of its longevity and vitality. Nevertheless, consider the hot button of this target market, because only about half of millionaire households have a current estate plan. In addition, the boomer generation shows signs of comprehending the enormity of its responsibilities; many boomers are coming to understand that an event as random as an illness or accident can completely destroy a life and lifestyle built on borrowing. Without adequate insurance in place, an unexpected reversal could wreak enormous dislocation and trauma. Ask the question again—"What would happen if something happened to you?"—and consider your top client households (maybe even your own). Broach this subject to a client household in the presence of both spouses and watch the body language of both parties. You'll get a sense of the receptivity and who feels more vulnerable.

Other Ways to Promote Your Practice

By promoting your team, your firm, and your knowledge, you will be able to drive business without seeming to be a self-promoter. Take the example of Clayton, a top wirehouse advisor and the lead principal of a team in a small Western city. As a fixture in his community for many years, he does little or no prospecting. Nevertheless, he pays for a prominent ad in the city's annual magazine and directory. The big ad stands as testimony to the reality that Clayton's practice is *the* financial advisory practice in town.

In his South Florida community, David makes sure that his team holds leadership positions in several major local charities. Most charities willingly publicize top givers, and David takes advantage of that fact. He reports that consistency is the key to reaping benefit from these efforts. Many advisors and business owners are short-term thinkers, he says. They will support a charity for a year or two in a big way, then lose their focus or reduce their commitment. David says that for a charitable involvement to work the commitment must be real, not just a public relations ploy, which is why he is actively involved in each of the charities he supports.

In affluent Beverly Hills, Jack and Tom (not their real names) head a successful team that runs a charity golf tournament at a prestigious country club. The project is a major effort, requiring Jack's attention year-round. He solicits donations from business partners as well as local companies, and recruits a celebrity host as well as pro golf stars. His team does little else in the way of advertising, because the tournament is so effective in raising the team's visibility.

Here are some ideas for generating referrals through promotion of your practice:

- *Public relations.* What are the media opportunities in your community for your practice? Is there a specific target market with its own newsletter, such as building contractors, a country club, or a medical group? Is there an opportunity to advertise or to contribute a regular column describing different advice issues? This is a potential use of your case studies as well.

- *Charitable activities.* What organizations and causes are most important to you and your team today? Can you improve your visibility and support to one or more specific organizations? Is there an annual event you can create or assume from someone else who wants to relinquish the job? What causes are most important to you and your top clients? Can they help to guide your mission?

If you have a good feel for the different scenarios and target markets for managed account prospects, let's now consider the *individual* attributes you want in a prospective client. First, the warning: Some people just aren't appropriate prospects for managed accounts. The biggest pitfall that claims many advisors who decide to use managed account solutions is their attempt to fit a square client peg into a round managed account hole.

Veteran advisor Mike's prospects have to be the right fit for managed accounts; otherwise, they don't become clients. His typical client is a middle-aged corporate executive. These individuals are interested in taking care of their business, are sophisticated, and don't have the interest or time to focus on their finances. Many did not have an investment strategy until they started working with Mike's firm. According to Mike, almost every new relationship must become a managed account, because he doesn't talk about stocks. Each client must have a financial plan that clearly identifies the client's risk tolerance and asset allocation. This plan is attached to and integrated with the managed account program. Many of his clients are affluent and are willing to have a professional manage their assets. "One thing we do for all of our clients is to create an organizational chart for their assets," Mike says. "We aren't only interested in the total amount; we want to know how the assets are invested in all the accounts."

Says successful advisor Keats, "The prospect has to have some degree of financial sophistication. Assets must be worth at least $1 million. We will take smaller accounts if we believe there is opportunity to grow the business, and for smaller accounts we will use mutual funds. In some instances, we use funds because only a small portion of assets is available to be managed; we might have a 40-year-old who is worth $6 million, but almost all of it is in stock options—this client really hasn't amassed anything of substance in a 401(k). For some clients, we use alternative investments and also suggest variable annuities for tax efficiency and to create a death benefit. Mutual funds will be used to mirror what would be in a managed account. If someone has $400,000, we can create a portfolio with a stable of six managers similar to what someone with $4 million would get." Keats has $125 million of assets under management and has been in the industry since 1981.

According to a recent industry study, one-third of all affluent investors say they are willing to fully delegate management of their assets to a professional advisor, and 17 percent claim to be fully discretionary—a role made much easier by the availability of so many online tools, like estate planning analyzers and Monte Carlo simulations. The remaining 50 percent want to have some degree of participation in the management process. Simply put, half of affluent investors are looking for validation but not to assume total control. Therefore, at some level, 83 percent of these individuals wanted a third party helping them manage their money.

Individuals who are very active, with busy careers, family lives, hobbies, and/or participation in civic and charitable projects, are all good candidates. Explain to these prospects that they will have more time to do what truly interests them, and they will have a more consistent method of financing these activities. These people want to spend more time with their families and have priorities beyond their money. It doesn't mean they aren't interested in making and preserving their capital; it means they are just as interested, if not more so, in what their money can do for them.

Look for these types of prospects. This type of profile shows they are responsible, grounded people with goals. The more goal-oriented they are, the more likely they will be attracted to the goal-oriented process of a managed account solution.

"The ideal client for a managed account is a husband-and-wife team," says advisor Gerry. "The husband is a former corporate executive, and they have money to invest that represents 30 to 40 percent of their overall estate." This profile falls below many firms' radar screens, he says.

Advisor Tip

WOOFing Down Managed Account Solutions

The profile of Harry's typical client is 55 to 75 years old, married, a highly compensated executive or retired executive with a sprinkling of entrepreneurship. He likes to call them "WOOFs," which stands for well-off older folks. Harry says their annual income is $75,000 to $100,000 and their average net worth (excluding home) is $1 million. "They are interested in paying a flat fee for a comprehensive financial plan," he says. "This process includes the following features: an investment portfolio with appropriate asset allocation, retirement security analysis, income tax reduction analysis, risk management analysis, survivor caregiving analysis (insurance), legal document review, and estate planning wealth transfer."

Steve believes the best targets for managed account solutions are the typical clients he has right now: business owners who didn't inherit the assets. "It's the entrepreneurs, in their mid-50s, sophisticated, married with kids," says Steve. "They should be in the high-net-worth category with $1 million to $10 million to invest." Steve will take any amount if there is promise of capturing more assets later. His business is built strictly on referrals, and he has significant relationships with CPA firms.

Chuck doesn't agree with Steve about referral business. Very little of Chuck's managed account business comes from referrals—by choice. "That's not to say you can't get good clients from others," Chuck says. "Most folks don't think about the potential land mine that they can be. One key issue to worry about with a referral is that if the relationship goes south, you can end up with egg on your face, as can the person who referred the prospect. What do you do if you simply don't like the person after you have them as a client? It isn't easy to just fire them!"

Chuck obtains much of his business through his extensive community activities, allowing him routine contact with a large number of wealthy individuals who are suitable for managed accounts. Several years ago, he wanted to develop a community approach to help him establish solid, long-term relationships. So, over the course of two years, he read a number of books on community leadership programs because he wanted to interface with high-level business executives who played an active role in community affairs. He quickly developed a database of business leaders and established a local chapter of a national leadership program to give high-level business executives the ability to participate in community affairs. He created several programs that allow business leaders to speak at area colleges on a variety of issues and also holds forums to address concerns faced by many of today's companies. Chuck does not introduce himself as a financial advisor, but rather as the director of a program whose goal is to improve the quality of the community.

The foregoing suggestions should provide you with a steady stream of referrals from current clients. However, you may decide, like Chuck, that you'd rather not rely on personal referrals to help build your practice. There are other ways to position yourself as a provider of managed account solutions, and we explore some of them in the next chapter.

CHAPTER
9

Positioning Yourself as a
Solutions Provider

*By cultivating mutually beneficial relationships with service providers,
allied professionals, and the media, you can develop a steady stream of
referrals to help grow your business.*

Your current clients are excellent sources of referrals and can help you
build your managed account business; however, they are not the only source.
The money management firms and other service providers you partner with
can be another excellent source, as can other professionals such as accountants and attorneys. Finally, you can develop a partnership of sorts with the
local media that can position you as a solutions provider in the public mind.
Let's take a look at each of these sources and how they can help drive prospects to your door.

Partner with Service Providers

Investment managers and fund companies compete for your attention, and
they can be great allies to help you build your business. One of the most
critical factors in presenting a new product or process, such as a managed
account solution, is the ability of a firm to promote it through advisors. This
means training the advisors in the specifics of the product itself as well as
helping them portray the product to the prospective client. You can benefit
from these efforts.

Consultants to affluent investors should search for helpful and suitable
partners in the process of reaching their market. A wholesaler can help you

with more than just personalized delivery of marketing materials. A good wholesaler can be a true business development partner.

"Banks build relationships with bank managers and regional office managers, all of whom can give referrals to advisors," says Lidiette Ratiani, director of investment consulting solutions with Wells Fargo Private Client Group. "These are warm leads, not cold calling, because these are satisfied and loyal customers of the bank with whom we've established a relationship based on trust. We are interested in helping the advisors we serve grow their practices."

Keats, a seasoned advisor, considers the wholesalers he works with his allies, not just product delivery people. "A wholesaler should provide value in terms of helping me grow my business through target marketing, for example, and assisting me with relationship management."

When you begin your search for managers, think of it as searching for a strategic alliance partner. You will need managers who can provide investment solutions for your clients. For example, large-cap value and large-cap growth managers are the most pervasive managers in the managed account world, and they are important components of most asset allocation solutions. Although you are not limited to these categories, they are a good place to start—and it's important to ally with a manager who can serve the needs of your clients not only now, but also in the future.

"The pioneers in our business focused on being an advisor to the client—that is, developing a special relationship among the client, the advisor, and the money management firm, with improved economics for everyone involved," says one top wirehouse executive. "But at the end of the day the concept of a single account flies out the window if the firm has only narrow product offerings. Advisors need to partner with firms with whom they can develop a personal relationship *and* provide their clients all of the products and services they need."

When you find the right managers, you need to create an incentive for a firm and its wholesaler to work with you. You may not be the largest managed account advisor or consultant in the area, but you may work in the same office with other advisors who also are interested in the same managers and need help, too. You may want to consider aligning with those advisors to leverage the wholesaler's time when visiting your office, especially if you are in the process of transitioning your business.

If you are a more experienced advisor, you may be interested in financial support for ongoing client appreciation meetings, for which the manager's economic support is helpful and also justified by the business you've done with the firm. Partnering with wholesalers for business development assistance is the highest and best use of their time. They see all of the best practices and marketing strategies being used by the most successful advisors. The best wholesalers are walking libraries of information for you.

"We have invested a lot in our field force to help financial advisors," says Chip Walker, managing director of Wachovia Securities. "We know advisors need to leverage their time, and having a wholesaler sit in with an advisor at a meeting or seminar can be really helpful, especially in the first few meetings when an advisor is just beginning to make the transition to managed accounts."

Skilled wholesalers put a tremendous amount of energy into helping advisors build their businesses. Because a good wholesaler has an incentive to keep your business growing, this person can also act as a coach if you have shared your business plan with him or her.

All of this value-added help notwithstanding, we are not suggesting that you should select a manager and wholesaler based solely on their business development programs. First and foremost, you need the talent and capability of the investment manager. All things being equal, though, why wouldn't you opt for the individuals who can give you the most assistance in capturing more assets?

The ideal arrangement for your practice would be to build an array of managers to cover the style boxes and asset classes that you need the most and, at the same time, be able to extract additional value from each of the managers—whether education, financial support, or expertise—and recognize the professional quid pro quo of working with the management firms and benefiting from their tools.

We interviewed a number of financial advisors and asked about their relationships with wholesalers and what they expect from them. Advisor Carroll says that the best partnership with wholesalers can be achieved when they:

- Provide outstanding service, communicate good *and* bad news, don't hide when the manager's style is out of favor, and tell advisors frankly what is happening.
- Agree to participate in client appreciation meetings when advisors need them.
- Provide other communications to the team on what is going on with the manager. Advisors need more due diligence on how the manager is performing in addition to the advisor firm's due-diligence process.
- Visit with each advisor two to four times per year.

"When selecting managers and working with wholesalers, one of the biggest issues is service support," says advisor Paul. "We make it a point to conduct business with people who help support ours. We let our firm do the initial screening because they are very good at it, and then we decide who is best to work with. Seminar support is critical for us."

Keats has valuable insight on how he feels wholesalers can help him build his business. "The wholesaling industry sometimes can be out of step with the times," he says. "We don't want to have multiple meetings with outside wholesalers. In fact, I limited myself to two meetings with wholesalers in my office all of last year. Even though I sometimes get six to eight calls a day from wholesalers, there is simply no time to meet. The really successful wholesaler has to talk about something that I don't know—things like client and asset retention practices, value propositions, and other unique business development tools. What can we do that is better than our competition? That is the question we want answered.

"The right way to get out there (for the wholesaler) is to find out who the top 25 producers are at each firm," he adds. "Tell them how they can grow their business strategically. Give them an architectural plan. Tell them how they can set up a quality review with a client. Go to these top people and tell them you are providing tools to grow a business. Don't confuse activity with productivity. Help us paint a vision of what it's like to be a client of ours. We call every client once per month and have a formal quarterly review. If a client calls with an administrative issue, we get back to them the same day. Here is the reality: People share experiences. If you see a really lousy movie or a great movie, you tell others about it. It's the same with referrals. If you create a client experience (wholesaler with producer or financial advisor with client), people will share the experience."

Advisor Mike says, "The great ideas we get from wholesalers are those that help us to find solutions for those clients with problems. These could be investment problems or retirement problems with suggestions or guidance that can be provided to the client. New business or prospecting ideas to get us through tough times in the market are great types of communications."

Chip Walker says Wachovia expects the money managers in its platform to provide as much support to financial advisors as possible. "We're not talking about golf balls or anything like that," he says. "We're talking about communication—keeping the financial advisors informed. If advisors have high-net-worth clients, the wholesaler can be there in a meeting or a seminar if need be. Field support of financial advisors is important."

David Wadley, senior vice president/national sales director and one of the most sought-after speakers from Phoenix's retail markets group, says, "The stellar wholesaler is a great public speaker. The financial advisor can use the wholesaler's speaking skills in seminars with clients to provide the educational bent. It's not a product sale; it's a learning process. We need to help advisors grow their business. We can do one-on-one meetings with their clients or sit in on team meetings and comment on how they are managing their business. We give them a resource to carry their business to the next level because we are visible."

Jim Miklas, senior vice president/investment consultant, and his internal partner, Taia Riley, internal investment consultant, both with Phoenix's retail markets group, have this to say about working with advisors: "We usually tell advisors, 'The reason we are here is to help you ask yourself some basic questions about your practice. Give us three critical objectives.' For example, one advisor said, 'Maintain current client base, annuitize and get new accounts, and capture net new money.' We send the advisor one great idea per week to help him with his business."

Both Miklas and Riley are discerning about those to whom they deliver their value-added service. "Who do we, as wholesalers, want to do business with? We try to avoid the performance-fixated advisors and, ideally, want to do business with advisors who like us as much as we like them."

Mary, a senior wholesaler with another investment management firm, tries to understand how managed accounts fit into the advisor's practice. "The key is understanding how the wholesaler can help the advisor develop a better practice," she says. "It doesn't matter if it is an established financial advisor or a rookie. The role of the wholesaler is changing. Before, we would tell advisors the story of why they should use managed accounts. Everyone knows that now. The more important question is how they are used. You can't get traction with an advisor when you discuss *why* (taxes, control issue, etc.). Focus on the *how*."

Mary says her goal is to help the advisor with each of the following:

- Examine the advisor's existing practice. What changes can be made? How can the practice be enhanced? What are the risks? What are the weaknesses?
- Help educate the advisor's clients on the managed account process. Move away from the transaction mentality.
- Retention, retention, retention. Bring assets in the door and keep them. Focus on the clients you already have and maintain a superior relationship.

Dan, an advisor who's been in the business for more than 10 years, explains how to partner effectively with wholesalers. "Not only do wholesalers have to provide us with new ideas when things are good, but they have to be available to do so when the markets are in bad shape, too," he says. "Communicate when there is a crisis! Give us advice on how to conduct better client meetings in challenging times and bring a manager to the meeting who has a great story. What does he or she do that is unique, and what are the steps in that process? Tell us more than, 'We buy great companies that have the best products.' The best wholesalers I've seen are not out of sight, out of mind when the markets reverse course."

Information is what advisor John values most in a wholesaler. "The best support we can receive is to get the inside track about the portfolio," he says. "In other words, provide us with a solid knowledge level about weightings on stocks and other key data changes about the portfolio. We also need to be kept up to speed about manager changes. We look for tools to use in client seminars and for assistance in writing client proposals. As an advisor, I'm not a research analyst; I'm a relationship manager. Sure, we can do the evaluation ourselves; however, it takes a significant amount of time and is quite difficult to do. If our wholesaling partner can look at a client's entire portfolio, evaluate it using Morningstar and other tools, and suggest the best fit with their company's products, we would have the golden goose egg."

Miklas discusses the literature and materials provided by many firms. "Some firms have excellent material for advisors, while others either have none or have information that is poorly presented," he says. "Advisors get inundated with right-brain stuff from their firms. Focus on the left brain. My partner and I provide concepts and value. What value means to us is giving support to advisors to help them make an impact on their practices."

Miklas and Riley also assist advisors with the investment process. "We help advisors with the firing component of manager evaluation," Jim says. "We help them set their boundaries with their investment policy program with managers—for example, three years' underperformance to the benchmark and the fund manager is gone, or he is advised that he is under probation for the next year and if things don't improve, then he's gone. We try to build expectations into the advisor's business. Here's another example: Get advisors to think about the concept of attribution. We can help them evaluate why the portfolio is underperforming. Is one stock driving 80 percent of the underperformance?"

Mary believes that advisors who take a holistic approach to the business are the most successful ones. She wants to establish relationships with advisors who present a host of global wealth management solutions to clients. In other words, she avoids the product pusher.

Advisor Mike also tells us, "Physical presence is important, too. We have 5,000 things in the hopper at one time, and we can't always communicate with our wholesalers in the most effective manner by phone. They need to be there."

Partner with Allied Professionals

There are journeymen stockbrokers, junior reps, and other advisors who are uncomfortable with the complexities of providing wealth management solutions. Since some advisors prefer to discuss only investments, they risk losing clients whose requirements exceed those of their limited focus. The potential for partnering with less sophisticated advisors is substantial, and one of the most significant growth opportunities for providers of managed account solutions.

Tim, an advisor we've known for many years, works with several very sophisticated ultra-high-net-worth families and has been successful in creating innovative portfolio solutions. He shares his expertise with a number of advisors who each typically have only one such client. Tim supports the advisors with his portfolio solutions while the advisors maintain the primary relationship. This account-sharing trend is powerful, and we've seen versions in which advisors tap into the expertise of other advisors because of specialized knowledge in 401(k) and pension investments, estate planning, business succession, concentrated stock liquidation, and charitable giving strategies. Imagine the power of your practice if you became known for a particular strategy and were able to market yourself through other advisors!

Talented professionals prefer the company of other professionals. The best accountants, lawyers, lenders, life agents, actuaries, family office directors, hedge fund managers, and private bankers all travel in the orbit of affluent clients and don't have time for marginal players. These colleagues are a significant source of potential referrals; cultivating them is time well spent. Invite them to your seminars, and arm them with concrete examples of how you have helped your clients. The best way to provide this information is with a case study. Once these other professionals have worked with you, they will acquire their own insight into your skills and process. Until then, the case study can represent you well.

Here is a checklist of requirements needed for generating referrals from other professionals:

- *Biography.* Prepare a professional biography that includes your background and experience. Your accomplishments should create confidence and be superior to those of an advisor who would benefit from bringing you into a client solution.
- *Profile.* This is an overview of you and your team, further supporting your capability to assist other advisors and their clients.
- *Your specialty.* Create an outline of your specific expertise, not a listing of the range of your services. You must have a particular specialty in order to position yourself relative to the generalist advisor.
- *An A-list.* This is a list of the advisors who have a positive impression of you and your specialty, and who might consider bringing you into a case.
- *A prospect list.* This contains names of advisors you don't know well who could be referral sources.
- *A contact plan.* You need a way to stay in touch with your list of advisor referral sources. How about a lunch meeting every quarter?
- *A collaboration plan.* Are there joint prospecting activities you can manage? Client seminars? Professional seminars for accounting professionals?
- *A prospecting plan.* How will you cultivate your list of prospective referring advisors? Do you have a newsletter or case studies of client solutions that you can share to keep your name in front of these advisors?
- *The specialist A-list.* These are professionals with whom you share clients today: accounting professionals for sure, but also estate attorneys, mortgage lenders, insurance agents, benefits consultants, and record keepers for retirement plans. For handy reference, sort this list by profession and by client.
- *The specialist prospect list.* These are professionals from the categories defined by the specialist A-list with whom you do not now share clients. Whom do you want to meet and get to know? What do you know about their practices? Sort this list by profession.

You can build a virtual team with centers of influence—CPAs, estate-planning attorneys, and business consultants. Consider doing this with your client's circle of professionals so you have a better picture of where that client's additional assets are.

Harry works with a certified elder law attorney who focuses on long-term care planning. Elder law is the legal practice of counseling older persons about the legal aspects of health and long-term care planning, public benefits, surrogate decision making, and the conservation, disposition, and administration of their estates. It also includes implementation of their decisions in these matters, the tax consequences, and the need for more sophisticated tax expertise. Having this expertise on board, Harry has the capabilities to specialize in this market.

Ron in Fairfield County, Connecticut, depends on skilled partners and says, "Our business requires knowledge in sales, trusts, taxes, and operations. It is very difficult for a one-, two-, or even three-person shop to have excellent command of all of these different skills. The larger the scale, the more experts you have in-house, the better you can serve clients. By being both detailed financial planners as well as discretionary money managers, we are afforded significant insights as to the needs of clients and the ability to act with speed when allocating or reallocating portfolios. Obviously, the greater the scale, the greater the value of the firm."

In *Practice Made Perfect*, Mark Tibergien and Rebecca Pomering of Moss Adams LLP explain how such arrangements should work:

> In a referral agreement, whether it's a formal joint venture or not, two parties formally combine their strengths to shore up each other's weaknesses and systematically capture more business. A CPA firm, for example, may want a referral agreement with a financial advisory firm so that it can deliver financial advice to its clients; or a financial advisor may seek a joint venture with a law firm to make legal advice and document preparation readily available to its clients. Usually one of the entities generates new business and the other provides expert services. Ideally the parties to the agreement would bring both strengths to the table, but that's rarely the case.

Tibergien and Pomering say the following key factors should be considered before entering into any agreement:

- How will the method of sale build on the strengths of each firm?
- How is your firm differentiated from others competing for the same type of clients?
- Can you realistically create business through such a proposition?
- Is an agreement of this type the best way to allocate your resources?

In addition to these philosophical concerns, there are practical issues that must be addressed as well:

- What is the function of each party to the agreement?
- Who is responsible for client introduction?
- Who is responsible for providing service?
- Who will handle billing and document collection?
- Who will handle dispute resolution?
- Who is responsible for quality control?
- How will you distribute the proceeds?

The authors suggest that such agreements be monitored regularly to make sure they are achieving what they were meant to achieve. "Eventually you may find that managing the relationship takes up more of your time and energy than you originally intended," they say. "Make sure the arrangement is right for your business."

Don't overlook teaming up with your fellow advisors. Teams are growing in importance, and many are specializing in wealth management. For example: You capture the assets; your partner does the asset allocation, monitoring, and performance reviews. Other members of your team can be adjunct specialists like analysts, computer experts, and marketing strategists.

Paul, a wirehouse training director and 20-year industry veteran, coaches advisors on the advantages behind developing a team of experts. "There is a huge difference between a team and just having strategic alliances," says Paul. "A team of skilled advisors is really a partnership. Working with an outside contact is more of a strategic alliance. The sole practitioner that gets referral business from a CPA or an attorney has challenges creating the real synergies needed for a highly successful wealth management practice. You can't develop sufficient leverage on this level."

Paul says teams will almost always outperform sole practitioners—in terms of average assets and production, "at least double," he says. Why? "Because of the ability to mesh talent into a cohesive approach to solving a client's life issues. Teams succeed because you have the right people doing the right things."

How can an advisor truly manage wealthy clients and be a stock selector at the same time? According to Paul, you can't. "Stock picking is a full-time job. Since portfolio managers are dedicated to combing the universe of stocks, how can an advisor build the structure and technological capacity to manage a portfolio?" He encourages advisors to look at the big picture. "Given all of the estate, trust, and insurance complexities that clients don't even want to think about, you'll need a team to build an integrated, successful practice. Our industry has ignored some key financial issues because we tell a client, 'We don't do that.' You have to think of your business as a team of doctors. You've all gone through medical school and now each of you subspecializes. You can then fully engage your clients in a systematic wealth management solution."

Bill and his partners have determined that they can manage 75 to 100 relationships to be effective. Beyond that, the capability of being a point person diminishes significantly. Bill developed a model team with his partners to operate the business horizontally, rather than vertically. This way, each partner knows the others' clients. Each partner's specialty or segment also can be presented to the client to focus on total wealth management services. The three general areas he and his partners focus on are public relations/ marketing, investment management (manager selection and asset allocation), and financial planning.

Advisor John says a team approach results in multiple levels of expertise. He partners with three advisors and employs one full-time and one part-time support associate. John's focus is on insurance and estate planning, and money management. A second partner focuses on 401(k)s, and the third has expertise in debt and credit issues. "It's not a good use of our time for all three associates to know the details of all of the clients," says John. "Our philosophy is to have a primary relationship manager (usually the person who landed the account). This person knows the intimate details of the client's financial situation."

Other successful advisors and consultants may be willing to be a mentor until you have transitioned to managed accounts, or at least to give you professional support along the way. If you are interested in this approach, try to locate someone who is inside your branch or someone outside your office. Lately, more firms are developing formal and informal mentoring programs for their advisors and are encouraging the veterans to lend a hand to rookies.

Gerry has a very successful wirehouse practice in Hartford, Connecticut, and is a fan of teaming up veterans with rookies. "For the new kids on the block, Wall Street can partner trainees with advisors who have been in the business for a while," he says. "You have to give the new consultant time to build relationships, given the competitive nature of this business."

Advisor Gary is emphatic about mentoring new advisors who are transitioning into the managed account business. "For those trying to build a plan, I say, 'Get yourself into a mentoring program. Have a senior advisor serve as your mentor,'" he counsels. "It is incumbent upon the firm to help the new advisor, too. Many training programs fail, which is why turnover is so high in some firms."

Don't overlook the advantages of hiring an industry coach or trainer if your firm does not support the training effort, or if you want to take your business to a higher level, or simply if you need someone to help keep you on track with a strict, disciplined approach. At the very least, think about retaining someone to help keep you accountable and motivated. It is an investment in your own future. Fees for coaches and trainers depend on the amount of time spent on each session, depth of coaching, in-person or telephone coaching, and how long you retain the coach.

All in all, possibilities to ally and partner with other professionals and colleagues who will take a keen interest in your business are myriad. Investigate the choices we've outlined in this chapter, and you might be surprised to discover a few ways not only to boost your business but to develop friendships and strong professional relationships along the way.

Partner with the Media

There are few sales tools more powerful than having an impartial, influential third party endorse you as an expert. Sure, you can tell the world—or a segment of the world—that you're an expert by buying media space and paying for an advertisement. But while ads can raise awareness, they lack credibility. Being quoted in news and feature stories, however, positions you as a person whose comments and insights are worthy of note.

Joseph Finora, a Long Island–based former Wall Street reporter and public relations executive (jfinora@optonline.net), says that it's never been easier to get quoted in the media because of all the financial web sites, talk shows, and publications regularly looking for financial experts. At the same time, it's never been more difficult to find the right place to say the kind of things that will position you as an expert. Joe suggests using a seasoned public relations (PR) professional to help you reap the benefits of a well-conceived media-relations program. Here are some pointers from Joe:

- Determine your publicity and public relations objective. How will a comprehensive media-relations program help? Stick with one or two financial themes and areas of knowledge (retirement, municipal bonds, and options are just three examples) and be prepared to stay with them for the long term. Offering yourself as an expert in one area, only to change course a year or two later, damages your credibility.

- There are no guarantees in media relations. That's why you should limit comments to subjects in which you're thoroughly knowledgeable. This reduces the possibility of error. If you are asked a question you feel uncomfortable answering, be honest and say you'd like to do some research. Offer to get back to the journalist or refer him or her to someone better qualified to respond. Providing an incorrect or misleading response can permanently damage your reputation.

- Seek professional PR help from someone who has worked successfully with other advisors or professionals such as attorneys and accountants. Ask at the chamber of commerce or speak with related professionals for a recommendation. Be sure the PR pro you're considering does not work for a direct or indirect competitor. Remember, bigger isn't necessarily better in public relations; a small firm with experienced principals can be extremely effective. Before making a choice, check references and examine track records. If you're not ready for a long-term arrangement, ask about individual projects. These can be a good way to get to know each other; six months is a reasonable time frame.

- While cultivating press relations can take time, after a few months you should be able to tell if your program is starting to work. If not, review what has and has not taken place on your behalf. Regular communication between client and media-relations representative is the key to success.

- Reporters crave news and timely insights, so make your comments newsworthy by being brief, making a point, and speaking plainly. Don't expect preferential editorial treatment (for example, having your picture taken or being quoted for saying something of little consequence) just because you advertise in the publication for which you're being interviewed. The editorial and advertising departments are separate; asking for editorial coverage because you advertise (or might advertise) is insulting to the editorial staff members who are trying to provide readers with unbiased reporting.

- Do not try to obtain favorable coverage by taking a reporter to lunch or sending a gift. All credible media outlets have strict policies against such practices. Ask in advance if you can pay for lunch. At the end of an interview, let the writer know you're available for follow-up questions, and be sure he or she has your telephone number and e-mail address. Do not ask to review the story or use the meeting to promote other aspects of your practice. Usually there is no time for either of these, and the reporter may consider such behavior amateurish or insulting.

- Above all, do not twist the truth, spin, or (let's use the plain, old-fashioned word) lie. Responsible journalists will double- and triple-check information before submitting their stories, because people are known to be less than reliable when providing information. Sometimes this inaccuracy is accidental; other times it's not. Stick to the facts.

There is a right way and there is a wrong way to try to establish a partnership with the media, and many financial advisors (and other professionals) go about it the wrong way. An editor we know at a national financial magazine relates this story about how he developed a partnership with a financial advisor. "I had been working the police beat for a large daily newspaper and got reassigned to the business desk," he says. "This was many years ago, and I knew nothing about business at the time. The day my first bylined story appeared, I received a call from an advisor in a local branch of a wirehouse. He said he'd noticed my byline and asked if I was new. I told him I was new to the business desk but not new to the paper, and he asked if I had ever covered business before. I said no, and fully expected him to point out an error in my story. Instead, he said that he realized newspapers were often understaffed—which is true—and that I might be asked to cover stories on topics I was not familiar with—which was also true. He suggested I take down his name and number and call him if I ever found myself grappling with a story I didn't understand—some sudden uptick or downturn in the markets, for instance, or some obscure point of economic policy. He said he would be happy to help me sort out the facts.

"Sure enough, a few days later I was assigned a story that had me baffled—the Federal Reserve Board had just issued some incomprehensible statement, or something along those lines—so I called up this advisor and asked him to help me put the story in terms that newspaper readers could understand. He was great. We spent about 20 minutes on the phone getting the wording just right, and as the conversation was wrapping up I asked him for his formal title, so I could credit him as a source. He said that he'd rather not be identified, and even though I assumed the reason had something to do with his firm's compliance department, I asked for an explanation. He said, 'I am trying to position myself as a retirement planning expert, and I would welcome the opportunity to be quoted whenever you're covering 401(k)s, pension plans, or any related issues. In the meantime, feel free to call whenever you have any business-related questions. I'm glad to oblige.'

"Not too long after that, I was assigned a retirement planning story, obviously a major issue that newspapers and magazines cover all the time. I interviewed this advisor and quoted him as a source—on the record, as we say in the business—and guess what? Immediately after the story was published, I was bombarded with phone calls from at least a dozen financial advisors—including some in my advisor's own firm!—all wanting to discuss the subject with me. Several even suggested I run another story quoting them on the same subject the following day! They just didn't get it, but that first advisor did."

What did the first advisor do right that all the others did wrong? A lot. For example:

- He reached out to the reporter and offered to share his financial expertise.
- He did not insist on being quoted every time he spoke with the reporter; on the contrary, he asked that his name only be used in conjunction with a specific subject.
- He did not call to comment on a story just published; rather, he positioned himself as a source in advance of the story assignment.
- He made it clear that he wished to establish a partnership with the reporter; he wasn't just looking for free publicity.

Our editor says that he is often amazed at the ineptitude some otherwise intelligent people can display when it comes to working with the media.

"I've had advisors submit stories with instructions that I was not allowed to change a single word," he says. "I've had advisors submit stories that were virtually identical to something I'd just published, thereby demonstrating that the person either wasn't reading my magazine or didn't understand that no publication wants to run the same story over and over. I've had advisors submit a story to me that had been published by a competitor only a month or two before. I even had one advisor submit a story with a cover letter that said, 'My writing is much more interesting than the boring stuff you usually publish.' I wonder if he was surprised when the story was rejected."

In the previous chapter, we mentioned that when properly edited, case studies could be suitable for publication. Editors and reporters are always on the lookout for new, fresh, interesting story ideas, and how you helped a client with a particular problem might be just what an editor is looking for. Don't expect your story to be published exactly as you've written it—that almost never happens—but understand it can serve as the foundation of a story that gets you press coverage.

Here are some suggestions for positioning yourself as a solutions provider in the eyes of the media:

- *Think locally.* While you may harbor fantasies of being interviewed or published by the *New York Times*, the *Wall Street Journal,* or some other major publication, the chances of that happening are pretty slim unless you have prior media credibility. Start with your local newspaper and work your way up.
- *Name, please.* If you are trying to get published in the local newspaper, don't just send story ideas to "business editor" or "business reporter." Mail addressed to a particular individual has a much greater chance of being read and reviewed than mail addressed to an anonymous title, because even the smallest newspapers gets a deluge of correspondence on a daily basis. To really stand out, mention a particular story or series of articles recently published by the reporter or editor. A little flattery never hurts, and such a move also shows that you read the publication and therefore probably have a pretty good idea of its target audience.
- *Be specific.* Suggesting that an editor consider a story about investments or retirement isn't going to go anywhere. Give the reporter a specific story angle, particularly one that hasn't been published before (or hasn't been published in a good long while), such as, "Retirees often have money in multiple accounts such as IRAs, 401(k)s, and similar vehicles, with no real understanding of which account to withdraw from first. Choosing the wrong account can have significant tax consequences."
- *Tell both sides.* If your suggestion is one-sided—"Variable annuities are perfect for everyone!"—then your pitch will come across as promotional and therefore journalistically unsound. There are benefits and

drawbacks to virtually everything, and by highlighting both the good and the bad you will show the editor that you understand the importance of objectivity.

- *Explain yourself.* Let the editor know why you should be used as a source for the story (other than the mere fact that you suggested it). Something like this should suffice: "Variable annuities can provide consumers with guaranteed income for life, but they're not the right choice for everyone. As a financial advisor, I've helped dozens of clients understand the intricacies of these products—and steered a few clients away from them—and I think your readers would benefit from knowing both the advantages and disadvantages of variable annuities."

- *Show your letters.* If you have a professional designation (Certified Financial Planner, Certified Investment Management Analyst, etc.), then use it. The fact that you took the time to earn the designation will enhance your credibility in the eyes of the media—and the public.

- *Follow up.* Treat a media source the same way you would a prospective client. After sending your story proposal, follow up with a phone call to make sure the appropriate editor received it and to see if he or she has any questions. Make this phone call personally; do not have a member of your support staff call on your behalf. Doing so may create the impression that you are too busy to talk to the press, or that you are sending out so many story proposals that you don't have time to follow up on them yourself.

- *Stay in touch.* Once you establish a relationship with a media contact, add that person to your newsletter mailing list. From time to time, follow up to see if the reporter is receiving it and finding it helpful.

Although the preceding tips have focused on establishing contact with newspapers, the same rules apply for radio, television, and magazines. Establishing a media presence is a great way to attract referrals. Depending on the circulation of the publication or the size of the radio/TV audience, you could receive anywhere from a few phone calls to scores of inquiries from prospective clients who read your comments or heard you speak and would like more information. Not all of these inquiries will come from people who would make good clients—in fact, most probably will not—but as you begin to become viewed in the public mind as a solutions provider, you will become better known and affluent clients will seek you out. The process takes time, but is well worth the investment.

No Time to Prospect? Hire a Rainmaker

Let us ask a blunt question: Are you an advisor or a salesperson? I know, everyone's a salesperson and the advisor/salesperson answer isn't necessarily either-or. But as the delivery of advice becomes more complex and requires more time for analysis and customer service, the time available for rainmaking shrinks. For many advisory practices, hiring a sales and marketing professional to promote and position the advisory practice with potential clients is a smart economic move. It frees the advisor to spend more time with valued clients while at the same time enabling a sales professional to concentrate on prospecting (which we know is a low priority for most advisors).

No matter how great a salesperson you are, someone else talking to others about what you do is more effective than you doing so on your own behalf. Many top advisors have hired full-time marketers to promote their practices. One advisor group on Florida's Gulf Coast was very impressed with a wholesaler from one of the team's investment companies. They took a deep breath, ponied up the cash from among the profits shared by the three principals, and took on the wholesaler. Used to working for a fairly low salary and sales-based incentive compensation, the wholesaler-turned-advocate for high-net-worth practices got right down to business creating leads and following up both prospects and referrals. He had nearly paid for himself within the first year.

Now that you've got prospective clients coming at you from all sides, what's to be done with them? Seminars are an efficient and effective way of getting your message across to a number of people at the same time. The next chapter features step-by-step instructions on how to run an effective seminar and turn clients into prospects.

C H A P T E R

10

Attracting and Retaining Clients

Seminars remain an effective marketing tactic in the sale of managed accounts. Here are proven techniques for staging a successful meeting and building your reputation.

In the preceding chapters, we examined ways to build your business through referrals from clients, service providers, allied professionals, and the media. Now that you've got a list of prospects, how do you go about converting them to clients? One time-tested method is by inviting them to a seminar and educating them about yourself, your practice, and the managed account solutions you can provide for them.

When managed accounts were first popularized in the late 1980s, many brokers who served high-net-worth clients were familiar with the seminar format, having used it to sell tax-sheltered investment products. Many of these brokers went on to discover that seminars were a great way to present managed account solutions. It was an ideal venue to showcase the advisor's skills and explain the relative complexity of the managed account process.

Back then, if you had the acumen and public speaking experience, a seminar was a powerful way to show an audience how knowledgeable you were. To this day, seminars remain the most effective method of promoting managed account solutions directly to affluent clients. Of course, when you say the word *seminar,* most people instantly envision a large crowd in an impersonal hotel meeting room, a speaker at the front flipping through PowerPoint slides, and an awkward lunch break with rubbery chicken and stilted conversation. This is *not* the sort of seminar we are talking about. A seminar to educate clients and prospects about managed account solutions could take place in your office or at a restaurant. We will talk about the opportune location a little later on.

Although there are numerous approaches to organizing an effective seminar, they all have one thing in common: Their purpose is to afford you an opportunity to have a personal interaction with clients and prospects. First, let's talk about those prospects—that is, your target market. Do they have enough money to invest in a managed account and the interest to use a real process to manage their wealth? In a "basics" seminar, you might simply introduce managed account solutions to investors who are unfamiliar with the process or who are currently mutual fund investors. Another audience could be investors who have a higher level of understanding, who may already have managed accounts with you, and from whom you might capture additional assets.

The Audience

There are a few key elements to all successful seminars. First, you need a homogeneous audience. Nothing is more difficult to maintain than a seminar where some attendees understand the topic while others have no idea what you are talking about. You will be ineffective at reaching a large percentage of your audience at either end of the spectrum. It's better to have a smaller audience whose members have issues in common. Homogeneity of the group is the first key to a successful seminar.

Don't ever be afraid of having too narrow an audience or too specific a focus. One of the first managed account seminar success stories Steve Gresham witnessed in his career was when he worked with preretirees from Procter & Gamble on behalf of advisors Steve and Lew at a wirehouse firm in Cincinnati. The audience was very specific: They worked at the same company, lived in the same town, and had a lot in common (especially their impending retirement), so the questions they asked during the seminar were all similar, and it was obvious that the answer to one person's question was applicable to many others in the audience. This particular seminar was more like a support group. Everyone sat at small tables for dinner, not in a big hotel conference room, and the conversation was kept tightly focused.

We've all attended seminars where one or two participants continue to ask basic questions while the others in the audience, having more knowledge on the subject, become visibly bored and very much annoyed. You won't be able to speak as personally and specifically to your audience if you have too much variety of attendees, and you will probably lose the opportunity to interact with the prospects most likely to become clients.

In addition to ensuring that the members of your audience have roughly the same literacy level in regard to the subject of the seminar, you should also give some thought to how many people should be in attendance. This is a hotly debated issue, but successful seminar advisors say the optimal size for a good managed account seminar experience is no more than 20 attendees.

Mark Pennington, a partner with Lord Abbett, says that when his firm sends managers to support financial advisors in seminars, they prefer to work with smaller groups. High-net-worth clients expect—and are entitled to receive—individual attention. "The client service model is incredibly important in this business, because when you are dealing with a client and their money you have to build trust," Pennington says. "We prefer to work with a very small, very elite group of people when we have investment discussions, and come in more as a facilitator of that discussion."

Somewhere between eight and 20 individuals is the perfect size, giving consideration to your goal of a homogeneous audience. Nobody sells much at a 300-person seminar. While the numbers sound terrific, you want to use your seminars as part of your sales process to give the investors a sense of who you are and how you work. The more you can personalize your message to them, the more they will feel as though you understand their needs and issues. Remember, your goal is to earn one-to-one appointments with the attendees.

You want to make the most efficient use of your prospects' time as well as your speaker's time and your own. It's better to have three programs in one day with audiences segmented according to their levels of interest and understanding rather than miss an opportunity and jam mismatched people into a single meeting. Many top advisors recommend multiple locations and multiple times for the same topic. This is particularly important when you are soliciting attendees for the seminar.

The Host

No matter the topic or the audience, you are always the seminar host. This is your opportunity to show leadership and present yourself as an authority on managed account solutions—even if you are not the person who will do most of the talking. Many service providers are willing to send managers and support staff to advisor seminars, and you may wish to limit your role to introducing the speaker to the audience. Such introductions should be brief but thorough. Make sure everyone in attendance knows who the speaker is and why he or she is qualified to address the topic at hand. Affluent investors are interested in working with people who have defined expertise.

The same rule applies when you are the primary or sole speaker, especially when addressing an audience of referrals. They may know something about you—a friend or colleague may have told them you're a great advisor— but that doesn't really tell them why they should listen to you (or trust you with their money). Tell them everything they need to know, and don't wait until the seminar to do it. Prove your expertise on paper beforehand, with either a biography, a published article, or other credentials such as a Certified Investment Management Analyst (CIMA) or Certified Investment Management Consultant (CIMC) designation. Review the prospecting tools outlined in Chapter 8, and make sure the people you invite to seminars have a copy of your brochure, the address of your web site, and a copy of your most recent newsletter or client bulletin. You will increase your chances of drawing a qualified and interested audience.

If you are new to managed account solutions, you might want your firm's managed accounts coordinator for the region to give the presentation, or perhaps a representative or wholesaler from a managed accounts firm. For a historic perspective, this is how E.F. Hutton did most of its training and promotion of managed accounts. Hutton's regional coordinators worked around the national branch system and gave client presentations for the brokers and advisors.

Frank Campanale, president of Campanale Consulting Group, was the man responsible for making sure that Hutton brokers knew how to explain the managed account process to clients. "We would attend meetings and seminars where clients were introduced to managed accounts and say, 'Here are all the things that we do. We have institutional-quality money managers and we can make them available to you. Ordinarily they would not be available to you unless you had $10 million to invest.' That got the clients' attention," Campanale recalls. "We would explain that we were offering the same approach that institutions used, and if it made sense for institutional clients, then it made even more sense for private clients. We did not teach advisors to sell a product; it was purely a conceptual sale. We were selling clients on the investment process—the product was incidental—and once they understood the logic and the benefits they would receive, they wanted to be a part of it."

Some of the most successful managed account seminar programs present the entire investment process. You can demonstrate the value of having an investment policy statement and the value of diversification of managers by asset class and investment style. Illustrate the historical interplay between value and growth styles and the efficient frontier among different portfolio choices. By showing the benefits, you are pointing out that a managed account solution is the vehicle of choice of other affluent individuals and major institutions.

The Location

Give considerable thought about where to hold your seminar, keeping in mind the professional nature and the exclusivity of the managed account solution for your audience. Remember, the typical affluent investor with a managed account has a net worth of more than $1 million. Your seminar is the first indication to them of your style, how you operate, and what you are like. You want to select a location that captures people's attention and creates a positive first impression of you.

If you work in a major city and seek to represent yourself to an upscale clientele, an exclusive club or restaurant would quickly set the stage for a serious message. However, there are advantages and disadvantages to a restaurant location. Restaurants can be very expensive because of the cost of food, of course, and you will need to consider adding wine to the bill and whether you should serve cocktails. This is the most expensive way of working with your prospects; however, you may find it necessary because your competition serves food and drinks.

On the plus side, offering a meal is a nice gesture and also one that may increase attendance, but on the minus side, food service can distract attendees from the conversation and serving alcohol may bring on a whole host of unforeseen problems. When weighing whether to opt for a restaurant location, consider the number of people who will be in attendance, how well you know them (a meal might be more appropriate for current clients than for prospects), and even what is going to be discussed (estate planning and long-term care needs may not be appropriate conversations over dinner). If you opt to forgo a complete meal, have simple refreshments on hand—snacks and soft drinks—because the last thing you want is someone rushing from the room in search of a glass of water.

An exclusive country club is a great location, too, because you have the added benefit of promoting your seminar to the members of the club by posting a notice, even if you're not a member.

One of the most successful seminars we've ever seen was held in the press box of an empty college football stadium. The advisor holding the seminar was an alumnus of the college; it was very unique, and everyone had a good time—and it was free! Another advisor we know was targeting the executives of a major corporation and determined that the best location for his seminar was at a nice hotel right around the corner from the company. It was incredibly easy for the attendees to walk over and not worry about driving and parking again.

Some advisors question whether to have a seminar in their office. While we have seen advisors use the office, it tends not to work as well for the newer audience because they are still in an educational mode, are not ready to commit, and may not feel comfortable arriving at your branch. You may need the perception of objectivity gained from an unrelated location, like a club.

Time of day is important, too. I've seen advisors who have tried to hold dinner seminars, only to fail because many on their invitation list had trains to catch after work and the restaurant did not serve the meals on time. Yet others in the same city have been successful with breakfast meetings because many individuals are willing to come in early but are not willing to stay late. I've seen advisors in the suburbs have successful dinner seminars because their prospects drive home and it's more convenient than mornings, when many people drop children at school. Choose a time that's appropriate for the people you wish to have attend. Retirees, for instance, may be more likely to attend an afternoon seminar but avoid one in the evening, while most working professionals would be unable to attend in the afternoon but might have time in the evening.

When considering the time and date of your seminar, watch the local newspapers for a few weeks to learn when other organizations hold their meetings. For instance, if the local chamber of commerce is an important organization in your area and it typically holds its meetings in the morning, take your cue from that fact. That organization picked that time for a reason.

What you really want is for your audience to be relaxed and not under a lot of pressure to leave. Roger, a successful advisor and branch manager in Buffalo, built his business with the breakfast seminar. He says people are very focused in the morning and he reports fewer cancellations. Because they have the greatest control over their day at the beginning, people tend to schedule the seminar first. When he began holding seminars on a frequent basis, his prospects and clients began bringing their friends and colleagues. They got to know the location and frequency of his weekly sessions.

The Invitation

As important as the location of your seminar is, the invitation you send is even more important, because it is your first overture to the prospect and plays a major role in determining how you and your practice are perceived. Ask yourself, if you received this invitation in the mail, would you be intrigued? Both the look and the feel need to speak directly to the target audience.

Let's start with the envelope, because that is the first thing your prospect will see. When people receive mail, either they open it or they don't—and they usually don't open mail that looks like an unwanted solicitation or mass-market advertising. They open the mail that looks professional. These days, every printer in every office has the capability to print an original address on an envelope. Use yours. Don't settle for just sticking a mailing label on an envelope, because that looks amateurish and slapdash. It goes without saying that the person's name, company, and address should be spelled correctly.

A coach we know advocates using a first-class stamp on all mailings, but we believe it's far more important to have the envelope look professional. Using a postage meter rather than a stamp conveys a sense of professionalism.

Successful seminar-givers report that it is not a bad idea to send a copy of the invitation to the prospect's home *and* place of business, because you never know who actually opens the mail in either location. There is also an added benefit for just the cost of another envelope and stamp: You get two chances to get the prospect's attention. Mailing seminar announcements to your prospect list is the least expensive advertising you can utilize. Treat each announcement as an advertisement for your services, so include your biography and other credentials. The recipient may not want to attend the seminar, but might need your services.

The invitation should explain precisely what the seminar is about, who will be presenting (their biographies and credentials), and what seminar attendees will learn. Be sure the benefits are spelled out clearly in the very beginning. For example, if your seminar topic is about the benefits of investing in separately managed accounts, your headline could be as straightforward as "Separately Managed Accounts: A Personal Strategy for Your Hard-Earned Money."

A savvy advisor we know listed all of the questions that would be answered at the seminar on his invitation to pique the interest of prospective attendees and help make it easy for them to determine the value of attending. You have nothing to lose; if the prospects don't see anything on your list that interests them, they aren't good prospects! Here are some questions you might wish to consider using:

- What is a separately managed account?
- What is an investment policy statement?
- What is asset allocation?
- How do you select a professional investment manager?
- How do you monitor the manager?
- What should be the benchmark of performance?
- Do I need more than one manager?
- What are the fees involved, and are they negotiable?
- How do I know how I'm doing?
- What are the tax benefits to me?

The invitation might say something like this: "Separately managed accounts are a revolutionary concept in investment management and the program of choice for affluent individuals and wealthy families, as well as public and private pension funds. These accounts are also available to individual clients of [insert the name of your firm] for amounts as low as $100,000. If you'd like to learn more about the advantages of separately managed accounts, and if you are an investor in mutual funds and securities and are ready for a comprehensive solution to your investment needs, we welcome your participation. This educational opportunity is being presented on the following dates at the following locations [insert at least two dates and two locations]." It's always better in a sales situation to give your prospects the choice of locations and times. When you call to make sure the prospect has received the invitation, you can ask, "Which meeting would you like to attend?" rather than asking, "Are you going to be there?" (See Appendix D for more helpful seminar ideas in the form of sample invitations and seminar checklists.)

Repetition is the key to success in using seminars for prospecting. For example, a recurring seminar program is a great way to introduce current clients to new investment managers. The seminar is presented on an ongoing basis, and it becomes a way to effectively utilize so-called drip marketing for prospects. Drip marketing is a consistent form of messaging done on a frequent basis to help brand your name and your services.

Again, the goal of the seminar is to introduce yourself and to showcase your skills in order to get a one-to-one meeting. The key to success becomes making the event an ongoing process—a part of your overall marketing strategy. If a prospect can't attend, but a colleague does and reports back to the original prospect about what a great seminar it was, it would be a shame if there were no repeat opportunity. Be sure to tell all of the attendees at the close of the meeting that you provide these seminars regularly, and that it's an educational service you offer. Also, give each attendee an invitation for a future program to pass on to a colleague or a friend.

The Topic

The examples we've cited refer to educational seminars—that is, seminars in which the primary focus is imparting information about products and services that you can provide to prospective clients. The choice of topic is up to you and whoever you decide to partner with (if anyone). You may wish to invite a money manager—or several—to speak to your audience.

One of the most common issues about manager seminars is whether to have multiple managers in a single program. Two managers can work well to reinforce issues around process so that you do not get lost in talking about performance records, which is strictly prohibited by compliance departments at some firms. Regardless of how closely the managers are aligned—that is, if their management styles are complementary—they will always reinforce the issues of process. They know that getting part of an overall solution is better than getting all of a client's assets and having that individual be overconcentrated in a particular style. All of the management styles you are likely to come across have already been through the experience of having too much concentration, and none of them wants to repeat that situation.

Make sure the manager or managers who speak at your event (based on your early knowledge of your attendee demographics) are potential hires by anyone in the audience. For example, what could be more of a misfit than presenting an aggressive growth manager to a group of retirees? Don't risk disenfranchising the audience by inappropriate manager selection.

Whether or not your attendees are new to managed account solutions, you need to establish your value early in the program. As the host, you must be crisp and articulate on the topic of manager selection and how managers have performed for you in the past. Provide a recap of the current market environment and the investment management consulting process so that attendees are very clear about what your added value is and will continue to be. Your goal is to convey confidence to your audience that you know what you're doing and that you would be a valuable advocate for them.

The goal of many seminars is to schedule one-on-one meetings with new qualified prospects. However, a terrific way to use the leverage of multiple clients already working with you is to bring them together on a common topic and show the group your appreciation for their business.

Client appreciation meetings are usually categorized in three ways: educational workshops, manager or market reviews, and pure appreciation social functions. Group client meetings show clients you care. Since most of them have multiple needs, you also get the opportunity to educate them in a group setting, taking advantage of the leverage that's created by the availability of an individual expert. They also get to meet other people like themselves.

For manager and market events, some of the most successful investment management firms we know hold annual client appreciation weekends. Invited guests include not only the chief investment officer of the firm holding forth on the market, but also top Wall Street analysts who visit throughout the weekend. Clients have opportunities to play golf and tennis at the local country club, and are treated to a special dinner on Friday night.

As for social functions, one of our biggest and most successful teams produces more than $7 million in revenue each year. The group was seeking a way to bring clients together more often. They tried a client appreciation event with a city museum, and it has become an annual event. We also know a very successful multimillion-dollar advisor team in Connecticut that organizes a barbeque every year for about 1,500 clients. The advisors take photographs and send the custom photos back to the clients with a thank-you note for their business. They maintain a yearbook of the event with pictures of all attendees at each yearly barbeque, which they keep in their office for prospective clients to flip through while they are waiting for their appointments. In other words, they try to create a family-type setting for their clients—a sense of community.

Sometimes advisors ask whether it's appropriate to bring clients together at one big event. On the basis of having fun or learning, it's always appropriate. Some have said that they fear clients will not like the lack of confidentiality, but you can always invite them and they may choose not to attend—and that's okay, too.

Appreciation gatherings can serve to educate your clients and keep the lines of communication open, and they are also an important client retention tool. For the most part, most wealthy people who came to you for advice generated their wealth through other means outside of investing. While your client may be relatively new to investing, he or she may be new to being wealthy, too.

These clients need to understand the components that will help with their overall wealth management, and as they become better acquainted with the topics and information in this area, they will become more comfortable—with you and with the managed account solution you are providing for them. Consequently, the easier it will be to discuss investment matters with them. It is extremely powerful for wealth management advisors to be in front of their clients to say, "We feel it's important for you to learn more about these particular areas of wealth management." The practical reality is: If you don't teach them, another advisor will.

We estimate that more than half of all affluent individuals want to learn the best ways to manage their money, but very few clients have the enthusiasm to take on more than one investment topic at a time. Advisors Richard and Jock stage topics they feel are important for their clients to understand and hold educational events throughout the year, year after year. Keeping clients on a continual educational track keeps them moving up the wealth management life cycle and learning curve.

Appreciation meetings don't have to be about investments. You might discover a topic that some of your affluent clients want to know more about. For example, Gary in Toledo knows many of his clients are interested in art and antiques. He found that by working with Sotheby's auction house, he was able to interact with key experts there, who were happy to come to Toledo and talk with his affluent clients over lunch about the art market or over cocktails in the evening about the wine market.

Gary also recognizes the charitable interests of wealthy individuals. Over the years he has tapped into his clients' desire to know more—and do more—in the area of family foundations. He has wine and cheese gatherings at his home to talk about charitable giving and the opportunities for his clients.

The Conclusion

After the delivery of your program, at which you can impart information that individuals can take with them, you need to make very clear how they can take the next step if they are interested in your services. Give them something personalized. If they have their own meeting agenda, notes, questionnaire, and a name tag you can clip to the seminar package, it shows you have taken the time to customize something for them. One successful advisor we know always includes a nice folder with pockets for information and a letter inside describing the advisor's initial new-client process—the first meeting with the client, how long it normally takes, financial information needed, and so on.

Include a questionnaire in the packet and ask seminar attendees to complete it. Here are some sample questions to ask:

- Did you find the seminar helpful?
- Was my approach appropriate to your level of understanding?
- Do you have any questions about the topic(s) discussed?
- Would you feel comfortable referring a friend or colleague to a future seminar of mine?
- Would you like to arrange a private meeting so that we can discuss the subject in greater detail?

All of these questions are important, of course, but the last one is most important. If a seminar participant says he or she would welcome a private meeting, then that is your opportunity to take action. Follow up personally by phone and arrange a mutually convenient time to meet. You are on your way to converting another prospect to a client!

11

Building on Your Success

Throughout the course of the client relationship, you will have multiple opportunities for capturing additional assets and building your managed account business.

Managed account solutions provide the discipline investors need to focus on the long term, and they also provide the basis on which the advisor and client build a relationship that lasts over years and decades. When you first transition your clients to managed accounts, you review the assets they hold with you and with others in order to determine the appropriate asset allocation. As your relationship with the client grows, many of them will ask you to manage more of their money.

"Once you sit down and go through the managed account process with clients and they understand how everything is integrated, and they receive a consolidated report every month with the gains and losses right there in front of them, then it's amazing how the additional money starts to show up," says Frank Campanale, president of Campanale Consulting Group. "Clients will say, 'Yes, this is exactly what I want.' But that will only happen after the advisor and his or her team demonstrates their ability to service their client relationships."

Mark Pennington, a partner at Lord Abbett, agrees. "When you take the time and make the effort to focus on client service, you find you will get not only more assets, but stickier assets," he says. "The relationship will last a long time."

During that time, you will have a number of opportunities to acquire additional assets. Let's review some of those opportunities in detail and examine how they can help you build your business.

Performance Reviews

Savvy advisors know their clients keep some assets elsewhere, so in your regular client review meetings you should ask your client for account statements for the assets held with other advisors. You need this information in order to recommend appropriate investments and informed allocations. Clients understand this, even if they are initially reluctant to put all of their assets with one advisor. Once they become familiar and comfortable with the managed account process, however, they will see the benefit of having an aggregated account and a consolidated statement. This is particularly important as clients are growing their wealth.

Account and performance reporting has developed into an asset-capture opportunity. Clients will volunteer additional assets that they want considered in a report because they like to see the entire picture of their holdings. Seldom would a bank or brokerage firm be willing to provide such a report if they didn't hold all the assets, yet many advisors use this as a strategy. They say, "If we knew about your other holdings, we could put them on your statement. Wouldn't that be convenient?" Many large clients at brokerage firms receive this benefit, which is a highly sought-after service requested by the affluent. This service is also offered by successful independent advisors.

"Most of our clients have all of their assets invested with us," says advisor Carroll. "The very first step in our process mandates that we know everything about our clients, including where they have their assets. If they don't tell us, we're unable to give an appropriate allocation strategy. Clients are almost always cooperative and provide us with other advisor statements, copies of trusts, wills, tax returns, and the like. This information also helps us to identify important issues such as a capital loss carryforward or whether clients are subject to the alternative minimum tax. We do recognize that once we get into the $20-plus million range, it is more likely investors will have multiple relationships with advisors. Still, we must know the details. We have one client who uses a bank, in addition to our group, to manage his assets. Every year we accompany the client to the bank to conduct a meeting with the manager there and review the entire portfolio."

Gerry's approach is to just "go for it." He says, "We want to know where everything is. We track out-of-custody assets, and we push the client to consolidate. It is important to be the quarterback. We try to get the client in front of our estate planning professionals whenever possible to help capture assets, and only focus on serious money. If individuals want a trading account, they can go somewhere else. We don't say this stuff to be lofty, but we want to be held accountable."

The asset-capture process involves determining why your clients might be motivated to give you additional assets. In many cases, a managed account solution removes any barriers. The concept of working with multiple managers, multiple asset classes, and multiple styles in a mutual fund advisory account, a unified managed account, or both, is that it is better to have all the assets in one place so you can develop a coherent investment solution for your clients.

You can explain to your client that it's important not to duplicate the efforts of other advisors or managers because doing so tends to reduce the value of the investment solution. You might want to say something like this to your clients: "If you go to another firm that offers managed account solutions and they also create an investment policy statement, putting you with multiple managers, multiple asset classes, and multiple styles, you may be deadening your overall potential return. If you have too many similar managers and styles, you'll end up with something resembling an index fund, and that will defeat the purpose of your investment goals. The goal, through your investment policy statement and the managed account process, is to create diversification for a better risk-adjusted return. In reality, you might be overdiversifying by placing your assets with various advisors and managers."

Account Upgrades

Some of the early success stories for capturing assets with managed accounts employed a simple feature: account minimums. Some advisors said to clients, "I know you have a number of mutual funds and securities, and that's a great strategy for the beginning investor and the initial stages of building wealth, but for me to better manage your wealth, at a certain point you earn the right to have a more customized portfolio. And this is possible when we have assets of $————." (You fill in the blank here.)

Eager to avail themselves of the higher level of service, some clients would produce assets enough to make the minimum. This phenomenon is reminiscent of the pre-money-fund days when investors would scrape together enough cash to buy a $10,000 Treasury bill. The exclusivity implied by a minimum is often a lure to affluent investors. A top advisor team we know has had a minimum account size for many years. Originally $1 million back in 1980, the minimum was so widely publicized that it became a status symbol to be a client of the group. When you told a friend you were a client, the friend now knew you were a millionaire!

A similar phenomenon is happening with hedge funds right now. These funds have high minimums, of course, but clients who express interest in them may not realize how high those minimums are. This is a perfect opportunity to educate the client and capture additional assets at the same time, for those clients for whom hedge funds are appropriate. For those not suited to hedge funds, you can still use the discussion as an opportunity to capture additional assets and recommend one of the lower-minimum hedge-type strategies discussed in Chapter 4.

Portfolio Expansion

Exposing a client to new asset classes provides yet another opportunity to capture additional assets. The goal of every advisor should be to create a solution that achieves the highest risk-adjusted return appropriate for every client.

Lidiette Ratiani, director of investment consulting solutions for Wells Fargo Private Client Group, says that when advisors sit down with clients to review their portfolios, they should also ask if the clients want to reevaluate their goals. This is a perfect time to inquire about additional assets. "Many advisors focus on market performance, or how the client's portfolio has performed against the S&P 500. That's how we taught investment professionals to speak to clients, and we created our own worst nightmare—because what the client really wants to know is, 'Will I achieve my goals? How far along am I?' Nine times out of 10, they're doing fine against the benchmarks, but that doesn't matter if they are not on track to achieve their goals; and if they're not, then it may be time to talk about further diversifying the portfolio by bringing in additional asset classes."

Successful advisor Bill explains how he uses new asset classes to capture more assets. "I call my clients up and say, 'We are going to help you more than we already do.' We generally know what they own and who has it, and we don't hesitate to ask for more of it. For example, if we have 10 to 20 percent of a client's assets, we'll ask the client to show us what else he owns to balance the allocation. If you are lucky, the guy on the other side is asleep at the wheel and you can capture those assets."

Portfolio Rebalancing

Perhaps the greatest challenge for advisors and consultants who create managed account solutions for clients using complementary asset classes and manager styles is that at any point in time, one manager, class, or style will perform better than the rest. Since performance of each sector is unpredictable, the only way to take advantage of this unpredictability is to expose clients to different asset classes and styles so that when one of them takes off, clients will already be in place to benefit. Generations of investors still try to hopscotch ahead of the next asset class, only to find themselves buying last year's winner.

Talk to clients about the opportunity to put additional assets to work and the concept of placing them with managers who are performing at different rates of speed. Rebalancing is a great way to take advantage of shifting market leadership and is also proof of your active management of client portfolios. For example, let's say a client's initial managed account solution consisted of 25 percent large-cap growth, 25 percent large-cap value, 25 percent small- to mid-cap core, and 25 percent small-cap core, and a market downdraft led to a drop in the large-cap growth allocation. Rather than shift money out of the other accounts, you could recommend that the client invest additional—that is, external—assets with the large-cap growth manager and bring up the percentage so that all allocations are equal again.

In other words, the performance of the value manager and the relative bad performance of the growth manager may have ended up with the account looking like 35 percent large-cap value and 15 percent large-cap growth. Rather than shift 10 percent out of the value fund to correct the imbalance, there is potential to get new money from your client to restore the growth allocation. Market changes, rebalancing, and shifting leadership style create the sense of opportunity so you can go back to your client and say, "We could take away from the more successful managers who are doing better by comparison, or we can shore up your account with extra cash."

Rebalancing is not always a function of market activity alone. Steve, a seasoned advisor in the Northeast, asks at every meeting whether the client's objectives have changed. Says Steve, "We want to be sure no personal event is overlooked, because it could require portfolio rebalancing." He captures more assets from clients simply by asking.

Many top advisors prepare their clients in advance for rebalancing opportunities, knowing that getting those clients to act in the moment can be difficult. Before the markets took a nosedive in 2000 and 2001, gung-ho investors were throwing their money at the Dow at 11,000. At 8,000 those same investors were reluctant to commit more money. That's human nature. But as professional advisors, we need to help our clients act more like institutions and move when the values are there.

Take an educational approach and teach your clients why this is a good time to put money to work. Here are some points you might want to pass on to them:

- At the start of every normal recession, few investors believe there is a recession.
- There's a point late in the recession when most investors acknowledge there is a recession.
- Profits decline, stocks decline, unemployment increases, consumer confidence declines, consumer spending slows.
- Observers start to believe that the recession will be deeper and longer than any similar period before.
- Every normal recession has some particularly dangerous features—for example, the 1970 stagflation, 1974 oil embargo, 1982 oil collapse, 1990 banking crisis.
- In the last three months of a recession, the pace of Federal Reserve easing accelerates.
- In the last three months of a recession, the stock market rallies.
- At the end of every normal recession, few believe the recession is over.

Take a look at the series of bear market charts in Figure 11.1 for some additional perspective.

Many investors *zig* when the markets *zag*. In the aftermath of the tragedy of September 11, 2001, when the markets plunged, the institutional investing

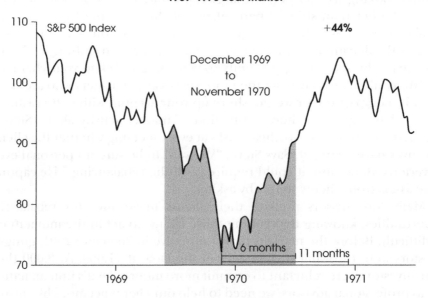

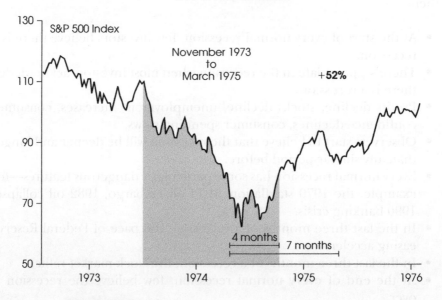

Figure 11.1   Bear Markets

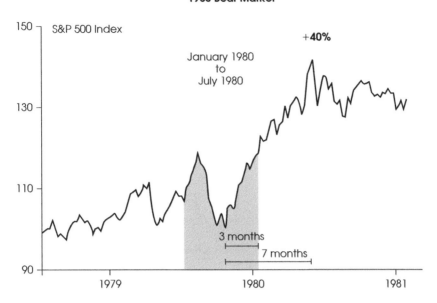

Figure 11.1   (Continued)

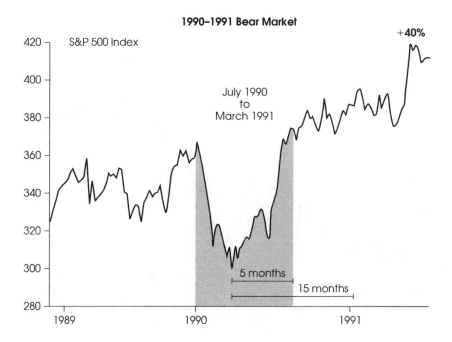

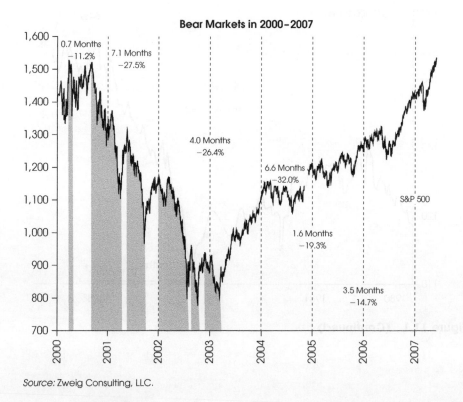

Source: Zweig Consulting, LLC.

Figure 11.1 **(Continued)**

community spent its cash on stocks, while individual investors ran to money funds and intermediate-term bonds. Institutions were moving with opportunity, while individuals reacted to their emotions.

Most affluent investors made their own wealth—about 80 percent are businesspeople in some form. The challenge of obtaining additional assets from these clients at the right time is that their businesses are tied to the economy, and many business owners will not be comfortable investing when the economy is not doing well.

The number one competitor you have in gathering more assets from affluent business owners is their business or practice. They don't want to take money out of their businesses when they think they might need it in a sagging economy. Human nature and events conspire against the business owner/investor. Owners might be reluctant to take money out of their businesses during a recession, but ask if they feel the market is a leading or lagging indicator. Of course, it's a leading indicator. When you look at the history of modern markets, whenever there has been a recession, the investors who waited until the end missed about half of the gain in the market.

Client Dissatisfaction

The typical $1 million client has three or four advisors, and that means the client is receiving three or four different levels of customer service. Make sure the level of service you provide is the best.

At an investment advisor seminar about a month after the September 11, 2001, attacks, the speaker asked the members of the audience to raise their hands if they had reached out to clients in the weeks that had passed since that horrible day. Only about one in four of the seminar attendees raised their hands. The speaker pointed to a man in the audience who hadn't raised his hand and asked, "Why haven't you called your clients?" The man sheepishly replied, "Because I wouldn't know what to tell them." A woman sitting nearby—one of the relative few who had raised their hands—spoke up and said, "Have them call me. I know what to tell them!"

So did another advisor we know, who used the event to trigger discussions among all of his managed account clients. "It's appropriate in this market environment for us to look at your original questionnaire and investment policy statement," he told them. "Let's talk about potential changes we might make and explore the possibility of getting you into the market in a more aggressive posture to take advantage of the drops." He told his clients that while the original questionnaire helped form the blueprint for an investment solution, that solution requires occasional maintenance, which can mean rebalancing the portfolio. (See Figure 11.2.)

Market dips and bounces provide opportunities to reinforce your value as a consultant. By providing a course of action—or inaction, if appropriate—you remind clients that you are watching the markets, as are the chosen managers.

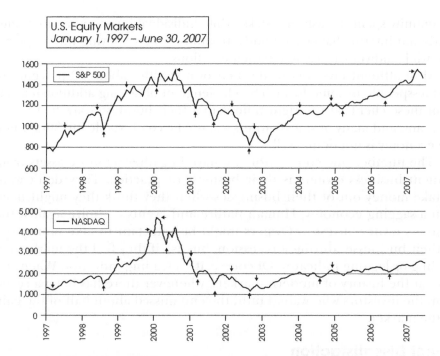

Figure 11.2   Don't Hide: Market Volatility Creates Opportunity for Proactive Communication
Source: Zweig Consulting, LLC.

The extra layer of supervision provided by you and your firm is comforting to your clients.

The number one reason why clients look for a new advisor is because their current advisor does not provide the level of customer service they expect—and deserve. If you know that your affluent clients have assets invested with other advisors, then discreetly ask about the quality of those relationships. You don't want to be perceived as trashing your competitors or suggesting that they are ineffectual or incompetent, so be sure to emphasize the quality of the relationship rather than the performance of the other accounts. For example, in a period of market turmoil, it's perfectly acceptable to ask, "What are your other advisors telling you?" Chances are the answer is, "Nothing!" Your clients will quickly realize which advisor is sensitive to their needs and which ones aren't, and that realization can pave the way to a discussion about the client investing more assets with you.

Lump-Sum Payouts (and Other Windfalls)

Some clients may suddenly find themselves with an infusion of cash all at once, whether it be from the sale of a home or business, an inheritance, or a bonus or profit-sharing distribution. Each of these events provides an opportunity for you to capture additional assets.

Sale of a Home

Many older clients encounter empty-nest syndrome: The kids have grown up and moved out to start lives of their own, and the clients find themselves with a house that's much too large for their needs. They may decide to sell their current property and buy a smaller, more manageable one (or even an apartment). The proceeds from the sale of the home could be significant. If you have a number of older, retired clients who own their homes, it may be worthwhile to establish an alliance with one or more real estate brokers in your area. Introducing clients to people who can help them sell their homes (which can be confusing and even traumatic for many people) will help strengthen your position as their trusted advisor and motivate them to invest their profit with you.

Sale of a Business

The sale of a business is a multifaceted, complex issue that many advisors get very excited about, only to become frustrated by the final result: There may not be a significant amount of cash to be captured. Why? Most businesses in the United States are small, and many have no end value. The entrepreneur's great dream is to build a successful company that can be sold to a giant like Microsoft.

The difficulty is that most small businesses—private practices like those of doctors, lawyers, and dentists—may not have sustainable revenues beyond the founder or principal. Even if the business is salable, most of the transactions are small, and many businesses are not sold outright but are transitioned to family members.

For you as an advisor, the potential sale of a closely held business can be lucrative, but you may have to help facilitate the sale. Simply waiting around for the transaction to occur, and assuming the client will come to you with the money, is misplaced confidence. Just as investment bankers are valuable rainmakers for their firms, the advisors who facilitate transactions may get the money because they get the first crack at it.

How many of your clients currently own a business that eventually will be sold? A good question to ask yourself is what your role might be in these types of transactions. If your target market is the small-business owner, you'll need to be conversant in the process by which they achieve equity. That may include helping them plan in advance of the sale how that equity will be realized. It is unlikely that you will be able to drive the sale of a business without working with centers of influence.

You need to know who will help with valuation, who will structure the terms of the sale, and who will fund it. It is possible that a business broker could help you facilitate a small transaction, but it might be too small to warrant a managed account and not worth your time. The typical small business in the United States is sold for between $500,000 and $2 million, so we are not talking about multimillion-dollar events. When the sale does involve a substantial amount of money, you need to be flexible because you want to structure a sound managed account solution, and you need to be vigilant about how the cash flows will arrive.

Distribution from Bonuses and Business Profits

Few affluent executives or business owners earn their wealth through salaries. Most capture the bulk of their compensation from performance bonuses or profit sharing. Typically, these prospects and clients use those big payments to fund their investments. You can capture additional assets by learning when these financial windfalls will occur.

If you are prospecting key salespeople or executives within a firm, you need to determine when their bonuses are paid. For the most part, after the books are sorted out at the end of the year, most businesses take a look at their financial situation and distribute bonuses at the first of the year. When do your clients earn their bonuses or take their distributions?

As we mentioned earlier, the number one competitor for the business owner's assets is the company. Talk to your small-business clients about building wealth outside of their businesses, as a hedge against the business not having the kind of value they expected when it is eventually sold. At best, it is an alternative strategy to what the clients are doing successfully on their own anyway. At worst, it is a hedge against their businesses being worth little or nothing.

Divorce

More than half of all marriages end in divorce in this country, so it is an event for which you should have a strategy. Do you have networking relationships with matrimonial attorneys?

In many cases, one or both of the two individuals in the divorce equation may not be entirely familiar with investments and finance. You want to be in a position to show that you are conversant with their issues and have sensitivity to people who find themselves in this situation. Understand that no matter what happens in the divorce, if you have a client couple, you will be forced to choose one side or the other.

"It's a highly challenging segment of the market," says Mark McLeland, first vice president of investments for the McLeland Group in Fort Worth, Texas. Part of Mark's practice is providing wealth management services for divorced clients. Mark has been an investment advisor for 20 years and has established networks with several matrimonial attorneys. "You have to build a tremendous level of trust with the client, given the emotional intensity of the situation. And it's not easy. In some cases, the client was never a decision maker in the investment process and suddenly has come into a substantial amount of liquid assets. With little or no financial background, your client needs a financial advocate, so guidance out of the starting gate is crucial.

Some clients are of the mind-set that they want to take the cash, buy a new house, and move on. The problem is that they don't realize that the $5 million they just received actually reduced their standard of living." Mark's formula for success has been to integrate his expertise with the highest level of trust in what is a niche but growing segment of the affluent market.

Inheritance

This is another area that requires sensitivity and discretion. Your clients may inherit a lump sum or annuity payments resulting from the death of a loved one, and many times they may initially decide they want to "do something special" with the money rather than pool it with their other investments. That may make sense emotionally, but not financially; pressuring the clients to invest their inheritance rather than spend it, however, puts you at risk of appearing insensitive.

One way to overcome this obstacle is to raise the issue when you are talking to clients about their own estate planning. Ask if they are named as anyone's beneficiary or if their financial situation would be changed by the death of a relative. By dealing with this matter objectively, within the context of the client's overall financial picture (both present and future), you acquire essential information for later use.

Say, for instance, that during the information-gathering stage you learn of a client who is the sole beneficiary of a parent's life insurance policy. That information will not affect the managed account solution you prepare for the client at the time, but it may have an impact later. When the parent dies, call the client to express your condolences and gently raise the issue from your previous discussion. You might say, "I am so sorry to hear of your father's passing, and I know this is an incredibly difficult time for you. Please let me know if there is anything I can do. I will call you again in a few weeks to see how you are doing, and at some point we should discuss how your inheritance will affect your current financial plan, but I know that's the last thing you want to think about right now and there is no need for immediate action. Right now, you should focus on yourself and your family. Let me know if I can help."

Your client will be impressed not only with the personal sentiments you've expressed, but also with the fact that you remembered a financial detail that may have been disclosed years before. You will have gone a long way toward reassuring them they are in safe hands with you, and you will have done so at a time when support and encouragement are most welcome and meaningful.

Keep the Future in Sight

By implementing these strategies for capturing additional assets, you will be working toward fulfilling your own personal and professional goals—establishing predictable revenue streams from ongoing fee-based income, building equity in your wealth management practice, saving for your own retirement, and so on—while helping your clients achieve their goals. Providing managed account solutions allows you to shift your focus from the day-to-day, transaction-oriented focus of many financial advisors to a long-term, future-based approach.

Throughout the course of this book we have shown you the many benefits of managed account solutions for both you and your clients, helped you determine whether managed account solutions are right for you and your practice, outlined steps for explaining the process to clients and transitioning them to managed accounts, and suggested ways to attract new clients and capture additional assets. This step-by-step approach will enable you to build your practice—and your future.

What will that future look like? We asked some of today's most successful money management executives to predict what tomorrow's managed account industry will look like. The next chapter examines what changes in the industry are under way now, how those changes will benefit the providers of managed account solutions, and why there has never been a better time to transition your practice.

12

The Future of Managed Account Solutions

Industry leaders present their visions of what the future holds for managed account solutions and the advisors who provide them.

The past five years have been a period of phenomenal growth for the managed account industry, and the next five years hold the promise of even greater growth and expansion as the U.S. baby-boom generation moves into retirement in significant numbers, spurring the greatest transfer of wealth in human history. To meet the changing money management needs of this massive audience—estimated at 79 million Americans, or more than one-fourth of the U.S. population—financial advisors and the firms that serve them will have to offer even more creative, flexible managed account solutions.

Changes are already under way. Let's take a look at some of the trends beginning to make themselves felt in the money management industry now, then ask today's leaders what they think tomorrow's managed account industry will look like.

Unified Managed Households: The Evolution of UMHs

In Chapter 2 we discussed how separately managed accounts (SMAs) and multi-discipline accounts (MDAs) evolved into unified managed accounts (UMAs). Despite the many advantages of UMAs, however, there are some limitations. One, most clients have assets that cannot be included in a UMA, such as real estate and tax-deferred retirement holdings. Two, most clients are part of households whose combined assets and investments should be considered in a comprehensive, holistic fashion. A high-net-worth couple, for instance, may each benefit from separate UMAs, but the couple has joint financial goals— saving for retirement, say, or for their children's college education—where a consolidated approach would be more appropriate. The fact that they may use different advisors for various assets makes the prospect of an integrated approach that much more difficult.

According to Randy Bullard, executive vice president of Placemark Investments, one of the managed account industry's largest providers of overlay portfolio management, "Many clients cannot or will not consolidate their assets with a single advisor. Taxable and nontaxable accounts, real estate holdings, limited partnerships, stock options, self-directed and advisor discretionary brokerage assets, as well as the complexities of the clients' wealth profiles, tax law, and trust and estate requirements will always require that clients have multiple legal registrations, usually spread across multiple unaffiliated financial institutions. While UMAs provide a rationale for consolidating a client's assets and delivering improved services on those assets, the legal and operational reality is that a UMA can never be more than a partial solution for addressing the complex needs of most clients. The unified managed household (UMH) provides a critical new way of thinking about how to better service the broader needs of such clients."

The Money Management Institute (MMI) has identified three essential elements of the UMH process:

1. *Household-level planning.* A UMH platform should support financial advisors in performing household-level asset allocation, asset placement, tax planning, and more advanced wealth management services across multiple accounts and product types.
2. *Household-level investment management.* Most clients have assets outside of the accounts they have with advisors (stock options being one example, and ownership of their primary residences being another), but movement in these assets can have a dramatic impact on the client's overall financial picture. For example, if a client realizes a taxable gain from the sale of a noninvestment asset, how can that gain be incorporated into the tax strategy the advisor has implemented for the client's other assets? For a UMH platform to work effectively, clients need advice at the household level, not just the individual level.
3. *Household-level reporting.* Many advisors already have the ability to generate household-level statements and performance reports for assets held with a single custodian, but to provide the client with a complete picture the advisor will need to incorporate assets held at multiple custodians, such as external bank accounts and retirement plan accounts.

Bullard notes that the level of industry collaboration and investment needed to make the fully integrated UMH concept a reality is intimidating, but not overwhelming, and the financial services industry has risen to such challenges before, most notably in the development of infrastructure to support equity markets and the distribution of mutual funds. "The unified managed household is not a product for sponsors and managers to develop and put on the shelf beside other products, but a road map for how the industry can evolve the business models and infrastructure used to deliver the greatest possible value to its clients."

James Patrick, managing director of Allianz Global Investors, observes, "UMAs and UMHs share the same goal of getting the clients away from themselves and focusing on their overall, long-term wealth management goals. There will need to be some regulatory changes and technological innovations for this to work, but I believe it will happen."

Distribution: Not Just for Wirehouses Anymore

"Bank trust organizations are sitting on enviable amounts of assets under management that tend to have much lower levels of turnover than the broker/dealer industry," states J. Reed Murphy, managing director of Bank of America's Consulting Services Group. "Combine this asset base with a highly specialized service model undergoing a cultural evolution toward open architecture, and you are presented with some phenomenal opportunities."

"People think of banks as sleeping giants in the managed account business, but banks have a phenomenal opportunity," says Lidiette Ratiani, director of investment consulting solutions for Wells Fargo Private Client Group. "Once they get beyond the concerns of short-term loss of profitability with regard to developing the necessary infrastructure, they should be well positioned to play a major role in managed accounts."

Wirehouses, with about 78 percent of SMA assets under management, continue to dominate the managed account industry, but bank market share is increasing. According to the MMI, "Positive trends are occurring as banks move into the SMA space. For example, the largest and more established programs are growing the fastest, which indicates that banks have been able to increase adoption of SMA products among clients and advisors within their wealth management divisions. In addition, banks are increasing their use of nonproprietary investment products." A recent study by the MMI and Dover Financial Research found that 70 percent of banks surveyed either had created or were developing plans to offer UMA capabilities.

"This isn't surprising in that bank trust departments have been in the managed account business for a long time," says Murphy. "In the past few years banking organizations have addressed cultural and fiduciary issues of control. Portfolio managers are now more willing to incorporate external investment managers, while trust officers realize that they can still fulfill or expand on their fiduciary responsibilities by providing more offerings to clients."

For most banks, the biggest obstacle to entering the MAS market is the lack of open architecture platforms, but MMI/Dover research reveals that many institutions are surmounting this obstacle by seeking the assistance of outside vendors. "A greater variety of SMA offerings is on the market to fit the varying needs of banks," the survey found. "In addition, more players have entered the marketplace. Specifically, trust accounting firms have developed SMA solutions to protect their client base. Value-added services such as training, education, and due diligence have become increasingly important as banks begin to roll out SMA programs and migrate toward open architecture."

Does Ratiani think banks may eventually rival wirehouses in MAS market share? "Absolutely. It's all about leverage and perception," she says. "We're all going after the same target market: people in the wealth accumulation phase or high-net-worth clients. Where wirehouses have a perceived advantage is with aggressive investors, while someone more conservative in nature will go to a bank."

Given the demographics of the baby boomers and the imminent transfer of retirement wealth, being perceived as conservative will be a boon. "Banks, either through their broker-dealers or through their trust departments, tend to have a higher trust factor than wirehouses. Bank reps are not viewed as salespeople, but rather as strong investment professionals."

Going Global: Overseas Interest in Managed Account Solutions

Nikko Cordial was the first firm to offer fee-based financial services to Japanese investors, in 1998, and the concept was enthusiastically received, according to Toshiya Shimizu, deputy president of Nikko Global Wrap Ltd. "The service was intended to dismiss any conflict of interest between investors and financial advisors by introducing the asset-based fee structure," he says, adding that both SMAs and mutual fund advisory accounts were offered. As a result, Japanese investors are rethinking their attitudes toward saving and investing.

"Investors had no patience. They used to sell when net asset values appreciated sharply and took their profits, so investors' average holding periods for mutual funds were very short," Shimizu says. "But that is changing. Investors are aware that they are paying too much in up-front commissions and that such commissions can significantly detract from their compound growth rate in the long run. They have become much more careful in selecting appropriate mutual funds, and increased competition among distributors—especially after banks entered the mutual fund business—has also helped investors' fund-selection process. We can easily find flagship funds of over one trillion yen these days, but that was not the case until recently."

Shimizu attributes the recent expansion of Japan's mutual fund market to rising interest in international diversification. "With Japan's limited natural resources, matured economy, and decreasing labor population, there are more growth opportunities outside Japan," he says. "Internationally diversified portfolios have in fact shown solid performance for the past five to six years."

Interest in the world beyond Japan is also why Nikko Global Wrap became the first member of the International Money Management Institute, a newly created organization based in London and designed specifically for firms offering managed solutions outside of the United States. Representatives from the United Kingdom and the Netherlands quickly followed. Tina Wilkinson, head of business development, asset management and services for BNP Paribas in the United Kingdom, believes that because regulation and taxation are still challenging issues across Europe, the more flexibility an advisor has, the greater likelihood he or she will be able to help clients achieve their financial goals. "To be successful in managing portfolios in this environment, advisors need good research analytics, online trading and management tools, and flexible access to and delivery of products," she says.

In Canada, the managed accounts industry is in its infancy. "Independent advisors are just beginning to benefit from access as industry assets top $35 billion," explains Lisa Langley, vice president of member services for Canada's Investment Dealers Association. "Tremendous opportunity exists in the marketplace for all participants in distribution, manufacturing, and advice provision for bundled asset management solutions." Martijn Duijnstee, senior vice president—investments for Fortis Private Investment Management in the Netherlands, is also a believer in MAS. "Managed accounts have changed the U.S. market," he says, "and they will change the international market." However, there are key differences between the two. European MAS providers must deal with multiple political and regulatory environments, and performance reporting is more challenging with multiple languages and multiple currencies.

Such challenges are not insurmountable, observes Mark Fetting, president of Legg Mason Funds. "Thus far there has not been the acceptance of the wrap account approach in international markets that there has been in the United States, part of the reason being that outside of the U.S. and the U.K. many individuals are unfamiliar with the concept and see no reason to change the way they're doing things," he says. "But that resistance will erode over time. The managed account approach will become an international phenomenon."

What the Leaders See Ahead

No doubt other changes will take place as more advisors, in the United States and around the world, opt to become providers of managed account solutions. We asked some of the industry's leading experts to predict what other changes they see taking place in the coming years, and here is what they said.

Richard "Dick" Schilffarth

"Fee-based will predominate."   I think we're going to see the needs-based concept ever expanding. All of our firms must be efficient, competent global custodians, because the market for financial advice is becoming increasingly international. There are 7,000 stocks in the United States, but 30,000 globally, and markets continue to expand. I think we will see hedge funds and private equity incorporated into investment consulting programs, and I see the dominant concept changing from transactions to fees. Look at brokerage firms today: The amount of fee-based revenue is still less than a third of total revenue. That will change. Also, I think we will see the return of regional firms. Right now firms are either huge or small, but we need midsize, regional firms.

Frank Campanale, President, Campanale Consulting Group

"Individual defined benefit plans."   We are going to be managing clients down to the allowance they get from their portfolio every week. Accounts will be structured with an eye toward building a defined benefit plan for individual clients. Today clients are saying, "I have this 401(k) but don't know if I have enough money to achieve my goals." Advisors will build specific defined benefit plans and say, "Your portfolio is going to have to grow at a rate of X percent a year in order to sustain you through retirement." We will create actuarial tables for the client and show how short-, medium-, and long-term investments will keep driving their portfolio toward that ultimate goal, a personal liability index for the client, and make sure that liability is fully funded.

Leonard Reinhart, President, Lockwood Financial

"Nothing left to chance."   The retiring baby boomer will force the biggest change in the way the financial services industry does business. The UMA will quickly transition to the UMH, which will support and be the catalyst for this change. The boomer who for the past 30 years wanted the best stock, the best fund, and the best manager will now be focused on absolute dollars with little concern for indexes, rankings, and so on. The almost-singular focus will be on living the lifestyle they are accustomed to without running out of money—and with not just a high degree of probability, but rather 100 percent certainty. Estate planning will take a backseat to the "30-year living plan," a documented plan that directs the investment management through all four phases of retirement, including disengagement and institutionalization. The high-net-worth boomers will not be satisfied leaving anything to chance; they are living through their parents' final years and are seeing firsthand what happens when there are no plans. To accomplish this, the industry will have to get more creative: Insurance with guaranteed living benefits needs to be brought into the UMH; just as the boomers made a lot of money on their homes by leveraging their buying power, they will learn to leverage their retirement investment portfolios; fixed income will play a smaller and smaller role in retirement planning and will be replaced by insurance and other derivative products; advisor transition strategies will have to be built into the 30-year living plan. The list will go on and on, and life as we know it in the financial services industry will be changed forever.

Charles Widger, Chairman and CEO, Brinker Capital

"Innovation through technology."   The industry has evolved to provide a portfolio of managed account solutions for advisors to deliver to investors—SMAs, mutual fund advisory programs, managed ETF programs, and now UMAs. In the developmental pipeline are unified managed household accounts and data standards for the communication of information among sponsor, managers, and custodians (the MMI is leading that charge on the data communications standards). Also just beginning to take root in the marketplace are managed mutual fund programs for 401(k) plan participants. Some qualified plan industry experts report that 80 percent of plan participants do not want responsibility for the management of their plan assets—they prefer to pay someone to do it for them. Technology will continue to play a vital role in improving the delivery and administration of managed accounts of all types. And one of the most important areas for innovation through technology is in training and educating advisors on managed accounts. Technology offers a cost-effective way of accomplishing this vital task. Overall, the outlook for growth is bright for managed accounts. This growth will witness continued evolution of the industry fueled by product and technology innovation, all to the benefit of advisors and investors.

Mark Pennington, Partner, Lord Abbett

"Articulating the cost of advice."   There are challenges on the horizon in trying to build customized investment solutions and economies of scale, but there have been some positive movements. If you look at technology, clearly standardization efforts are great when you are trying to build scale—it doesn't work if you speak different languages. So, standardization in technology will be a big help. Another issue is articulating the cost of advice and the cost of investment management, so the industry can price itself and bring complete transparency and unbundling of fees. Then, customers can determine if they want to pay for all services, or just some.

Chip Walker, Managing Director, Wachovia Securities

"Personalized progress monitors, not quarterly reports."   Traditionally, managed account solutions have been growth vehicles, but now we're looking at ways to provide income as well as growth within our managed account platform. Clients are used to managed accounts for growth; now we need to get them used to managed accounts for income that may last 30 years or more. We need to look beyond traditional fixed-income investments to alternatives such as emerging market debt, real estate investment trusts, and high-yield investments. Currently, those things are available in mutual funds and they're becoming available in exchange-traded funds (ETFs), but I'm not aware of high-yield or emerging market debt in separately managed accounts. I think there is an opportunity for asset managers and firms to deliver income solutions, and I think we are going to see a transition away from traditional performance reporting to a progress monitor. It will take a while to change—clients are used to quarterly reports vis-à-vis an index—but as we provide more flexible, customized account services, clients will see the value of personalized progress monitors.

Lidiette Ratiani, Director of Investment Consulting Solutions, Wells Fargo Private Client Group

"Changing mind-sets."   From a product perspective, UMAs and UMHs are here and now, but from a technology standpoint, some tools will have to be developed to make these work more efficiently. Enhancements will be developed that will streamline many processes, such as capturing data, opening accounts, tracking portfolios, rebalancing, inclusion of more risk-management products, and others. I also think both clients and advisors will focus more on progress toward individual goals rather than investment performance. As an industry, we needed some method to benchmark ourselves, and we taught investment professionals to focus on the hot dot, but most clients don't care about that. What they really want to know is, "How close am I to achieving my goals?" I don't think they care about external benchmarks; that's something *we* care about, and we are going to have to change advisors' mind-sets—but you can't change those mind-sets unless you change the compensation structure. I think that will happen, though, over time.

J. Reed Murphy, Managing Director, Bank of America

"Increased transparency."   Technological advances are allowing more holistic implementation of advice through UMAs. As we add more investment vehicle types, our industry will expand from a managed account to a managed solutions paradigm. This is and will provide an enhanced opportunity to segment costs of the underlying investment vehicle from the advice services being provided. Clients and regulators are also demanding and will continue to demand more transparency of costs. While this will present more challenges around advisory and nonadvisory issues, those who can separate and communicate the costs of advice from the investment vehicles and the benefits of this transparency will have a competitive advantage.

Ed Blodgett, Director, Private Client Group, Brandes Investment Partners, L.P.

"The advisor's critical role."   The fundamental problem facing investors is that their own survival instincts tend to make them overreact to short-term events in the marketplace. The advisor's critical role, then, is to build a long-term plan that helps clients resist their urge to respond to the markets, or to go along crowd behavior, or to jump into whatever is popular, or to believe whatever the media is currently touting as the latest and greatest. If, through their careful planning, advisors can help clients determine ahead of time how they will respond to the changing marketplace, they may be in a position to add tremendous value. Clients can benefit from their advisor's steady guidance.

Furthermore, the advisor's value is not dependent on the direction of the market—if anything, an advisor's value may even increase during times of difficulty. The advisor's guidance can spell the difference between long-term success and failure. Not only that, but the advisor's critical role, based on an in-depth knowledge of the client's desires, predilections, and attitudes, can't be commoditized and can't be outsourced. Trends and fads may come and go, and markets will rise and fall, but through it all a good advisor's steady counsel can remain invaluable.

Larry Sinsimer, Managing Director, Eaton Vance

"More opportunities to customize."   In the past, investors were categorized and their solutions determined by the amount of money they had to invest. With the advent of the UMA, a client with $50,000 can have the same asset allocation and diversification as a client with $5 million. Clearly the wealthier client will have more opportunity to customize, but time and again asset allocation has been shown to be the primary mover in investors' success or failure to meet their financial goals.

Mark Fetting, President, Legg Mason Funds

"Active interest in passive investment."   More likely than not we'll have tougher times, potentially bumpier, and if so I think we will see people start to move more toward index funds, ETFs, and other types of passive investment. There will be a shakeout for those who rely on active management, with a shift toward active management of alternative investments and more common use of passive strategies for traditional investments. Also, I think there will be changes in the fixed-income marketplace. Right now, the fixed-income side doesn't lend itself as readily to a managed account approach as the equity side, but as boomers move into retirement they are going to focus more on fixed income and we are going to have to find a way to deliver fixed-income managed account solutions.

Jay Link, Managing Director, Morgan Stanley

"Solving needs through our clients' eyes."   As an industry, we've done a good job at building and selling products and designing managed account program silos. As a result, we often require clients to choose a silo rather than help them create integrated, simple, holistic life solutions. As technology evolves, we will be able to seamlessly address highly specific needs and preferences, with an endless variety of investment structures, tax optimization, and customized income management, all in a way that is easy to follow, track, and understand. Surely, clients will expect this from us, because it's the way they think about their financial lives.

James Patrick, Managing Director, Allianz Global Investors

"The walls are coming down."   I think the walls are going to be completely down over the next few years, and clients are going to be driven by the best vehicle that serves their investment needs. If a client wants access to a particular type of market exposure, it could be in dozens of formats, and he or she will choose the one that's most appropriate. The physical structure will not drive investment decisions as it has in the past. Also, there will be an evolution in terms of tax-management capabilities, so the advisor's ability to serve clients will be enhanced—the tax and regulatory tail will no longer wag the investment dog. The nickel-and-diming of fees has been a tough thing to get through, but I think the wave of the future will be advisors charging fees the way a doctor does—on a case-by-case basis, depending on the complexity of the client's needs. That's how institutions do it, that's what happens in the mortgage industry, and I think that's what financial advisors will do.

James Tracy, Executive Vice President, Smith Barney Consulting Group

"Enhancement at all levels."   We will see a refining of all existing programs and enhancements at all levels, and we will be in an environment where we will provide greater efficiency to clients through UMAs and multistrategy portfolios. There will be a greater emphasis on embedded advice, such as asset allocation–driven managed accounts, and I think clients will come to value advice and research at a much greater level than they're valuing them today. We will also see an environment where the focus will be on retirement income solutions as opposed to equity accumulation. The changing demographics and changing needs of the investor will drive a demand for more wealth advisory services, more wealth management, and a greater focus on lifestyle decisions and lifestyle planning.

Valerie Petrone Corradini, National Sales Manager, Barclays Global Investors

"Client-centered solutions."   There will be much greater emphasis on open-architecture platforms for firms that are motivated, but this has to be a top-down initiative because retrofitting technology platforms is an immense task. Right now, mutual funds are perfectly fine in their own silos—separately managed accounts, same thing—but as reps move toward becoming registered investment advisors they will find open architecture an eye-opening experience, and that will be very important for the industry. Firms will unwind their fee-based brokerage platforms—and there will be more of a focus on truly advice-driven, client-centered solutions. Also, firms will find ways to capitalize on the hedge fund rush and will take more interest in ETFs and index management as they look to source alpha and beta separately. I think we will see an explosion and then a contraction, because some firms will realize they would rather partner to provide these types of investments. ETFs require a lot of due diligence, a lot of research, and a lot of advisor education about how to speak to clients, because with index investing the performance component is removed from the discussion. You're not picking an index to outperform; the challenge is to pick the right index to match the client's needs and expectations. Some sponsor firms that provide ETFs make an issue over cost, so the industry will have to be reeducated to understand that the fiduciary advisor is not responsible for delivering the *cheapest* solution possible; they are responsible for delivering the *best* solution possible, and they will have to understand how to explain that choice.

Mark Tibergien, Partner, Moss Adams LLP

"An oversupply of clients, an undersupply of solid advisory firms."   The financial advisory business is moving from adolescence to adulthood, bringing with it a new set of challenges and a new set of opportunities. The irrefutable fact is that all firms are wrestling with margin pressures, a squeeze on time, the lack of qualified talent, more rigorous compliance oversight, and competitive threats that will force them to rethink their current operating model. The big question is whether their individual strategies are still relevant and are structured right for the next phase of their business lives. What got them here won't get them there. As a result, we will likely see more mergers of practices rather than outright acquisitions, and we will see more firms add professional management with the skills and experience to direct a more complex organization with many moving parts. The good news is that for the next five years at least, there is an oversupply of clients and an undersupply of solid advisory firms. Those who take control of their destinies rather than reacting to the plethora of opportunities will likely be the noticeably superior financial advisory businesses.

Kevin Hunt, Chairman, The Money Management Institute

"The legacy lives on."   The coming years will see the creation of unique products and services to suit the needs of clients, but the real issue will be the enduring legacy of the managed account movement itself. This culture was created when a group of people from diverse backgrounds—investment management, distribution, and technology—came together in a spirit of cooperation and realized that, by working together, they could change the landscape and offer individual clients a level of quality and service that had not been available to them previously. They discovered the strength and power of working collectively to solve problems and serve clients, and they serve as mentors to the next generation of managed account solution providers. The standard has been set for professionals from all areas of the financial services industry to come together, tackle complex issues, and provide solutions that benefit clients, advisors, and sponsors. Over the years the products and services will change and evolve, but the cooperative spirit of the managed account movement will endure.

This Isn't Your Father's Advisory Practice

This book opened on a promising note—the greatest wealth transfer in human history is about to begin as baby boomers are poised to enter retirement, and many of them are going to turn to financial advisors for assistance—but it closes on a cautionary one. Yes, there are more people with more money seeking financial advice than ever before, but that doesn't mean every advisor will reap the rewards of this seismic demographic shift.

The protracted and painful decline of the U.S. automobile industry will illustrate our point. At one time General Motors was the largest automaker in the world; today, it's a shadow of its former self. Why? Have people stopped buying cars? Of course not. But there came a point when consumers wanted a different type of vehicle than Detroit could provide. By the time the giant automakers were able to respond to the changing marketplace, their customers had already grown accustomed to buying vehicles from other manufacturers—manufacturers that could give them what they couldn't get from the Big Four (yes, there were four at the time, and they were big . . . at the time).

Many financial advisory firms are in the same situation now that U.S. automakers were in then, with one key difference: The automakers had little advance notice that massive change was about to befall them. Financial advisors do, if for no other reason than because we've just told you!

The decline of the American automobile industry can be traced to the Arab oil embargo of the early 1970s. Automakers (along with the rest of Americans) were unprepared for the sudden disruption in the fuel supply. Gas prices soared, long lines stretched from service stations, and frustrated consumers demanded more fuel-efficient vehicles. Overnight, it seems, Americans stopped viewing their large, luxurious automobiles as kings of the road and started seeing them as unwieldy gas-guzzlers. The market was ready for something new, but dealer showrooms were stocked with the same old thing.

The major automakers were not stupid. They had assessed the situation and concluded that the political crisis would be short-lived and the interest in fuel-efficient foreign cars would be nothing but a passing fad. They were half-right.

The Arab oil embargo lasted eight months.

Consumers buy fuel-efficient foreign cars to this day.

Toyota is now the No. 1 automaker in the world.

Detroit's market dominance had gone unchallenged for so long that it seemed unfeasible those automakers could lose it, although trouble had been brewing even before the OPEC crisis. Quality had been declining and owner dissatisfaction increasing, but Detroit automakers had grown complacent and unresponsive. They believed they owned the market, and the market would accept whatever they offered. They simply weren't interested in building fuel-efficient vehicles, which had a more slender profit margin than the luxury cars Americans had been buying before the embargo. The automakers did not see the system as broken, so they saw no need to fi x it, by golly.

Eventually, however, they realized they would have to give the car-buying public what it wanted if they were to stop surrendering market share to foreign competitors, and they spent millions of dollars on advertising to reposition themselves in the eyes of consumers. All of the messages had essentially the same theme: We listened. We learned. We've changed.

"Have You Driven a Ford Lately?"

"This Isn't Your Father's Oldsmobile."

"Putting You First Keeps Us First."

But by the time the automakers responded to the changing marketplace, it was too late. The tipping point became their tripping point. Sadly, the same may soon be said of some advisors.

In Chapter 6 we noted that fear of change was preventing many advisors from becoming providers of managed account solutions. Chip Walker of Wachovia Securities expounded on this theme when we interviewed him for this book. "A lot of financial advisors have built their practices a certain way and they see no reason to change," Chip told us. "These advisors are accustomed to the relationship the way it is now, their clients are accustomed to the relationship the way it is now, and more than anything else this is a relationship business. Some advisors fear that by injecting change into the mix they may be asking for trouble. They're comfortable with where they are, and they're uncomfortable with the thought of change."

The advisors Chip describes, like the U.S. automakers that once dominated the market, apparently believe that the approach that brought them success in the past will continue to bring them success in the future. History suggests this will not be the case.

We're not trying to imply that you will lose your clients overnight if you decide not to become a provider of managed account solutions. Americans didn't stop driving their Fords, Chevys, and Buicks in 1974 just because the price of gas soared to 55 cents a gallon. Rather, the oil embargo awakened Americans to a vulnerability they'd not known before, and when it came time to trade in that gas-guzzler, many opted for vehicles that made them feel a little less vulnerable.

There is an interesting parallel in the financial advisory world at this very moment. A recent survey by industry guru Russ Prince found that 89 percent of millionaire households feel they are vulnerable to a financial reversal, yet only 15 percent of advisors were aware that their clients harbored such fears.

Think about that: An overwhelmingly high number of affluent clients who should feel financially secure instead feel vulnerable, and an overwhelmingly high number of their advisors are completely unaware of it. Two questions spring immediately to mind:

If someone with $1 million feels financially insecure, then how is someone with half that amount likely to feel?

If advisors don't know that their high-net-worth clients feel vulnerable, why don't they know?

Advisors aren't asking. Clients aren't telling. But it seems reasonable to conclude that, at some point, these clients will realize they should feel less vulnerable than they do, and that maybe the problem isn't with their finances, but with their financial advisors. Maybe there is another advisor who can provide the feeling of security that their current advisor cannot. Maybe they will turn to you. (Maybe they will turn *from* you.)

Outsourcing investment management will free up your time to focus on clients, find out what's really on their minds, and provide the appropriate solutions. You can be the advisor who raises the issues that clients are reluctant to bring up. You can be the advisor who provides them with the security they seek—and deserve. But if you wait until the marketplace forces you to change, it may be too late.

Remember, Toyota didn't wait until the Arab oil embargo to start manufacturing fuel-efficient cars; it began building them long before and, when it saw an opportunity, it was well positioned to act. By transitioning your practice to managed account solutions *now*, you will be well positioned to capture a sizable share of the largest wealth transfer in human history. You'll be in the driver's seat, easing your clients down the road to prosperity. Enjoy the ride!

APPENDIX A

Sample Business Plan

BUSINESS PLAN 2006
GROW 15

Goals

15% Production Increase to $840,000
15 New Households
$15 Million in New Assets
$100,000 More in Fee-Based Business

These break down to $2,500 per day, 1.25 households per month, $1,250,000 new assets per month, and $8,333 in fee-based business per month.

Activities to Accomplish These

15 Dials Every Day
15 Points Every Day
15 Prospects on List at All Times
(Later in year, see if I can even increase these and shoot for 20 a day, which should bring me over $1 million.)

Spend time each day in thinking from the client's perspective. (What if it really was all about them?)

Accountability for Activities

Weekly: No week can end without the dials and points being caught up. If it means working late or working Saturdays, then that's what it takes. Trust the activity level. Add another level of accountability to someone else.

Changes

No nonbusiness Internet use during day.
Work standing up and at kneeling chair.
Light lunches.
Two-hour block every weekend or Friday to do planning for next week.
Add a belief system component to the affirmations, including the "state" questions.

Prepare appointments 24 hours in advance.

Focus on QII activities well in advance, from taxes to mailings to newspaper articles.

Actually have prospecting activities.

Systematize more activities so that I can hand them off to other people.

Keep investment themes, campaigns, and client service ideas in front of me.

Continue

Quiet time, affirmations, and tapes/CDs every morning.

Read business plan every morning.

Exercise before I come in (once back is okay).

Not concerned about what time I come in.

Meeting people in the community.

Lunches with COIs and others I know to explain how I can help people.

Meet with fee-based clients semiannually.

Technology

Learn how to work from home and from other remote locations.

Practice and get good at that.

Get keyboard for Treo.

Get new laptop if necessary.

Get ACT working and migrate broker's Ally stuff over.

Get approval for all technology with firm.

Mental Sharpness and Sales Skills

Memorize 50 great quotes, stories, and analogies about investing.

Read the investing and sales books on my list.

Staffing

Solve problem of staffing when _____ is out, especially telephone answering, keeping up with work in process, and checking with home office.

Make sure _____ is adequately compensated.

Areas to Improve

Order execution to eliminate errors.

Less discounting.

Quality of client relationships (i.e., no people who disrespect me or don't understand my position or our relationship).

Time with mega-wealthy clients who have done little business.

Referrals.

Prospects.

Keeping up with adult children of clients.

Regular monthly letters to clients.

Organization.

Throwing things away.

Reading.

Consistency of process and systems.

Learn, get questions answered.

To Explore Further

Teaching and training.

Web site.

Newsletter.

E-mail system to people—Constant Contact.
Helping Lukacs with names of people.
Reward for activities.
Client service system.
Develop five-year plan in all areas.

Marketing Plans

Referrals

Ask for referrals until I have built up my list of 15 prospects.
Promote referrals through conversations and mailings.
In conversations with parents, make notes of information about adult kids.
Have a newsletter, so that I can ask who they know who would like to receive it.

COIs

Meet with one per week.
Have a developed program to discuss with them.
Mail to COIs monthly.

Client Upgrades

Make a pipeline list of who has money elsewhere.
Look through clients' assets for dead assets.
Consider cross-selling ideas, such as life insurance and long-term care.
Attempt to meet with my top five low-producing clients to see what else I might do.

Friend Referrals

Meet with people I know to get to know them better and to tell them what I do, so that when they know others, they can suggest a meeting.
Mail them my newsletter.
Help them by giving them referrals or ideas when I can.

LIFE PLAN 2006
GOALS

Physically Fit

230 pounds and toned (lose 15% of weight).
Exercise every day.
Stretch every day.
Lift weights three times a week.
Go through TMP fitness paperwork and regimen.
Finish Dr. Cooper tests.
Schedule exercise activities with friends and kids.
Take walks and hikes whenever I want to.
Change eating habits:
Three vegetables or fruit in every meal.
Get bulk from the vegetables or fruits.
Avoid fast foods.
Avoid red meat.
Avoid fried foods.
Avoid processed carbohydrates and sugars.
Plan ahead.
Lots of water every day.
Lots of salads.
When anxious, find a substitute for eating: Drink water, take a walk, read a book.
Reward: New car, with CD player, XM radio, AM/FM, tape player.

Strong Marriage

Lots of time talking.
Work through things when needed.
Give card or something daily.
Reread my notes.
Read books.
Attend marriage seminars.
Take great trips.
Work around home.
Watch out for key points, such as clean kitchen and bedroom.
Help her on business.
Take stress off her.

Significant Parenting by Transferring Value to Kids

Spend time with them.
Plan trips ahead of time to Northern California.
Use time when they're home, knowing that it takes quantity of time to open them up.
Contact one of them every day.
Have all current addresses, phone numbers, and so on.
Show them how special they are with CDs, cards, and letters.
Accountability for Amber and York.

Significant Life Strategies

Continue TMP.
Continue and improve High Ground.
Look for other church opportunities.
Read and study the literature.
Work with other people.
One page of book per week.
Review roles weekly.

Others

Friendships and develop friends database.
Be better at working around home.
Be excellent at throwing things away and organizing things.
Confront fears about tackling things I've never done before.

Changes

Reduce TV to one hour per day.
Read 50 books this year.
Keep nonbusiness tasks on Treo.

Daily Stats Worksheet— Promote Referrals!

Date: ___/___/___

Excellent Day

- QT and goals (especially Wanda!).
- Call list prepared before day starts.
- Motivational tape/CD + affirmations.
- Make a managed money presentation.
- Do 30 minutes exercise.
- Review business plan to implement.
- Train a person for results.
- Promote a referral.
- Develop one system.
- Eat right.
- Review roles and QII activities.
- Prepare investment list.
- Review 12-month calendar.
- Prepare for an appointment.
- Set an appointment.
- Make 10 client/prospect contacts _____.
- Do 10 dials _____.
- COI contact.
- $2,500 gross ($840k!) _____.
- Appreciate/encourage someone.
- Do something special for VIP 20.
- Client meeting.
- Client project.
- Present written client recommendations.
- Run an asset allocation.
- Schedule a seminar.
- Get expense reimbursement.
- Write a client/prospect mass letter.
- Run a mailing.
- Five more client contacts.
- One quality prospect added to list.
- Prospect contact.
- Plan with _____.
- Review one-inch client statements.
- Clean up office.
- Spend 30 minutes on knowledge (p/t).
- Throw away eight inches of stuff.
- Back up data.
- Post results.
- Prepare call list for next day.
- Clear desk and end day ritual.
- Wild card _____.
- Research a question.

Client Contacts

1 2 3 4 5 6 7 8 9 10 11 12 13 14 15 16
17 18 19 20 21 22 23 24 25 26 27 28
29 30 31 32 33 34 35 36 37 38 39 40

Business Today

Referrals Requested/Received

_____

_____

New Prospects/Source

_____

_____

COIs Contacted

_____

Managed Money/Trails

_____

_____

New Clients

Assets Brought In

_____

IPG Monthly Goal Tracking Worksheet

Name: _____   Month:_____

Goals for Month

1.
2.
3.
4.
5.

Marketing Activities

1.
2.
3.
4.
5.

Personal Development Activities

1.
2.
3.
4.
5.

Action Plan

1.
2.
3.
4.
5.

Top Five Prospects/Opportunities for This Month

1.
2.
3.
4.
5.

# of prospects on list:
# of inches of paperwork thrown out:
Preparation done in advance (1–10 rating):

Manager Evaluation Formulas and Ratios

Standard Deviation Formula

Measures the volatility of the manager's return relative to the average return.

$$\sigma = \sqrt{\sigma^2} = \sqrt{\frac{\sum\limits_{i=1}^{n}(x_i - \bar{x})^2}{n}}$$

σ = Standard deviation

Σ = Summation graphic

x_i = Sample return

$\bar{x}$ = Sample average return

n = Number of observations

Beta Formula

Measures risk relative to a market index.

$$\beta_i = \frac{\text{Cov}_{i,\,market}\,\sigma_i\sigma_{market}}{\sigma_{market}} = \frac{\text{Cov}_{i,\,market}\,\sigma_i}{\sigma_{market}}$$

$$\text{Cov}_{i,\ market} = \text{Covariance of asset } i \text{ to the market}$$

$$\sigma_i = \text{Standard deviation of asset } i$$

$$\sigma_{market} = \text{Standard deviation of asset market}$$

Market index always $= 1.0$

Alpha Formula

Measures a portfolio's return in excess of the market return adjusted for risk.

$$\text{Alpha} = \text{Excess return} - [\text{Beta} \times (\text{Benchmark} - \text{Treasury})]$$

R² Formula

Measures how closely a portfolio's return tracks a given index.

$$R^2 = \frac{\beta^2 \sigma M^2}{\sigma_p^2}$$

$\beta = \text{Beta}$

$\sigma_M^2 = \text{Standard deviation of the market}$

$\sigma_p^2 = \text{Standard deviation of the portfolio}$

Sharpe Ratio

Ratio of portfolio excess return relative to standard deviation; one measure of risk-adjusted returns.

$$\text{Sharpe Ratio} = \frac{\bar{r}_p - \bar{r}_f}{\sigma_p}$$

$\bar{r}_p = \text{Expected return of the portfolio}$

$\bar{r}_f = \text{Expected return of risk-free asset}$

$\sigma_p = \text{Standard deviation of the portfolio}$

Sortino Ratio

Measures downside variability in relation to the minimal acceptable return (MAR); one measure of risk-adjusted returns.

$$\text{Sortino Ratio} = \frac{MAR}{\sqrt{\int_{\infty}^{m} (m - r_A)^2 f(r_A) dr_A}}$$

m = Return on index

r_A = Return on asset A

$f(r_A)$ = Probability distribution function of returns on asset A

dr_A = Downside risk of asset A

Treynor Ratio

Ratio of portfolio excess return to beta; one measure of risk-adjusted returns.

$$\text{Treynor Ratio} = \frac{\bar{r}_p - \bar{r}_f}{\beta_p}$$

$\bar{r}_p$ = Expected return of the portfolio

$\bar{r}_f$ = Expected return of risk-free asset

β_p = Beta of the portfolio

Sample Investment Policy Statement

INVESTMENT POLICY STATEMENT

High Net Worth Individual/Family Wealth
(Client)

Approved on (Date)

This investment policy statement should be reviewed and updated at least annually. Any change to this policy should be communicated in writing on a timely basis to all interested parties.

This Investment Policy Statement (IPS) has been prepared by Fiduciary360. It is intended to serve as an example of the type of information that would be included in a comprehensive IPS. Investment Advisors are advised to have legal counsel review their IPS before it is approved. Visit Fiduciary360's web site at www.fi360.com.

Executive Summary

Type of Client:	Taxable, Individual
Current Assets:	$650,000
Time Horizon:	Greater than 5 years
Modeled Return:	8.0%
Modeled Loss:	−9.4% (Probability level of 5%)
Asset Allocation:	

	Lower Limit	Strategic Allocation	Upper Limit
Domestic Large-Cap Equity			
Blend	5%	10%	15%
Growth	5	10	15
Value	5	10	15
Mid-Cap Equity	5	10	15
Small-Cap Equity	5	10	15
International Equity	5	10	15
Intermediate-Term Fixed Income	30	35	40
Cash Equivalent	0	5	10

Purpose

The purpose of this Investment Policy Statement (IPS) is to assist the Client and Investment Advisor (Advisor) in effectively supervising, monitoring, and evaluating the investment of the Client's Portfolio (Portfolio). The Client's investment program is defined in the various sections of the IPS by:

1. Stating in a written document the Client's attitudes, expectations, objectives, and guidelines for the investment of all assets.
2. Setting forth an investment structure for managing the Client's Portfolio. This structure includes various asset classes, investment management styles, asset allocations, and acceptable ranges that, in total, are expected to produce an appropriate level of overall diversification and total investment return over the investment time horizon.
3. Encouraging effective communications between the Client and the Advisor.
4. Establishing formal criteria to select, monitor, evaluate, and compare the performance of money managers on a regular basis.
5. Complying with all applicable fiduciary, prudence, and due diligence requirements experienced investment professionals would utilize; and with all applicable laws, rules, and regulations from various local, state, federal, and international political entities that may impact the Client's assets.

Background

This IPS has been prepared for John and Mary HNW Client (Client), a taxable entity. The assets covered by this IPS currently total approximately $650,000 in market value, but the Client's net worth is estimated to be $1,225,000. Assets not covered by this IPS include:

1. Corporate-sponsored defined contribution programs, where both the husband and wife participate (combined, valued at $350,000); and
2. A vacation condo valued at $225,000.

Statement of Objectives

This IPS describes the prudent investment process the Advisor deems appropriate for the Client's situation. The Client desires to maximize returns within prudent levels of risk, and to meet the following stated investment objectives:

Advisor lists investment objectives:

1. Retire with sufficient assets to support a lifestyle of _____.
2. Provide college tuition to grandchildren, etc.

Time Horizon

The investment guidelines are based upon an investment horizon of greater than five years; therefore, interim fluctuations should be viewed with appropriate perspective. Short-term liquidity requirements are anticipated to be minimal.

Risk Tolerances

The Client recognizes and acknowledges some risk must be assumed in order to achieve long-term investment objectives, and there are uncertainties and complexities associated with contemporary investment markets.

In establishing the risk tolerances for this IPS, the Client's ability to withstand short- and intermediate-term variability was considered. The Client's prospects for the future, current financial condition, and several other factors suggest collectively some interim fluctuations in market value and rates of return may be tolerated in order to achieve the longer-term objectives.

Expected Return

In general, the Client would like the assets to earn at least a targeted return of 8.0%. It is understood that an average return of 8.0% will require superior manager performance to: (1) retain principal value; and, (2) purchasing power. Furthermore, the objective is to earn a long-term rate of return at least 5.5% greater than the rate of inflation as measured by the Consumer Price Index (CPI).

Asset Class Preferences

The Client understands long-term investment performance, in large part, is primarily a function of asset class mix. The Client has reviewed the long-term performance characteristics of the broad asset classes, focusing on balancing the risks and rewards.

History shows that while interest-generating investments such as bond portfolios have the advantage of relative stability of principal value, they provide little opportunity for real long-term capital growth due to their susceptibility to inflation. On the other hand, equity investments, such as common stocks, clearly have a significantly higher expected return, but have the disadvantage of much greater year-by-year variability of return. From an investment decision-making point of view, this year-by-year variability may be worth accepting, provided the time horizon for the equity portion of the portfolio is sufficiently long (five years or greater).

The following eight asset classes were selected and ranked in ascending order of "risk" (least to most).

Money Market (MM)
Intermediate Bond (IB)
Large Cap Value (LCV)
Large Cap Blend (LCB)
Large Cap Growth (LCG)
Mid Cap Blend (MCB)
Small Cap Blend (SCB)
International Equity (IE)

The Client has considered the following asset classes for inclusion in the asset mix, but has decided to exclude these asset classes at the present time:

Global Fixed Income
Real Estate

Rebalancing of Strategic Allocation

The percentage allocation to each asset class may vary as much as plus or minus 5% depending upon market conditions. When necessary and/ or available, cash inflows/outflows will be deployed in a manner consistent with the strategic asset allocation of the Portfolio. If there are no cash flows, the allocation of the Portfolio will be reviewed quarterly.

If the Advisor judges cash flows to be insufficient to bring the Portfolio within the strategic allocation ranges, the Client shall decide whether to effect transactions to bring the strategic allocation within the threshold ranges **(Strategic Allocation)**.

Duties and Responsibilities

Investment Advisor

The Client has retained an objective, third-party Advisor to assist the Client in managing the investments. The Advisor will be responsible for guiding the Client through a disciplined and rigorous investment process. As a fiduciary to the Client, the primary responsibilities of the Advisor are:

1. Prepare and maintain this investment policy statement.
2. Provide sufficient asset classes with different and distinct risk/return profiles so that the Client can prudently diversify the Portfolio.
3. Prudently select investment options.
4. Control and account for all investment expenses.
5. Monitor and supervise all service vendors and investment options.
6. Avoid prohibited transactions and conflicts of interest.

Investment Managers

As distinguished from the Advisor, who is responsible for *managing* the investment process, investment managers are responsible for *making* investment decisions (security selection and price decisions). The specific duties and responsibilities of each investment manager are:

1. Manage the assets under their supervision in accordance with the guidelines and objectives outlined in their respective Service Agreements, Prospectus, or Trust Agreement.
2. Exercise full investment discretion with regard to buying, managing, and selling assets held in the portfolios.
3. If managing a separate account (as opposed to a mutual fund or a commingled account), seek approval from the Client prior to purchasing and/or implementing the following securities and transactions:
   - Letter stock and other unregistered securities; commodities and other commodity contracts; and short sales or margin transactions.
   - Securities lending; pledging or hypothecating securities.

- Investments in the equity securities of any company with a record of less than three years of continuous operation, including the operation of any predecessor.
- Investments for the purpose of exercising control of management.

4. Vote promptly all proxies and related actions in a manner consistent with the long-term interests and objectives of the Portfolio as described in this IPS. Each investment manager shall keep detailed records of the voting of proxies and related actions and will comply with all applicable regulatory obligations.

5. Communicate to the Client all significant changes pertaining to the fund it manages or the firm itself. Changes in ownership, organizational structure, financial condition, and professional staff are examples of changes to the firm of interest to the Client.

6. Effect all transactions for the Portfolio subject "to best price and execution." If a manager utilizes brokerage from the Portfolio assets to effect "soft dollar" transactions, detailed records will be kept and communicated to the Client.

7. Use the same care, skill, prudence, and due diligence under the circumstances then prevailing that experienced investment professionals—acting in a like capacity and fully familiar with such matters—would use in like activities for like Portfolios with like aims in accordance and compliance with the Uniform Prudent Investor Act and all applicable laws, rules, and regulations.

8. If managing a separate account (as opposed to a mutual fund or a commingled account), acknowledge co-fiduciary responsibility by signing and returning a copy of this IPS.

Custodian

Custodians are responsible for the safekeeping of the Portfolio's assets. The specific duties and responsibilities of the custodian are:

1. Maintain separate accounts by legal registration.
2. Value the holdings.
3. Collect all income and dividends owed to the Portfolio.
4. Settle all transactions (buy-sell orders) initiated by the Investment Manager.
5. Provide monthly reports that detail transactions, cash flows, securities held and their current value, and change in value of each security and the overall portfolio since the previous report.

Investment Manager Selection

The Advisor will apply the following due diligence criteria in selecting each money manager or mutual fund.

A suggested minimum due diligence process would include the following:

1. **Regulatory oversight:** *Each investment option should be managed by: (a) a bank, (b) an insurance company, (c) a registered investment company (mutual fund), or (d) a registered investment adviser.*
2. **Minimum track record:** *Each investment option should have at least three years of history so that performance statistics can be properly calculated.*
3. **Stability of the organization:** *The same portfolio management team should be in place for at least two years.*
4. **Assets in the product:** *Each investment option should have at least $75 million under management (for mutual funds—can include assets in related share classes).*
5. **Holdings consistent with style:** *At least 80% of the underlying securities should be consistent with the broad asset class.*
6. **Correlation to style or peer group:** *Each investment option should be highly correlated to the asset class being implemented.*
7. **Expense ratios/fees:** *Fees should not be in the bottom quartile (most expensive) of the peer group.*
8. **Performance relative to assumed risk:** *The investment option's risk-adjusted performance (Alpha and/or Sharpe Ratio) should be evaluated against the peer group median manager's risk-adjusted performance.*
9. **Performance relative to peer group:** *Each investment option's performance should be evaluated against the peer group's median manager return, for 1-, 3-, and 5-year cumulative periods.*

Control Procedures

Performance Objectives

The Client acknowledges fluctuating rates of return characterize the securities markets, particularly during short-term time periods. Recognizing that short-term fluctuations may cause variations in performance, the Advisor intends to evaluate manager performance from a long-term perspective.

The Client is aware the ongoing review and analysis of the investment managers is just as important as the due diligence implemented during the manager selection process. The performance of the investment managers will be monitored on an ongoing basis and it is at the Client's discretion to take corrective action by replacing a manager if they deem it appropriate at any time.

On a timely basis, but not less than quarterly, the Advisor will meet with the Client to review whether each manager continues to conform to the search criteria outlined in the previous section; specifically:

1. The manager's adherence to the Portfolio's investment guidelines;
2. Material changes in the manager's organization, investment philosophy, and/or personnel; and,
3. Any legal, SEC, and/or other regulatory agency proceedings affecting the manager.

The Advisor has determined that it is in the best interest of the Client that performance objectives be established for each investment manager. Manager performance will be evaluated in terms of an appropriate market index (e.g., the S&P 500 stock index for large-cap domestic equity manager) and the relevant peer group (e.g., the large-cap growth mutual fund universe for a large-cap growth mutual fund).

Asset Class	Index	Peer Group
Large-Cap Equity		
Blend	S&P 500	Large-Cap Blend
Growth	Russell 200 Growth	Large-Cap Growth
Value	Russell 200 Value	Large-Cap Value
Mid-Cap Equity	S&P 400	Mid-Cap Blend
Small-Cap Equity	Russell 2000	Small-Cap Blend
International Equity	MSCI EAFE	Foreign Stock
Fixed Income		
Intermediate-term Bond	Lehman Brothers Gov't/ Credit Intermediate	Intermediate-term Bond
Money Market	90-day T-Bills	Money Market Database

A manager may be placed on a "Watchlist" and a thorough *review* and *analysis* of the investment manager may be conducted, when:

1. A manager performs below median for their peer group over a 1-, 3-, and/or 5-year cumulative period.
2. A manager's 3-year risk adjusted return (Alpha and/or Sharpe) falls below the peer group's median risk adjusted return.
3. There is a change in the professionals managing the portfolio.
4. There is a significant decrease in the product's assets.
5. There is an indication the manager is deviating from his/her stated style and/or strategy.
6. There is an increase in the product's fees and expenses.
7. Any extraordinary event occurs that may interfere with the manager's ability to fulfill their role in the future.

A manager evaluation may include the following steps:

1. A letter to the manager asking for an analysis of their underperformance.
2. An analysis of recent transactions, holdings, and portfolio characteristics to determine the cause for underperformance or to check for a change in style.
3. A meeting with the manager, which may be conducted on-site, to gain insight into organizational changes and any changes in strategy or discipline.

The decision to retain or terminate a manager cannot be made by a formula. It is the Client's confidence in the manager's ability to perform in the future that ultimately determines the retention of a manager.

Measuring Costs

The Advisor will review with the Client, at least annually, all costs associated with the management of the Portfolio's investment program, including:

1. Expense ratios of each investment option against the appropriate peer group.
2. Custody fees: The holding of the assets, collection of the income, and disbursement of payments.
3. Whether the manager is demonstrating attention to "best execution" in trading securities.

Investment Policy Review

The Advisor will review this IPS with the Client at least annually to determine whether stated investment objectives are still relevant, and the continued feasibility of achieving the same. It is not expected that the IPS will change frequently. In particular, short-term changes in the financial markets should not require adjustments to the IPS.

Prepared: Approved:

_____   _____
Advisor   Client

Date _____   Date _____

APPENDIX D

Seminar Checklist and Sample Invitations

Seminars can be a very effective way to educate and strengthen relationships with existing clients, introduce prospective clients to new ideas, and show both groups the benefits of working with you. The following checklist can help you plan your event and serve as a guide in organizing seminars as well as client appreciation meetings.

First Things First

Date and Time

- Plan ahead: Pick a date three months ahead to give you ample time to prepare, schedule speakers, and send invitations, and to give your invitees time to reserve the date on their calendars. Check the calendar for potential conflicts such as national or religious holidays, school vacations, and busy times for certain business owner clients.
- Timing: Consider your clients' work and family schedules when setting the time of day. To maximize attendance, try to select the most convenient time for your invitees.
- Duration: When planning the length of your event, design your seminar agenda to allow for guests to arrive, food to be served (if applicable), and speakers to present. Leave time for questions when speakers are finished and time for you to close out the event (recap the topics covered, suggest action steps, and, most important, thank guests for coming).

- Speakers: Make sure speakers arrive early for their portion of the meeting. Reinforce your time frame and the format that you would like them to follow.

Location

- Accessibility: Select a location that is suitable for the type of event you want to host. Find a place that will be convenient for your guests to travel to.
- Directions: Be sure to provide written directions to your location.
- Parking: Make sure there is adequate parking and, if your seminar is to be held at night, make sure the area is well lighted.
- Room: Pick a room that is private so that your group will not be distracted by others who are not part of your event. Select a room and table setup that are appropriate to the size of your event and create the atmosphere that you want for the seminar.
- Contact person: Establish an on-site contact person to help with details (room setup, menu selections, audiovisual arrangements, etc.) before and during your seminar.

Seminar Checklist

Three Months Before

☐ Choose date and reserve location.
☐ Reserve speakers and determine topics.
☐ Draft agenda and seminar invitations (see samples provided on the following pages).
☐ Submit agenda and invitation to compliance for approval.
☐ Compile list of invitees.
☐ Hold a staff meeting to discuss the seminar, prepare a checklist, and assign responsibilities.

Two Months Before

☐ Mail seminar invitations.

One Month Before

☐ Touch base with speakers or special guests to finalize topics, materials, and equipment.
☐ Order any special materials.
☐ Select menu and convey delivery/serving instructions.
☐ Arrange for any special equipment in room for speakers and you.
☐ Draft your presentation, accompanying materials, and host remarks.
☐ Submit presentation and materials to compliance for approval.
☐ Confirm status of RSVPs and place follow-up calls and/or send reminder notes.

Two Weeks Before

☐ Finalize agenda and confirm speakers.
☐ Finalize all presentations and written materials/handouts.
☐ Place final follow-up calls and/or send notes to invitees who have not yet responded.

Three Days Before

☐ Reconfirm location, equipment, and menu and provide final head counts.
☐ Draft seminar follow-up letter and submit to compliance.

One Day Before

☐ Place reminder phone calls to attendees with reservations (if desired).
☐ Assemble all materials for distribution to attendees.
☐ Make name tags and place cards (if desired).

One Hour Before

☐ Arrive at least 45 minutes to an hour early to coordinate final details, test equipment, and greet speakers.
☐ Make sure a staff member is on hand to greet people, direct guests to the right room, and provide general assistance.
☐ Set out materials and handouts for attendees.

At Conclusion

☐ Schedule appointments with seminar attendees at the end of your seminar—be sure to bring your calendar!

One Day After

☐ Send follow-up letters to attendees to thank them for their participation and reinforce seminar concepts and action steps. Include any educational pieces that are appropriate, as well as your business card.

Sample: Client Seminar Invitation

XYZ Financial Group

cordially invites you . . .

to attend an investment seminar

The Benefits of Managed Money

Hosted by:

Larry Smith

Senior Vice President
XYZ Financial Group

Guest Speaker:

Mike Adams
Financial Advisor
Smith, Jones & Wilson

Wednesday, September 24, 2008

6:00 P.M.

Location:

Four Seasons Hotel
100 Main Street
New York, NY
(555) 555-1234

Your guests with reservations are welcome. Seating is limited.
For reservations please call Mary at (555) 555-0000 before
September 10, 2008.

Sample: Client Seminar Invitation/Multiple Hosts and Speakers

XYZ Financial Group

cordially invites you …

to attend an investment seminar

The Benefits of Managed Money

Hosted by:

Larry Smith   Chris Brown

Senior Vice President   Senior Vice President
XYZ Financial Group   XYZ Financial Group

Guest Speakers:

Mike Adams   Sara Peterson

Financial Advisor   Portfolio Manager
Smith, Jones & Wilson   Acme Investment
                             Management

Wednesday, September 24, 2008

6:00 P.M.

Location:

The Ritz Carlton
100 Main Street
New York, NY
(555) 555-1234

Your guests with reservations are welcome. Seating is limited.
For reservations please call Mary at (555) 555-0000 before
September 10, 2008.

Sample: Client Seminar Invitation Wording

> *"Are you one of the best money managers in the country?"*

Neither Am I—

Come see
Sara Peterson, *Portfolio Manager*
and why using professional managers
could benefit you.

The Benefits of Managed Money

Hosted by:

John Morris

September 24, 2008
6:00 P.M.

Location:

The Manhattan Club
100 Main Street
New York, NY
(555) 555-1234

Sample: Client Appreciation Meeting

XYZ Financial Group

cordially invites you ...

to their Client Appreciation Dinner

Featuring Guest Speaker:

Michael Adams

Financial Advisor
Smith, Jones & Wilson

Wednesday, September 24, 2008

6:00 P.M.

Location:

Morton's
100 Main Street
New York, NY
(555) 555-1234

Your guests with reservations are welcome. Seating is limited.
For reservations please call Mary at (555) 555-0000 before
September 10, 2008.

Sample: Client Appreciation Meeting

Mr. William Donovan, Jr.
requests the honor of your presence for a
Black Tie evening of Client Appreciation

featuring a piano performance
by Elise Taylor

Saturday, the fourth of October
Two thousand and eight
at seven o'clock
La Chinoiseue
Windsor Court Hotel

Twenty-third Floor
Westport, Connecticut

Music by Myrage

Please RSVP by calling Pamela Jones at
(860) 555-1234 by September 16, 2008

Advisor's Resource Guide

Here's a sampling of the various sources to help with your marketing plans, business development activities, and training objectives. We've obtained the names of these popular services and products from advisors across the country. Take a look and check out the resources you feel will best suit you. We've categorized the listing to make it easier to search.

Industry Organizations

It's vital to join such industry associations as the Investment Management Consultants Association, National Association of Personal Financial Advisors (NAPFA), Financial Planning Association (FPA), or others that will provide not only educational courseware, continuing education credits, and conferences for networking and learning, but also marketing help and professional designations (such as CFA, CFP, CIMC, and CIMA) to give you a higher level of knowledge, credibility, and professionalism. Taking an active part in these types of organizations will differentiate you from the crowd. Here is a partial listing:

- The Money Management Institute (MMI), 1140 Connecticut Avenue NW, Washington, DC 20036; telephone: (202) 822-4949; www.moneyinstitute.com
- Investment Management Consultants Association (IMCA), 9101 East Kenyon Avenue, Suite 3000, Denver, CO 80237; telephone: (303) 770-3377; www.imca.org
- Financial Planning Association (FPA), Atlanta • Denver • Washington, DC; telephone: (800) 322-4237, (404) 845-0011; www.fpanet.org
- College for Financial Planning, 6161 South Syracuse Way, Greenwood Village, CO 80111; telephone: (800) 237-9990; www.fp.edu
- American College, 270 South Bryn Mawr Avenue, Bryn Mawr, PA 19010-2196; telephone: (888) 263-7265; www.amercoll.edu
- National Association of Insurance and Financial Advisors (NAIFA), 2901 Telestar Court, PO Box 12012, Falls Church, VA 22042; telephone: (703) 770-8100; www.naifa.org

- National Association of Investment Professionals (NAIP), 12664 Emmer Place, Suite 201, St. Paul, MN 55124; telephone: (952) 322-NAIP, (952) 322-6247; www.naip.com
- National Association of Philanthropic Planners, 176 West Logan Street, #434, Noblesville, IN 46060; telephone: (800) 342-6215; www.napp.net
- Center for Fiduciary Studies, Don Trone, 2004 East Carson Street, Pittsburgh, PA 15203; telephone: (412) 390-5080; www.fi360.com

Industry Periodicals

Other resources to help you learn more about managed accounts and the investment process are such popular industry trade publications as the following (most are free to the trade):

- *Financial Advisor*—www.financialadvisormagazine.com
- *Financial Planning*—www.financial-planning.com
- *Investment Advisor*—www.investmentadvisor.com
- *Investment News*—www.investmentnews.com
- *Journal of Financial Planning*—www.journalfp.net
- *On Wall Street*—www.onwallstreet.com
- *Pensions & Investments*—www.pionline.com
- *Plan Sponsor*—www.plansponsor.com
- *Registered Representative*—www.registeredrep.com
- *Research*—www.researchmag.com
- *Senior Consultant News Journal*—www.srconsultant.com
- *Wealth Manager*—www.wealthmanagermag.com

Books

Bachrach, Bill. *Values-Based Financial Planning: The Art of Creating an Inspiring Financial Strategy.* Aim High Publishers, 2000.

Bachrach, Bill. *Values-Based Selling: The Art of Building High-Trust Client Relationships.* Bachrach & Associates, 1996.

Bernstein, Peter. *Against the Gods: The Remarkable Story of Risk.* New York: John Wiley & Sons, 1998.

Bogle, John. *Character Counts.* New York: McGraw-Hill, 2002.

Cates, Bill. *Unlimited Referrals.* Referral Coach International, 1996.

Chambers, Larry. *Credibility Marketing: Build Your Business by Becoming a Recognized Expert.* New York: Kaplan Publishing, 2001.

Chambers, Larry. *The Guide to Financial Public Relations: How to Stand Out in the Midst of Competitive Clutter.* CRC, 1999.

Gerber, Michael E. *The E-Myth Revisited.* New York: HarperCollins, 1995.

Gibson, Roger C. *Asset Allocation.* New York: McGraw-Hill, 2000.

Graham, Benjamin, and David Dodd. *The Intelligent Investor.* New York: Collins, 2005.

Gresham, Stephen D. *Advisor for Life.* Hoboken, NJ: John Wiley & Sons, 2007.

Gresham, Stephen D., and Evan Cooper. *Attract and Retain the Affluent Investor: Winning Tactics for Today's Financial Advisor.* Chicago: Dearborn Trade, 2001.

Katz, Deena B. *Deena Katz on Practice Management.* New York: Bloomberg Press, 1999.

LeBlanc, Sydney. *History of Managed Accounts.* Washington, DC: Money Management Institute, 2002.

Levin, Ross. *The Wealth Management Index.* New York: Irwin/McGraw-Hill, 1997.

Levitt, Theodore. *The Marketing Imagination.* Free Press, 1986.

Loewe, Raymond D. *New Strategies for College Funding: An Advisor's Guide.* Hoboken, NJ: John Wiley & Sons, 2002.

Moeller, Steve. *Effort-Less Marketing for Financial Advisors: 5 Steps to a Super-Profitable Business and Wonderful Life.* American Business Visions, 1999.

Peterson, Peter G. *Gray Dawn.* New York: Random House, 1999.

Prince, Russ Alan, and Karen Maru File. *High-Net-Worth Psychology.* Fairfield, CT: HNW Press, 1999.

Prince, Russ Alan, and Brett Van Borte. *Rainmaker.* Erlanger, KY: National Underwriter Co., 2006.

Pusateri, Leo J. *Mirror, Mirror on the Wall: Am I the Most Valued of Them All?* Buffalo, NY: Pusateri Consulting and Training, 2001.

Ries, Al, and Jack Trout. *Positioning: The Battle for Your Mind.* New York: McGraw-Hill, 2000.

Rowland, Mary. *Best Practices for Financial Advisors.* New York: Bloomberg Press, 1997.

Sprinkel, Kay, and Alan Wendroff. *High Impact Philanthropy: How Donors, Boards, and Nonprofit Organizations Can Transform Communities.* Hoboken, NJ: John Wiley & Sons, 2001.

Stanley, Thomas J. *Marketing to the Affluent.* New York: McGraw-Hill, 1988.

Stanley, Thomas J. *Networking with the Affluent and Their Advisors.* Burr Ridge, IL: Irwin Professional Publishing, 1993.

Stenner, Thane. *True Wealth: An Expert Guide for High-Net-Worth Individuals (and Their Advisors).* True Wealth Publishing, 2002.

Tibergien, Mark C., and Owen Dahl. *How to Value, Buy, or Sell a Financial Advisory Practice.* New York: Bloomberg Press, 2006.

Tibergien, Mark C., and Rebecca Pomering. *Practice Made Perfect: The Discipline of Business Management for Financial Advisors.* New York: Bloomberg Press, 2005.

Trone, Donald B., and William R. Allbright. *Procedural Prudence: The Fiduciary's Handbook for Management of Retirement Plan Assets.* Veale & Associates, 1990.

Trone, Donald B., William R. Allbright, and Philip R. Taylor. *The Management of Investment Decisions.* New York: McGraw-Hill, 1995.

Ware, Jim. *The Psychology of Money.* Hoboken, NJ: John Wiley & Sons, 2000.

Weiss, Alan. *How to Acquire Clients: Powerful Techniques for the Successful Practitioner.*

Ziesenheim, Ken. *Understanding ERISA: A Compact Guide to the Landmark Act.*

Online Marketing and Training Solutions

A number of excellent online sources are also available. Some are free; some are subscriber based. Among the most popular are www.horsesmouth.com, www.stockbrokerpro.com, www.theprogresscenter.com, www.morningstar advisor.com,www.fncnet.com,www.sionline.com, www.brokerville.com, and www.pbstraining.com.

Contact Management Tools

Allied Financial Software, Inc.
    www.software4advisors.com

AS&A brokersoft
    www.brokersoft.com

Broker's Ally
    www.brokersally.com

CRM Software
    www.junxurei.com

E-Z Data, Inc.
    www.ez-data.com

Financial Planning Consultants, Inc.
    www.financialsoftware.com

Fugent, Inc.
    www.fugent.com

National Datamax, Inc.
    www.nationaldatamax.com

North American Software, Inc. (NASI)
www.nasoftware.com

Springwater Software
www.springwatersoftware.com

Mailing Lists

Harris InfoSource
www.harrisinfo.com

W.S. Ponton, Inc.
www.wsponton.com

D&B Small Business Solutions
www.dnb.com

D&B Sales & Marketing Solutions
www.zapdata.com

infoUSA.com, Inc.
www.infousa.com

DMG
www.leaddogs.com

Judy Diamond Associates, Inc.
www.judydiamond.com

Trainers and Coaches

Steve Moeller, American Business Visions, LLC
www.businessvisions.com

Bill Bachrach, AM Enterprises
www.amehigh.com

Leo Pusateri, Pusateri Consulting and Training, LLC
www.pusatericonsulting.com

Steve Saenz, Paragon Resources, Inc.
www.paragonresources.com

Bill Good Marketing, Inc.
www.billgood.com

Industry Consultants

Don Trone, Fiduciary360
www.fi360.com

Index

Printed and bound by CPI Group (UK) Ltd, Croydon, CR0 4YY

16/04/2025